CW00820836

THE

STARKEY

SACRIFICE

The Allied Bombing of Le Portel 1943

MICHAEL CUMMING

SUTTON PUBLISHING LIMITED

First published in 1996 by
Sutton Publishing Limited · Phoenix Mill
Thrupp · Stroud · Gloucestershire · GL5 2BU

Copyright © Michael Cumming, 1996

All rights reserved. No part of this publication may be reproduced, stored in a
retrieval system, or transmitted, in any form or by any means, electronic,
mechanical, photocopying, recording or otherwise, without the prior permission of
the publisher and copyright holder

The author has asserted the moral right to be identified as the author of this work

British Library Cataloguing in Publication Data
A catalogue record for this book is available from the British Library

ISBN 0-7509-1253-7

By the same author:
Pathfinder Cranswick
The Powerless Ones: Gliding in Peace and War

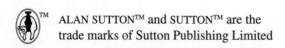
ALAN SUTTON™ and SUTTON™ are the
trade marks of Sutton Publishing Limited

Typeset in 10/12 Plantin Light.
Typesetting and origination by
Sutton Publishing Limited.
Printed in Great Britain by
Butler & Tanner, Frome, Somerset

CONTENTS

Dedication

To the victims, named or unidentified, who died for France in the bombardment of Le Portel on 4, 8 and 9 September 1943 . . . and to all others, members of the armed forces and civilians too, who lost their lives in the course of *Operation Starkey*, 16 August–9 September 1943.

ACKNOWLEDGEMENTS

But for my son and daughter-in-law, Richard and Dawn, buying a copy of the Pas de Calais daily newspaper to improve their understanding of the French language, this focus on *Operation Starkey* and its consequential impact on the town of Le Portel would never have been started . . . and without the continuing encouragement of my wife, Rita, it would never have been finished. It might then have been a further fifty years before someone else became sufficiently absorbed to research in depth the circumstances surrounding the destruction of this French seaside resort by Anglo-American bombing on 4, 8 and 9 September 1943 in the closing hours of a wartime strategy that was certainly a revelation to me: *Operation Starkey*. At that time, the invasion of Normandy was nine months away and the end of the Second World War a distant hope in an uncertain future.

The newspaper article that attracted my family's attention was the latest of many references to the long-unexplained bombardment of Le Portel, just south of Boulogne in the Pas de Calais region of northern France. The indication that the present inhabitants were still looking for answers was the catalyst for the painstaking investigation which has resulted in this book. Over the years, patient efforts by people associated with the Pas de Calais newspaper *La Voix du Nord* and by others working with the historical society in Le Portel, the *Cercle Historique Portelois*, has brought to light a good deal of information – and speculation too. I commend those individuals and their endeavours when acknowledging that those articles have been invaluable in piecing together this first comprehensive, stand-alone account of the tragedy. I am fortunate in being able to introduce a fresh dimension with the presentation of key facts that are entirely new to the subject: material obtained only through the facility for detailed examination of documents produced at the time within the British War Cabinet, War Office, Admiralty, Air Ministry and the US Eighth Air Force based in Britain. The inclusion of such once-secret material does more than produce answers to specific questions; it provides a greater understanding of the reason why Le Portel unexpectedly became a target area . . . and why the bombing by night and by day unfortunately caused so much destruction, so many deaths, so many injuries and so many painful memories – memories that remain so vivid even after more than fifty years.

My thanks are due to many people on both sides of what we call respectively the English Channel and *La Manche*: to friends old and new who have helped by providing information or pointers to extend my knowledge of that scarcely known *Operation Starkey* and the much less-known (to those outside France) '*bombardement du Portel*'. In France, where my initial objective was simply to 'test the water' for an article that would pay tribute to the remarkable reconstruction post-war of Le Portel, I will single out individuals in the sequence of my contact with them: Louis Bourgain-Godin, to whom I first mentioned the possibility of examining wartime records held in Britain to see what they might unfold; Jean-Pierre Painset, who opened up his file of personal international correspondence on the bombardment and shared my interest in the rebuilding of the town; Marie-Jo Duval and her parents for their warm hospitality and eager assistance, which included the loan of post-bombardment photographs from the family's collection; Gabriel Duval (Père Césaire, *Franciscain*) for guiding me through an incredible wealth of documentation he has assembled on his native town of Le Portel and its people; staff at Le Portel Town Hall, Boulogne-sur-Mer Municipal Library and the Pas de Calais archives in Arras for unearthing original papers 'at the drop of a hat'; Charles Merette and Ernest MacKenna, survivors of the bombings, who relived their experiences for me – individually underlining the telling fact that *if* any advance warning for the people of Le Portel was intended by the Allies, it could have been much better handled; Laurent Feutry, Mayor of Le Portel, for his personal interest in this research and allowing reproduction from official correspondence and other material relative to the town's affairs during and after the war; Guy Bataille, whose three volume history of wartime Boulogne is a model of objective reporting by a vigilant participant; *La Voix du Nord*, an unrivalled source of contemporary reporting and photography, extracts from whose files are reproduced with their sanction; and of course Gérard Pirot, representing the annual magazine produced by the *Cercle Historique Portelois*, who has kindly agreed to the inclusion of passages from various articles that capture so well the experiences of the Portelois before, during and after the bombardment. As a faithful, vibrant and lasting record of a town and its people from early times, *CHP* must be hard to equal, inside or outside France.

In Britain, where the most obvious sources of information were aviation-related, Ian Willsher was understandably the first 'port of call'; a friend for many years, since he read *Pathfinder Cranswick* which came out in the early 1960s, he was my entrée to a number of key contacts both in 35 Squadron (which was Alec Cranswick's) and others who were in, or associated with, Pathfinder Force around the time of *Operation Starkey*. Ron Curtis DSO, DFC and Bar was my 'instructor' in Mosquito matters (he flew with 109 Squadron) as well as introducing me to John Hooper for a 'training course' on Oboe; and Des Lander DFC (35 Squadron) provided background on so many complex aspects of target-marking and bombing that became second nature to Halifax pilots. Staff at the Public Record Office and the Imperial War Museum were ever-helpful; so, as well as formally noting that Crown copyright material in the Public Record Office is reproduced by permission of the Controller of Her Majesty's Stationery Office, I am pleased to salute the care and attention displayed by staff members when handling research enquiries from what seems to be a never-ending procession of visitors.

Having revealed my sources and registered my gratitude for their assistance with much pleasure, I realize that I could be doing them an injustice if I did not make it clear that any errors of fact which may have slipped into the text will be mine – inadvertently mine. Equally, any misinterpretation of facts made available through those official and personal sources will also be mine.

Some may argue that highlighting a wartime incident so long afterwards is an unnecessary reopening of old wounds – however unique the occurrence. I beg to differ. To do so may not make any material difference to the town and the citizens of Le Portel, or to the relatives and friends of those who suffered in that ferocious bombardment, but at least now the record is complete. Surely that must be justification enough for the desire to produce a definitive account of the *Starkey*-linked events of the summer of 1943 – events that some readers may find more emotive, now that the full story is known, than even was the case when the events were happening all those years ago.

Michael Cumming
London 1996

ABBREVIATIONS

AA	Anti-Aircraft
AFC	Air Force Cross
AOC-in-C	Air Officer Commanding-in-Chief
AP	Aiming Point
AWAS	Air Warfare Analysis Section
BC	Bomber Command
CD	Coastal Defence
CHP	*Cercle Historique Portelois*
CIU	Central Interpretation Unit
COS	Chiefs of Staff
COSSAC	Chief of Staff to Supreme Allied Commander
DFC	Distinguished Flying Cross
DFM	Distinguished Flying Medal
DSO	Distinguished Service Order
H2S	Air to ground mapping radar
HBM	*Habitations à Bon Marché*
HE	High Explosives
HQ	Headquarters
LCS	London Controlling Section
MPI	Mean Point of Impact
ORB	Operations Record Book (RAF Units)
ORS	Operational Research Section
OTU	Operational Training Unit
PFF	Pathfinder Force (No. 8 Group, RAF)
PRO	Public Record Office
PWE	Political Warfare Executive
RCAF	Royal Canadian Air Force
SOE	Special Operations Executive
STO	*Le Service du Travail Obligatoire*
TI	Target Indicator
TRE	Telecommunications Research Establishment
USAAF	US Army Air Force
VC	Victoria Cross
VCAS	Vice-Chief of Air Staff
WIDU	Wireless Intelligence Development Unit

Chapter One

Assault on Boulogne

How many times have you wondered about the reason for a particular street having a particular name? In countries around the world, holiday centres especially can provide a fascinating guessing game for visitors wandering through a town in search of a meal or somewhere to spend the night.

In Europe, the French are zealous about commemorating heroes from history: seafarers, military leaders, religious figures and civic dignitaries have their names justly perpetuated in this manner. All these and many others are to be found in the familiar blue-and-white street signs in broad, tree-lined boulevards, trim residential areas and picturesque alleys crammed with tiny shops to tempt the bargain-hunters.

Typical in following this well-established practice in the Pas de Calais region of northern France is Le Portel, once a bustling fishing port, now a seaside resort, a couple of miles south of the gateway town of Boulogne from which it gained its name. By comparison, this was the 'little port' – 'Portel' expressing the diminutive back in the Middle Ages.

Visitors will have no trouble with de Gaulle, Foch, Leclerc and so on, and certainly not with Rue Jean Mermoz – just down the road and within Boulogne. Unusually, the municipal authorities have themselves provided a brief explanation, which therefore negates the guessing game: '*célèbre aviateur*' has been added to differentiate this Jean Mermoz from others of the same name.

In the streets of Le Portel itself are remembered admirals, generals, clerics and mayors of bygone days. Indeed, it seems as if every street recalls someone, noteworthy or otherwise. But what about one, close to the market-place – a street with a date rather than a name?

There is a de Gaulle, a Foch and a Leclerc in many a French town (in some there is possibly a Jean Mermoz too), but it is safe to say that nowhere but Le Portel is there an Avenue du 8 Septembre. It is a unique identification ensuring that this date will never ever be allowed to lapse from the memory of future generations of Portelois.

What is so memorable about 8 September that it is important enough to be stamped indelibly into the hearts and minds of the people of Le Portel? To find the reason it is necessary to go back to events that occurred during the Second World War when this region was under Nazi occupation, and then to decide which was the year. Could it be 1940, the first September beneath German rule? If not, could the year be a later one – and remembered for what reason? In fact, enquiries show that the date commemorates a bombing . . . a bombing that has long defied explanation among the survivors.

Being so close to Boulogne, a key port in an exceptionally heavily defended area – there was probably none more so than the Pas de Calais – Le Portel expected its share of damage and casualties under Allied attack. In reality the resort was scarcely touched: 6 dead, 7 hurt and 15 homes destroyed in the space of three years.[1]

Then, one cloudless night, in bright moonlight, for reasons that have remained unclear to the townspeople for more than fifty years, one particularly savage air-raid devastated the town. The bombers were Allied planes – 'friendly' bombers, if that is not too much of a contradiction in terms – and the attack was in two phases, although to the people of Le Portel it probably appeared as a single event. Each attack was on a separate objective: one target was to the north-east of the town, the other to the south-west. Each onslaught was timed to last 15 minutes and separated by just 30 minutes. As with all military operations, the planners judged the timing as all-important.

The planes were carrying maximum bomb loads to achieve maximum effect within the twin target areas. Compared with an attack against the enemy heartland, this was a short trip from the twenty-nine airfields involved that were scattered around the English countryside as far north as the Yorkshire Dales. Even so, all were comfortably within a 300 mile radius. This meant that less fuel was required so there was room for more bombs without upsetting flight performance.

An estimated 5,500 people were in Le Portel that night – no-one had carried out a head count lately. No one was counting either when the bombs began falling, but the planes unloosed one bomb every second on average, the smallest the weight of a hefty man, the biggest nicknamed Blockbuster and tipping the scales at close on 2 tons. To those on the ground, which rocked and rolled with each fresh explosion, the rate was even more numbing because the bombing peaked in each of the two phases.

There was utter bewilderment when daylight came. Yet death and destruction continued, just as death and destruction had preceded. Daytime raids of 8 and 9 September created an awesome lethal sandwich around the savagery of the intervening night, that unforgettable night of 8 September.

Looking back on those events, it must have appeared to the townspeople that on 4 September by day and on the 8th and 9th by day, Allied planes must have homed-in quite deliberately on Le Portel. The results were relatively minor, however, when compared with the night attack on the 8th. It was this that caused the most casualties and the worst damage – hence this date for the street name.

Some 235 aircraft were overhead that night, their crews coming from British, Canadian, New Zealand and Polish squadrons – plus a further 5 aircraft, the crews of which were carrying out the US Air Force's first night bombing mission since arriving on British soil. The day raid was the Americans' speciality: this was the kind of mission that best suited their planes, their tactics and their crews.

Returning to the commemoration date on the street nameplate, what was the year? Was it September 1944 perhaps, three months after the Allies landed in Normandy, when the Germans were still hanging on grimly in the Pas de Calais and the Allies were having to battle for every fresh inch of its valuable coastline? At that crucial stage there could have been just cause to bomb targets close to Le Portel.

No, these bombings took place the previous year – in September 1943 – when no invasion was in being and none in prospect, at least none that became public knowledge at the time. Nevertheless, when the bombs were crashing down on this seaside resort 2 miles south of Boulogne, Allied ships were certainly gathering in the English Channel. They were all set to head for the sandy beaches between Boulogne and Le Touquet, a 12 mile stretch that had been so popular pre-war with British holiday-makers and remains an attraction today.

Under the protection of an air umbrella and with destroyers at their sides, those ships were still some miles off the French coast when daylight forced the total evacuation of Le Portel. The aerial bombardment that night of 8 September 1943 had been so appalling, so crushing, that it was impossible for any level of human life to be maintained in the stricken town. There was no gas, no electricity, no water, no negotiable roads and no ease of movement. There was hardly a building that had not been hit; hardly a family which had not suffered personal loss. Some 500 Portelois lost their lives and many hundreds more were injured – unfortunate victims of Allied bombing on enemy-occupied territory in one of the most bizarre episodes of the war. In the late afternoon of 22 September 1944, when the liberating Canadian soldiers accepted the surrender of a last-ditch garrison in the vicinity, Le Portel was still empty – a ghost town. There was no-one to greet the battle-weary troops nor flags waving in welcome, just the tattered remnants of window curtains fluttering gently in the breeze a year and more after the bombs.

At the outbreak of war, Le Portel had a population of roughly 8,500, but by the time the bombers came it had been reduced progressively. Many had left for England in the family fishing boats when the Germans came early in the summer of 1940. Still more dispersed subsequently for other reasons: some quietly disappearing when an opportunity arose, joining the Resistance and going 'underground' or simply moving out of the district; while others were interned for acts against the enemy or deported for forced labour.

With its back against the wall, Britain had prepared to meet the same invading forces which had swamped the countries on the other side of the Channel. Boulogne fell to the Germans on 25 May 1940, and as summer progressed the port became one of the key assembly areas for the waiting landing craft. However, Hitler's *Operation Sealion* was put off – he had other matters on his mind. The RAF's fighters put the *Luftwaffe* to flight and the war took a different course: civilians in the opposing capital cities found themselves in the front line when the bombs fell on London and Berlin.

Soon the war was engulfing more countries: Germany invaded Russia on 22 June 1941, but 20 degrees of frost that winter put a stop to its plans to reach Moscow; and Japan attacked Pearl Harbour on 7 December 1941, which brought America into the hostilities. That 'day of infamy' opened up a huge new reservoir of men and machines, hardware and hope, no doubt advancing the time appreciably when once-alone Britain could consider going on the offensive.

The new year, 1942, was still not the time, however. Britain had lost the battlecruiser *Repulse* and the battleship *Prince of Wales* off Malaya, and seen three crack German ships – *Scharnhorst, Gneisenau* and *Prinz Eugen* – escape up the Channel from Brest to fight another day. The turning point in Britain's fortunes would come later in the year with the Afrika Korps in retreat in the Middle East and Allied landings at Algiers, Oran and Casablanca. In the air war, American bombers from Britain made their first strike against Germany with a daylight attack on the port of Wilhelmshaven. The tide was shifting, but any real thoughts of an early land offensive in Northern Europe were plainly premature – the Allied leaders were clear on that.

In the Pas de Calais, the occupying forces further strengthened their defences, for this was surely one of the most obvious areas for an Allied invasion. Elsewhere in France there had been probing efforts on various scales: the bold raid on St Nazaire, the ill-fated landing at Dieppe and the cheeky 'Cockleshell Heroes' penetration of the Gironde river by Royal Marine commandos in November 1942. It seemed to be a time when it was 'best to be seen to be doing something' – 'doing something' kept the enemy on their toes across the water and kept up morale on the home front.

The truth of the matter was that even with the Americans' war arsenal now becoming available to boost the preparations for an Allied foothold in Europe, 1943 was still going to be too early for this to be a serious possibility. Half-measures were no use: the planning teams were hard at work deciding the minimum requirements to achieve success; success not only in the initial landings, but in the hours, days and weeks to follow when the enemy would be moving his forces around for counter-attacks.

Prime Minister Winston Churchill acknowledged that an invasion of the Continent was out of the question for the time being.* It was necessary to plan for a landing around mid-1944, this being the earliest time for the necessary men and equipment to become available. Nonetheless, much could be done in 1943 to pave the way for the eventual operations which would help to create a free Europe after prolonged Nazi domination.

It was at this point that Lt-Gen. Frederick Morgan came on the scene, a man who, it must have seemed, carried the future of the western world on his shoulders. He was Chief of Staff to the Supreme Commander (Designate) – COSSAC, when the 'A' for 'Allied' was introduced to make it clear whose future supreme commander it meant.

Since the spring of 1943, Morgan had been engaged on a triple task within the framework of the Allies' intentions to defeat the German fighting forces in north-west Europe as soon as practicable. He had to make the enemy think that the Allies

---

* He was on record stating that 'no important x-Channel enterprise is possible this year'; it was nevertheless 'highly important that this fact should not become widely known'.[2] Landing craft were needed for the Mediterranean theatre of operations, and as yet the arrival of American troops in the UK was no more than a trickle.

had every intention of getting back on the Continent in 1943; he had to plan for an actual re-entry with whatever forces were to hand should the occupying forces' grip weaken sufficiently to present this opportunity; and he had to prepare for 'the real thing': a full-scale assault against the Continent with a target date of 1 May 1944.[3]

Although these were three separate activities there was common ground, literally as well as figuratively. As the weeks progressed, so would the strength and effectiveness of the ground formations available to cross the Channel. So, planning for the ultimate invasion, he would be able to adapt as necessary if there was an earlier requirement. There was an ever-present possibility, however remote, that there might be some form of uprising, led from within the armed forces, to oust the Nazi leadership. It could be sparked by a reversal of fortunes: perhaps by incessant bombing, but more likely by the inevitability of defeat. If there was any suggestion of disintegration and a consequent loosening of the Germans' hold on the occupied countries, this could be the time to strike – no matter how weak the Allied punch. As for getting the Germans to think that there really would be cross-Channel action on a big scale in 1943, much of the thinking necessary for a real invasion could also be put to use in dreaming up a pretend landing, while guarding against giving away too much about the precise locations and methods.

COSSAC was required to produce 'an elaborate camouflage and deception scheme extending over the whole summer with a view to pinning the enemy in the West and keeping alive the expectation of large scale cross-Channel operations in 1943', this concept having been agreed when Churchill and US President Franklin D Roosevelt, with their chiefs of staff, met for the Casablanca Conference at the beginning of that year. The scheme would include 'at least one amphibious feint with the object of bringing on an air battle employing the Metropolitan Royal Air Force and the US 8th Air Force'.[4] Morgan's team, which was headquartered in Norfolk House, St James's Square, London SW1, came up with a three-part scheme: besides an amphibious feint to draw the German air force into the skies by threatening an imminent large-scale landing in the Pas de Calais, it also featured separate but coordinated deception operations directed towards Brittany and Norway.* Both of these would play a part in deluding the German military hierarchy, however, the operation planned closest to home, aimed at the Pas de Calais region of northern France, would absorb the most manpower, utilize the greatest diversity of weapons and set the biggest challenge in inter-service cooperative effort. It would also receive Churchill's personal attention.

As then visualized and outlined on 24 May 1943 in a document addressed to the Secretary of the Chiefs of Staff Committee (the top-ranking officers of Britain's armed forces), this plan was designed to take place during the period August–September 1943 and involve the Army, Navy, RAF and US Army Air Force (USAAF) in preparations 'consistent with an assault on Boulogne'.[5] Referring to the directive instructing him also to plan an operation for 1943 in the event of German

---

* *Operation Wadham*: to convince the enemy that a large-scale American operation is being prepared to capture the Brest Peninsula in the early autumn. Culminating date 30 September 1943. *Operation Tindall*: to mount a major deceptive threat aimed at Stavanger to pin down German forces in Norway during the summer and early autumn. Culminating date 12 to 18 September 1943.[6]

disintegration, Lt-Gen. Morgan wrote that 'every effort is being made to plan the feint operation, outlined above, in such a way that it could actually be carried out should the circumstances be propitious'.[7]

As a threat, it was progressive: it could be allowed to build up or stopped at will. Nonetheless, Morgan proposed an immediate start on the assembly and training of a naval assault force in the Portsmouth area; the largest possible concentration of landing craft in ports along the Hampshire, Sussex and Kent coasts by 1 September; vehicles to be embarked as if for a genuine operation; air effort to force German fighters into combat in circumstances favourable to the Allies; minesweeping to clear paths across the Channel for the invasion armada; and bombing and shelling of coast defences likely to oppose approaching vessels.

It was an ambitious plan: British and Canadian troops, in their thousands, to be ready to go into the assembly areas; two huge R-class battleships – among the biggest warships afloat anywhere on the seven seas – to turn their massive guns against German coastal batteries with a dozen destroyers as their escort and that of the Boulogne-bound armada; some 15,000 fighter sorties for defensive and offensive operations; 3,000 sorties by medium and heavy bombers during daylight – and as many by night. As for the assault, if it came to it, beach landings were planned between Audresselles and Ambleteuse, 6 miles north of Boulogne, and between the River Brone and Hardelot, 7 miles south of Boulogne, with subsidiary attacks by seaborne commandos, Royal Marines units and paratroops. The resort of Le Portel was targeted for a further landing by sea, the aim being to prevent, if possible, the demolition of the port of Boulogne before the pincer movement by the two main forces could seize it.[8] After the landings, the invasion force was to be built up so as to be able to sweep north to Calais to gain a second port, and to establish airbases and communications across the entire area. It would then move on towards Antwerp via Béthune, Tournai and Alost.

The operation had to have a codename – to help preserve secrecy and to identify it in discussions and in documents without disclosing the nature of the operation. An intelligence subcommittee within the War Cabinet coordinated the responsibility for issuing such names. And no codenames were allocated for any operations of importance without prior approval of the Prime Minister.

In an exchange of correspondence with his Chief of Staff, Lt-Gen. Sir Hastings Ismay, Winston Churchill insisted that:

operations in which large numbers of men may lose their lives ought not to be described by code words which imply a boastful or over-confident sentiment such as *Triumphant,* or conversely which are calculated to invest the plan with an air of despondency, such as *Woebetide, Massacre, Jumble, Trouble, Fidget, Flimsy, Pathetic* and *Jaundice.*

It was the Prime Minister's view, too, that code words should not be 'ordinary words often used in other connections, such as *Flood, Smooth, Sudden, Supreme, Fullforce* and *Fullspeed*', or those of living people, ministers of the crown or military commanders, for example *Bracken* (an allusion to Brendan Bracken, Minister of Information).

In a personal memo to Ismay he wrote that intelligent thought would readily supply an unlimited number of well-sounding names 'which do not suggest the character of the operation or disparage it in any way and do not enable some widow or mother to say that her son was killed in an operation called *Bunnyhug* or *Ballyhoo*'.[9]

He was 'rather fond of making up his own code words for new operations and projects', so when it came to casting an experienced eye over the efforts of others he was understandably critical. Hence, out of four lists compiled for his perusal by no lesser worthies than the Inter-Service Security Board (77 names, from *Bandleader* to *Whizzbang*), the Admiralty (75), the Air Ministry (19) and the Joint Planning Staff (25, plus a further 20 'handed over for use by the Prime Minister and not yet used'), Churchill was quick to strike through the suggestions *Triumphant*, *Massacre*, *Trouble* and *Jumble* (which came respectively from each of those four lists), along with various others that he judged to be unsuitable.

When the Prime Minister was put in the picture about Lt-Gen. Morgan's three deception operations, in a set of briefing papers in which all three had been brought together under the umbrella designation of *Operation Cockade*, the Pas de Calais, Brittany and Norway feints were identified only as Operations A, B and C. The codenames preselected for them were in an accompanying sealed envelope, and were accepted without call for change.[10] So it was that *Operation Starkey* received Churchillian consent to become stamped forever on Morgan's bold thrust – albeit only on paper at that stage – for the Belgian port of Antwerp, via the Channel port of Boulogne, occupied by the Germans since three summers ago.

What were the attractions of this part of the Continent in the summer of 1943? Morgan's planners identified several factors advantageous to the Allies which would be equally obvious to the Germans: the approaches were shorter and safer; a large port needed to be seized early on; there were suitable areas nearby for an assault; and there was a considerable extent of sheltered anchorage if the weather were to turn nasty. All these pointed to the region astride Boulogne as being the most suitable assault area, so a threat to it would be most likely to influence the enemy in the way that *Starkey* intended for deception purposes.[11]

The three coastal areas designated in the assault phase in Morgan's 26 June 1943 Appreciation for Outline Plan were Beaches 110 to the north (Audresselles/Ambleteuse), 116 to the south (River Brone/Hardelot) and 113 at Le Portel. The first two promised wide expanses to land sufficient numbers of troops to gain a firm foothold, whereas 113 at Le Portel, closer to Boulogne than the others, posed two problems: there was a rocky outcrop at the southern end which limited to 800 yards the length available for landing vehicles; and its exits led inland through a built-up area, so this was not a suitable spot to set up a beach maintenance area. It was more appropriate for the smaller, special-purpose operation written into the plan.[12]

What about the Germans' defence positions? The whole area had come under photographic reconnaissance surveillance, so it was now familiar territory via the sharply detailed prints that came from the RAF's cameras. Careful observation showed that there were 16 guns certainly, with a further 4 very probably, able to bring effective fire to bear on the Dover/Folkestone area; in addition, there were 13 fixed guns and an estimated 12 railway guns that could possibly be brought to bear on that area.[13] Morgan's team was in no doubt that this part of the Pas de Calais was daunting in the extreme. The Allies knew it, the Germans knew it – so this gave even greater strength to the deception motive within *Starkey*.*

The planners had done their 'homework' by assessing the dispositions of enemy forces in France and the Low Countries; forecasting the minimum forces remaining in the event of heavy commitments in Russia and the Mediterranean during the summer of 1943; and, of course, estimating the enemy's air effort in the Pas de Calais during August and September. This was the period that the calendar had dictated: it could not be sooner – there was insufficient time – and it could not be later because the weather, critical to air and sea operations, could turn against them. The last two weeks in August and the first two in September were likely to provide the most suitable weather conditions, both for air fighting and for night bombing.[14]

The plan would commence with operations intended to cause maximum disruption and disturbance to the enemy's defence organization in the Pas de Calais, as if preparatory to an assault landing astride Boulogne. Then, if followed through successfully, there would be opportunities for air-to-air fighting culminating in a major battle in the skies above the Channel.[15] At sea, in this final stage between 8 and 14 September, ships large and small would form a threatening armada, the presence of which would by now be obvious to the enemy. Opposing gun batteries would be the target for heavy bombers. However, whether or not the ships were to be crammed with troops was a decision that would have to wait – Lt-Gen. Morgan had left the options open.

It was, as he had told the Chiefs of Staff on 24 May 1943, a plan in which the feint operation could be carried out, 'should the circumstances' be propitious to do so. Circumstances, together with the decisions of his seniors, would determine what would happen now to *Operation Starkey*.

---

* An assessment in the Appreciation for Outline Plan left in no doubt the magnitude of the task facing an Allied invasion force in the summer of 1943. The Pas de Calais coastline was 'the most heavily fortified (particularly in long range and coastal artillery) and the most strongly held sector of the whole coast of France'. No assault against it could be attempted 'without considerable prior bombardment both from the air and from the sea'.[16] However, though the enemy strength would be far too great for the Allies to contemplate an assault, against opposition, with the currently limited resources in battle-trained troops and the landing craft to carry them, such resources *were* viewed as adequate in the event of a prior enemy collapse or withdrawal.

Chapter Two

Safeguard for Civilians

Deception plans were never universally accepted as necessary, desirable or even marginally helpful to the Allied war effort, whatever the intention, whatever the scale. Critics were quick to describe them as play-acting and time-wasting despite, as experience was gained, their value either as diversionary tactics or as tools to mislead.

In the War Office, as the first indications of the extent of Lt-Gen. Morgan's cross-Channel deception operation became known among his fellow red-tabbed senior officers, the comment on file from one brigadier to another drew a comparison with the Dieppe landing in August 1942. He noted that there was a:

> school of thought which considers that Dieppe was a howling success because we were able to bring the GAF [German air force] into the air and shoot down 200 German aircraft at the expense of 100 of our own (plus, of course, 5,000-odd good soldiers).

He concluded, stiffly but understandably, that Dieppe-type operations were considered not to be 'in the general interest'. The equal-ranking colleague responded with the somewhat apprehensive comment: 'I hope, like you, that we shall not have to pay so high a cost to give verisimilitude to a deception plan.'[1]

There was no place in Morgan's plan for losses on any scale simply to give the appearance of truth or reality. It was a plan that would not only receive the highest-ranking approval within the armed forces, but also have top-ranking leadership. From the RAF would come the AOC-in-C of Fighter Command, and from the US 8th Air Force the Commanding General, in collaboration. The naval and military commanders would be the nominees respectively of the C-in-C, Portsmouth, and the C-in-C, Home Forces. The proposal that Fighter Command's chief should control the operation was not unexpected – after all, here was an amphibious feint so designed as to draw the enemy into intensive air fighting with several air battles in prospect, even an 'Armageddon-of-the-Air'. By building up the threat of an imminent large-scale landing in the Pas de Calais area, Morgan reckoned on some fourteen days of fierce aerial combat. This timespan was not just one he had plucked out of the air. He was more formal in his choice of words when presenting the plan to the Chiefs of Staff, but to mount such a threat for any shorter period was a bait that was unlikely to be swallowed; and to maintain the pretence for any longer would, he acknowledged, 'tend to prolong unduly the diversion of the heavy bombing effort'.[2]

He was convinced that the German air force was now in such urgent need of conserving its strength that it would only be brought to battle by the threat of an imminent invasion of the Continent. To give the Allied fighters the greatest advantage, the threat must be mounted against the region which he was proposing, the Pas de Calais, which was so heavily fortified that an operation would require considerable preparatory naval and air action against the defences. To be realistic, he explained, the feint 'must have preparations similar in character though not necessarily in degree'.

Morgan recognized the limitations in resources and in time – this was the reason for a single amphibious feint and not 'at least one', which was the term used in the instructions he was required to follow. Also, though, he knew there was much to be learned in readiness for the real landings the following year, to which he was by now heavily committed.

He noted that in framing these plans he had endeavoured to the utmost, consistent with conveying a reasonably realistic picture to the enemy, to avoid interruption of the training of Army formations that was so urgently necessary if the Allies were to be ready for 1944.

However, there was one opportunity 'to kill two birds with one stone', and this related to the inclusion of large numbers of troops, principally from the Canadian army, for whom *Operation Starkey* would be a valuable practical test.

It was fundamental to the plan that soldiers, vehicles, weapons and supplies should be seen to be massing in coastal regions, ready to go into the landing craft that surely the enemy reconnaissance aircraft could not miss. Here was the means to carry out something that had never been done before, something that would need to be done in reality. With Morgan's deception operation there was the built-in facility to move a 'complete army' from its many scattered bases and concentrate them in forward positions as if poised for cross-Channel operations.[3]

Nevertheless, there were aspects of the overall scheme which were likely to be less well received. For example, there was the provisional estimate of 3,000 day bombing sorties by the Americans and 3,000 at night by the British. Would any planes be left for anything else? There were also the international political consequences to be considered: what would be the reaction of the resistance groups and of the Germans to what they would call an Allied failure to invade France?

The Chiefs of Staff, whose approval of the scheme would be required before it could be implemented, agreed that the general concept seemed sound, although the emphasis on bombing targets related to the Pas de Calais area was questionable. American bombers by day and the British by night were pursuing an agreed and declared policy of attacks against specific categories of objective; allowing first-priority targets a rest would give the enemy valuable breathing space. Better not be too specific too early – that was the view. The air commanders could work out later what division of bombing capability was appropriate in the light of changing circumstances in the progress of *Starkey* from its present form through subsequent stages to its culmination some three months ahead.

As for the political repercussions of a feint, patriot organizations had to be kept in the picture – any premature uprising could be counter-productive – and the enemy must not be allowed to make capital out of any apparent reversal. The Germans would certainly argue that the Allies had intended to land in large numbers and that enemy superiority had forced their return with their tail between their legs. The impact of propaganda of that nature, broadcast around the world, could harm the Allies' credibility enormously. It should not – it must not – happen. On these touchy points Morgan's team was to seek advice from the specialists in the Special Operations Executive (SOE) and the Political Warfare Executive (PWE).

Above all, *Starkey* called for realism – and if any opportunities appeared to be lacking in the paperwork, others reading it were ready to produce further proposals. The assembly ports would be subjected to heavy air attack, it was thought, so why not evacuate the civilian population from adjacent areas? The Chief of Combined Operations, Lord Louis Mountbatten, weighed in too: he suggested that the Royal Marine Heavy Siege Regiment, which operated the 14 inch long-range guns on the south-east coast, should be made available to throw in their effort.

It was on the subject of gun power, as it happened, that Morgan's plan came under early fire itself. He had proposed including battleships to bombard the German coast artillery in the closing stages, to provide a sufficiently convincing and patently effective display of force. At a meeting of the Chiefs of Staff Committee on 8 June 1943, he recalled the fierce air battle that had been brought on by the move of the *Scharnhorst* and *Gneisenau*, two of the Germans' biggest warships, when making their dash up the Channel from Brest. However, the Navy's Chief of Staff, Admiral of the Fleet Sir Dudley Pound, was clearly unhappy about putting his capital ships at risk in such a venture. In measured tones, the minutes of the meeting were to reflect that 'this proposal would require very careful consideration before the employment of battleships in the Channel could be sanctioned'.

There was another top-level group keeping an eye on *Starkey*, and this was the Joint Planning Staff. A week or so after the Chiefs of Staff meeting when doubts were cast about the wisdom of putting the two R-class battleships into the arena, the Joint Planning Staff – having examined Morgan's plan 'as instructed' – made 'one general point' which clarified the base on which the detailed planning of *Starkey* would henceforth proceed. The object of the plan was to:

convince the enemy that a large scale landing in the Pas de Calais area is imminent and to bring the German Air Force to battle. There is no intention of converting *Starkey* into an actual landing if sudden German disintegration appears to be imminent. Entirely separate plans are being made for the possibility of an emergency return to the Continent.

The planning of *Operation Starkey* is accordingly being limited to purely deceptive measures involving no plans for a re-entry into the Continent'.[4]

The declared intent was crystal clear: so far as *Starkey* was concerned, the plan was to be a pure deception – realism without reality and shorn of all motive for re-entering the Continent. The planned landings astride Boulogne, the intended seizure of the ports of Boulogne and Calais, and the onward thrust into Belgium and the prize of Antwerp were thus written-out, disappearing and never again to surface in this or any other form. Planned as a ruse that could be turned to reality, *Starkey* would now be solely a stratagem, a means of deceiving the enemy, a pretence in which the only semblance of truth would be the ships, the planes and the men in whatever quantity was either desirable or available.

The turning point had come. The scale of contribution that the deception operation was said to need came under further scrutiny, and the obvious conclusion was that support was weakening for the plan in its original presentation. It was said that it 'may not be possible' to provide assault-trained troops, and 'we do not consider that these will be necessary'; diverting 'a considerable portion of our heavy bombing effort' would have 'a very serious impact on our strategic bombing plan', and 'we recommend a convincing concentration in the small ports on the south coast rather than grouping shipping at Southampton and in the Thames' . . . 'So much may happen between now and September'. The Joint Planning Staff did concede, however, that the operation 'will be a most valuable and necessary troop-rehearsal' for the full-scale assault the following year.[5]

So *Starkey* was to proceed, and the tone of explanatory communiqués to be released after the event was occupying Col. John H Bevan, who ran the London Controlling Section, an organization set up in Whitehall in October 1941 to plan stratagems to deceive the enemy about Allied operations against the Third Reich and elsewhere. Bevan had in mind taking newspaper editors into the planners' confidence about a fortnight before the 'invasion' to explain that this was a full dress rehearsal, but to insist that no reference should be made until its completion. In a statement then, it would be stressed that all three services actively cooperated, that valuable lessons had been learned, that no attempt had been made to effect a landing and that no such landing had ever been contemplated.[6]

Regarding political repercussions, the PWE and SOE were busy preparing comprehensive plans to counter the risks inherent in the deception operation; the greater the realism, the stronger the incentive for a premature rising by members of the underground. This would be 'most unfortunate' because not only would German reprisals disrupt those subversive organizations but also, when the time came for the real landings in 1944, there would be reluctance on the part of the patriots to support them.[7] There were ways to overcome this risk, of course, notably with the use of leaflets dropped from aircraft and in coded messages sent by radio. Additionally, the PWE and SOE would be considering the effects on the inhabitants of the areas surrounding military targets that would be submitted to intensified bombing.

Even this early on, as Chief of Combined Operations Lord Louis Mountbatten communicated to the Prime Minister on 19 June 1943, *Starkey* was about to involve active participation as well as detailed planning. Arrangements were in hand for gunboats and coastal craft to carry men and equipment to survey the proposed landing sites, particularly to confirm the state of the beaches between Audresselles and Ambleteuse and from the River Brone to Hardelot. A 'future programme of raids' by Combined Ops teams included mounting a number of small-scale reconnaissance raids against less strongly defended localities on the French coast. The immediate object was to capture prisoners and obtain intelligence. These operations were 'planned in consultation with Gen. Morgan and formed an integral part of his deception scheme,' Lord Louis stated.[8]

Sir Dudley Pound's earlier concern about using battleships brought the matter to a head during a meeting of the Chiefs of Staff Committee on 21 June 1943. He was 'strongly opposed' to their use in the Channel; in the normal course of events, ships so valuable and so vulnerable as these would have been employed in confined waters only as a desperate venture. He would use them if necessary in a genuine operation, but 'it was wrong to endanger them merely in support of a feint'.

He took account of the fact that those particular battleships belonged to a class (R-class) which was now obsolescent. However, this would not justify the risks to their crews, nor would it prevent the Germans from claiming a great success if they were sunk, an event which would be hard to explain to the British public. Certainly, Pound would have had in mind the fact that such a loss in home waters would appear even harder to sustain than those earlier in the Far East.

A further unwelcome broadside came in the form of an update on the availability of real and dummy troop-carrying craft. In devising the plan, Morgan considered that the magnitude of the threat was wholly dependent on the presence of an adequate number of landing craft. Now he learned that their numbers 'were not likely to be achieved in full'. By the time this meeting closed, members had opted to hold back, until nearer the time of the actual operation, a decision on two significant factors. They deferred 'the possibility and desirability' of diverting bombing effort from its primary strategic task; and they deferred whether to proceed 'to extremes' by sailing the expedition or committing two battleships. However, there was no deferring the substance of the message that would come through loud and clear on completion of the operation – it should be presented, the Chiefs of Staff agreed, as having been a full dress rehearsal for an invasion of the Continent.[9]

On the directions of the Chiefs of Staff Committee of the British War Cabinet, Gen. Morgan now issued a thirteen-page document with twelve appendices and five maps detailing the background, purpose and implementation stages of *Operation Starkey*.[10] It was addressed to the C-in-Cs within the armed forces who were to be responsible for progressing the operation and to the Americans' commanding general in their European theatre of operations. They were 'to give effect to the plan for *Operation Starkey* as set forth in the annexures'. It was already 26 June 1943, and by the first day in September the largest possible number of landing craft should be in the Channel. Quite deliberately, they were to be visible to the enemy and their existence made known to them as a planned leakage of information.

The appearance of troop-carrying vessels gathering in the British ports facing the Continent would be sufficient, it was expected, to encourage the German air force to mount a series of attacks and thereby provoke the air battles that were a key element in the deception plan. Subsequent phases would provide further opportunities to help demolish the enemy's air strength by means of a combination of air-to-air and air-to-ground assaults. If that failed to work there was the ultimate threat made clear by ordering the ships to set sail.

By mid-July, however, with scarcely more than a month to go before launching the early stages, Morgan was becoming aware that much of the muscle he had intended to put behind *Starkey* was weakening, particularly in respect of sea and air power to be put at his disposal.

He must now assume that no battleships would be available; and although the heavy night bombing could 'probably' be met without prejudicing the air bombardment of Germany, the Americans were firmly opposed to side-stepping their heavy day bombers from the role already intended and agreed for them. The

USAAF was out to destroy German industry; any diversion prejudicing this task was unacceptable. On top of this dilution, Morgan already knew the view of the Chief of Air Staff, Sir Charles Portal, on RAF Bomber Command's contribution. In the tempered phrases of the administrators whose task it was to record for posterity the discussions and the decisions of the formal meetings of the great and the good, 'General Morgan in his plan should not count on a large diversion of the bomber effort'.[11]

Disregarding the eventual extent of this effort, the potential risk to the French people living around the selected military objectives was a subject which was alive among the comparatively few senior officers whose responsibilities required them to know of *Starkey*.

Within Air Ministry and among their RAF colleagues at COSSAC HQ, for example, reference was made to the long-existing ban on bombing targets in, or close to, built-up areas which might result in civilians being killed or injured. It was necessary to ensure 'that the targets selected for the final plan do not contravene any existing orders or alternatively that special authority is obtained for them to be bombed'.[12]

The Director of Bomber Operations noted the next day that:

the precise selection of targets must, of course, be left to the detailed planners at the time. It will be necessary for the COSSAC staff to obtain authority, well before the operation, for the attack of targets in populated areas where there is undue risk of casualties to civilians.

Britain's bombardment policy in respect of British, Allied and neutral territory occupied by the enemy was on file for ease of reference. It was defined in a letter which the Assistant Chief of Air Staff (Policy) addressed to the senior officers in charge of the Army Cooperation, Bomber, Coastal, Fighter, Flying Training, Technical and Maintenance Commands operating from Britain; to those in charge of RAF operations in Northern Ireland, and the Middle East and India Commands; and to those in charge of RAF operations in Aden, Egypt, Iraq, Levant, Malta, West Africa and the Western Desert.[13]

Bombardment was to be confined to military objectives and must be subject to specified general principles:

that the intentional bombardment of civilian populations, as such, was forbidden; that it must be possible to identify the objective; that the attack must be made with reasonable care to avoid undue loss of civilian life in the vicinity of the target; that, if any doubt existed as to the possibility of accurate bombing and if a large error would involve the risk of serious damage to a populated area, no attack was to be made; and that the provisions of Red Cross conventions were to be observed.

Further defined was the term 'military objectives' able to be attacked. Military in its widest sense was to include all armed forces of the enemy. They were stated to be naval auxiliaries, troop transports and military supply ships; military works and fortifications; military establishments and depots, including barracks, camps, billets and naval dockyards (where definitely established as in use or occupation by Axis forces); aerodromes, whether designated military or civil; and stores, dumps and military supplies.

The Assistant Chief of Air Staff's letter, which filled four pages, went on to identify further military objectives, including rail transportation in occupied France, Holland and Belgium, and objectives in the Channel Islands. It also specified the conduct of air warfare against German, Italian and Japanese territory.

The risk to French lives had been raised within the fortnight previous to this letter when, at a meeting of the Chiefs of Staff Committee on 16 October 1942, it was reported that the Foreign Secretary 'considered that the bombing of military and industrial targets in Occupied France would be unlikely to produce grave reactions, provided that it was not unduly costly in civilian lives'.

As for *Starkey*, which was not contemplated until some months after that comment and the subsequent promulgation of the bombardment policy, the Chiefs of Staff would themselves insist that particular steps be taken to safeguard the French population in the ensuing bombing. This was to turn out to be a costly component of the deception operation – an aerial assault that certainly did not have the unqualified support of RAF Bomber Command's chief, Air Chief Marshal Sir Arthur Harris, for whom the entire deception plan was no more than an academic study, 'at best a piece of harmless play-acting'.[14]

While Harris could have been considered correct in his use of the term 'play-acting', as events turned out he was wrong to call the plan 'harmless'. Lives were to be lost – some of his own men among them – and the effect on a French seaside resort, just south of Boulogne, would become catastrophic.

Chapter Three

A Piece of Play-Acting

Top brass was gleaming as never before when Air Marshal Sir Trafford Leigh-Mallory, AOC-in-C, RAF Fighter Command, chaired the first conference dedicated to *Operation Starkey*, which took place at his HQ on 7 July 1943. Gen. Eaker was there – commanding general of the US 8th Air Force; Brig-Gen. Hansell was there – he came from the COSSAC HQ; Admiral Sir Charles Little, C-in-C, Portsmouth, was there – the Navy's top representative; and so was the Army's, Gen. Sir Bernard Paget, General Officer C-in-C, 21st Army Group.[1]

Gen. Morgan was otherwise engaged. He was within a week of forwarding his far-reaching plan for the 1944 landings, centred on 'the Norman beaches about Bayeux', as he put it. He considered this to be the only area that assured 'a reasonable chance of success on 1 May 1944', given the limitations in resources imposed on him.[2]

Heading the 'pecking order' was another general, a lieutenant-general, two major-generals, a brigadier-general and two brigadiers; two admirals and a commodore; two air marshals, two air vice-marshals and an air commodore. Fighter Command's top man was in the chair. His opposite number – 'Bomber' Harris – was missing. He was represented, however, by a wing commander, the only person junior in rank to him in air force blue being a section officer in the Women's Auxiliary Air Force. In other respects, though, she very much had the edge on Harris's wing commander: Section Officer Lady Freeman was no lowly administrator – she was the personal assistant to Fighter Command's AOC-in-C, and to all intents and purposes he was running *Starkey*.

Outlining the objective, Leigh-Mallory insisted that *Starkey* was not a deception plan (to make this fact perfectly clear to all present, 'not' was underlined in the minutes); it was a rehearsal for invasion with the definite object of (1) deceiving the enemy into thinking that invasion was imminent, and (2) inflicting the greatest possible damage on the German Air Force. *Starkey* was an important part of the agreed strategical plan for 1943 and an essential rehearsal for invasion in 1944. Reference to *Starkey* 'as a deception plan must, therefore, be assiduously avoided'.[3]

As the preparations gathered momentum and Harris discovered precisely what the planners intended to be RAF Bomber Command's role in these activities, his anger increased and in a flurry of cypher messages to Air Ministry it became abundantly clear why he had chosen to send only the wing commander to that initial conference.*

---

* The root of this anger is revealed in an exchange of correspondence between Harris and the Chief of Air Staff, Air Chief Marshal Sir Charles Portal, in which it emerges that both Harris and his opposite number with the US 8th Air Force were 'very disturbed' that inevitably *Starkey* would cause a 'fearful diversion' from their joint offensive at 'possibly the most vital stage of the bomber war'. Harris wrote that he realized *Starkey* was 'only a paper plan, still to be blessed by the Chiefs of Staff', but it was 'just the

As soon as he had become aware of the preliminary discussions on *Starkey*, Harris had protested 'strongly and repeatedly' to the Chief of Air Staff against any suggestions to divert the bomber offensive to support this plan, 'which at best is a piece of harmless play-acting'. He received, he said, an assurance that it was 'just possible that the heavy bombers would be used for deception purposes to a small extent', but that this was extremely unlikely and that he, the Chief of Air Staff, would strongly oppose any such diversions when the time came. Furthermore, 'only the most extraordinary combination of unexpected circumstances will result in any substantial diversion of heavy bombers from your present plans'. It was on this understanding, Harris stormed, that he had sent a junior representative to attend, 'for liaison purposes', meetings of the Operational Planning Section at Fighter Command HQ.[4]

Harris referred to possible targets having been suggested at those meetings. Bomber Command's Operational Research Section (ORS) had examined those targets and informed Fighter Command that none was in the least suitable for heavy bombers. He heard nothing further and assumed – in view of the Chief of Air Staff's assurances and the 'obvious unsuitability' of those targets – that Bomber Command would not be called upon to take any active part in the operation.

The examination by Bomber Command's specialists related to planned attacks on specified enemy coastal batteries in the Pas de Calais.[5] Their appreciation of the bombing effort necessary to neutralize those gun positions was based on a number of premises: that Bomber Command's entire force would be used; that the most suitable bombs were 500 and 1,000 pounders; that the average bombing error of the whole force was half a mile; that 75 per cent of bombs despatched would be effectively aimed at the correct target; and that the defences could be considered 'neutralized' when all guns were more or less severely damaged.**

The conclusions must have been none too comforting to those planning *Starkey*. Four of the gun batteries were judged invulnerable to bombing attacks – Wimereux/La Trésorerie, Cap Gris-Nez/Haringzelles, Cap Blanc-Nez/Noires Mottes and Calais/Chalet Beutin – all mounted in turrets within concrete casemates. Around 7 per cent of the defences would be neutralized in one raid by 750 aircraft. Of the more important guns, 14 per cent could be neutralized by suitable arrangement of Aiming Points (APs), but the aggregate percentage neutralization would still remain at 7 per cent. With the exception of those four batteries, the

---

sort of thing an idle Army dotes on and, with nothing more serious to do, they may well – through this paper planning – get a foot in the door and thereafter insist upon going on with it'. Portal considered that it was 'madness to commit ourselves at this stage' to divert bombers from the combined plan prescribed by the Combined Chiefs of Staff when meeting with Roosevelt and Churchill at Casablanca in January 1943. Portal would always 'strongly oppose' the use of heavy bombers for deception purposes 'unless such employment seems to be more profitable to the war in general than carrying on with the combined bomber plan'.[6]

** An agreed statement following discussions between top-ranking members of the RAF and the USAAF, and *Starkey* planners from Norfolk House, reflected the importance of recognizing 'not that the bombardment should be on such a scale as to neutralize the enemy defences but rather to persuade the enemy of our intention to assault'.[7]

complete defensive system would be neutralized, from the material damage point of view, by 11,000 sorties involving 15 full-scale raids. If that was not condemnation enough, there was the sting that came in the tail: the letter signed over Harris's name by Gp Capt. N.W.D. Marwood-Elton insisted that

> the effort involved, a maximum effort on three nights under present tentative arrangements, is quite out of proportion to any results which may be achieved, particularly as in any case three batteries, listed as 'Most Important' will not be affected.

Morgan 'considerably reduced' the original estimate of heavy bomber effort required, reporting to the Chiefs of Staff that the main factor in this reduction was the decision to drop from the plan the proposed bombardment of enemy long-range artillery by the two battleships, assisted by a heavy scale of bombing, both on the nights prior to the naval bombardment and in daylight simultaneous with the naval bombardment. He explained that he would now ask only for a 'reasonably heavy effort' from the RAF's night bombing force. This would be directed against enemy coastal artillery in the Cap Gris-Nez/Boulogne area during the last two nights of the operation, with the object of reducing the effective fire of this artillery against the assault convoy.[8]

He regarded this revised bombing effort as a necessary measure to complete the impression that a large-scale landing was imminent. It meant materially damaging the batteries, knocking out their communications and their living quarters, and making morale suffer. To put figures on his needs in this respect, Morgan gave 'two to three hundred sorties' as his main requirement from Bomber Command, these attacks to be against enemy coastal batteries on both of the last two nights of the operation. As if trying to appease 'Bomber' Harris's wrath to some extent, Morgan noted that the targets were coastal ones requiring no penetration: 'It is suggested that the effort should be met with comparatively little diminution of Bomber Command's main effort.'[9]

Air Ministry had initially advised Harris that the effort to be made available by Bomber Command for *Starkey* was agreed as being up to 50 sorties on any night from 25/26 August to 5/6 September (though any postponement could extend that commitment to the night of 13/14 September), as well as 200 and 300 sorties respectively on coastal targets on the last two nights before the final day of the operation. If there was a decision to postpone the final day after the first of those two bombardments had been launched, it might be necessary to repeat the effort of the first night. Those requirements concluded with a request for Harris 'to confirm your preparedness to participate in the above operation up to the scales of effort mentioned'.[10]

It was that requirement that prompted Harris to launch an attack of his own: an explosion of words and phrases. Following on his 'play-acting' diatribe, he signalled the Vice-Chief of Air Staff that standing-by fifty serviceable aircraft and crews a night for almost three weeks would cause 'a fatal reduction' in his bombing effort, amounting to at least 350 sorties or well over 1,000 tons of bombs, in addition to seriously reducing the concentration over his targets and increasing casualty rates.

As for the commitment on the last two nights, amounting to 200 and 300 sorties respectively and subject to postponement and repetition, this would absorb the entire effort of Bomber Command for a week.[11]

By now the sizzling fuse on his anger was shortening appreciably. There was no hiding his feelings as he went on to protest vehemently against what he called 'this intolerable diversion at the peak of the bomber offensive and during the most vital time of year'. The Berlin raids had just been initiated, and these were now to 'go by the board' in order to allow participation in 'a comparatively futile operation'. He had never personally been consulted by the AOC-in-C Fighter Command on this plan, and Bomber Command didn't even possess AOC-in-C Fighter Command's final plan.

Harris would not let the matter rest. Later that same afternoon he signalled Air Ministry again, as before copying the text of this message to the Chief of Air Staff as well as to the Vice-Chief of Air Staff. As far as Bomber Command was concerned, Harris considered *Starkey* to have been 'an academical study of possibilities for future real operations'. It was 'the more astonishing' to receive a signal on 25 August, dated 24 August, to participate from 25 August. He argued that it was 'a cardinal Service principle of Command' that as a commander involved in a combined plan he should be set a definite task and he decide whether it was feasible; if so, he was the one who should decide what force and method was required to achieve the object in view. It was an entirely new departure that 'while still protesting the impracticability of the targets suggested I should be arbitrarily informed of the number of sorties I am to hold in readiness and employ against targets not yet decided or agreed'. Conducting an operation on such lines was 'merely turning my Command into a Maintenance Unit to supply on demand a number of aircraft to be employed as, and when and how AOC-in-C Fighter Command considers fit and appropriate'. Harris assumed that this was not the intention although it was, he pointed out, the effect of the instructions issued.[12]

When the Chiefs of Staff Committee met on 26 August 1943, the Vice-Chief of Air Staff reported that it was always the intention that the contribution from Bomber Command should not be allowed to prejudice the conduct of the bomber offensive against Germany. The subject had been re-examined and this was now the proposal:

> The effort up to the night of 5/6 September to be provided from Operational Training Unit resources and from the Wellington squadrons which are not suitable for major operations against Germany. If the culminating phase of *Operation Starkey* be postponed, that commitment may extend up to the night of 13/14 September.

> The effort on the penultimate night to be provided from OTU resources and Wellington squadrons up to the limit which the AOC-in-C Bomber Command can find possible at the time.

> The effort on the ultimate night to be provided from OTU resources, Wellington squadrons and Stirling squadrons up to the limit which the AOC-in-C Bomber Command finds possible – not less than 200 sorties.

If the final day of operations be postponed after the first of those two bombardments has been launched, it may be necessary to repeat the effort of the penultimate night.

The AOC-in-C Fighter Command accepted these arrangements, subject to the right to make representations to the Chiefs of Staff for more heavy bomber support should the trend of operations so require.[13]

The Vice-Chief of Air Staff, Air Marshal Sir Douglas Evill, went on to summarize the situation by noting that there were few objectives in the selected area which could be effectively attacked by night bombers. Nevertheless, it was agreed that some night bombing was essential to the success of the operation. Since there were few suitable objectives and a high degree of accuracy was not essential, the effort required during the preliminary period could be provided by the OTUs. Even so, this would leave some 300 sorties to be found from the heavy bomber force during the last two nights.[14]

Subsequently, Air Ministry spelled out the revised requirements in a message to Harris's command HQ, repeated to HQ Fighter Command and COSSAC (Air Branch), and marked for the attention of the AOC-in-Cs, adding that HQ No. 11 Group [the AOC of which was Air Force Commander] would indicate to HQ Bomber Command the target areas to be attacked and the effects that those attacks were required to produce. If the Culminating Phase final day was to be postponed after the first of the two bombardments had been launched, the AOC-in-C Fighter Command would attempt to give 48 hours' notice of that postponement. This substitution of Air Ministry's orders to Harris was 'the result of further examination of the plan'.[15]

Thus the bitter controversy on the heavy bombers' role in *Starkey* ended in the inevitable compromise with COSSAC himself, Gen. Morgan, minuted as having advised the Chiefs of Staff Committee that the revised bombing programme was acceptable, and that he did not think that it would 'materially detract' from the realism of the operation.[16]

But how far was this deception plan to be allowed to go in terms of the risk factor with consequential casualties from the bombing component, even though the extent of the bombing was now considerably weakened from first intentions? It was Sir Douglas Evill who raised the subject among the Chiefs of Staff, first by recalling the continuing restrictions that had been imposed by the War Cabinet in respect of bombing activities over occupied territory, and then by going on record that he would find out whether *Starkey* was likely to conflict with the rules laid down.

No time was lost. The importance of avoiding risk to the civilian population was brought to the attention of the AOC-in-C, Fighter Command, who was running *Starkey*, in an Air Ministry cypher message on 24 August 1943, repeated to COSSAC (Air Branch), RAF Bomber Command and the US 8th Air Force. It called for their confirmation that when conducting *Starkey* bombing operations it was the intention to adhere rigidly to the existing policy governing bombardment of objectives in occupied territories. They were reminded of the documentary source of this policy: Air Ministry letter C.S. 15803/A.S.P.1, dated 29 October 1942 (see Chapter Two). Then there was the clear instruction that if planned operations involved any divergence from that policy, 'you are requested to forward immediately a list of targets for which specific clearance is required, stating in each case the importance of the particular targets and the form of attack to be applied'.[17]

There were precedents familiar to the upper echelons of the USAAF in Britain which had sought clearance earlier in the summer regarding proposed targets in occupied countries. Acting for the Foreign Office, the PWE was involved in radio and leaflet warnings ahead of daylight bombings in France initially, with subsequent action on similar lines in Belgium and Holland, the terms of the warning being agreed in consultation with the respective governments. Leaflet drops over a town did not necessarily indicate an impending raid, but to bomb in advance of an intended paper snowfall was expressly forbidden. Once authorization was given, 'all possible measures' were to be taken to keep 'to an absolute minimum' the risk of casualties to the civilian population consistent with ensuring the effectiveness of the attacks.[18]

With *Starkey*, the outcome of the Air Ministry's action was the compilation and submission of up to eleven lists of main kinds of objective that the planners had already selected as targets for attack during the operation, the sequence of the lists following approximately the proposed phases of the operation. The listings were hand-delivered to Whitehall from Fighter Command HQ at Stanmore, Middlesex, under cover of a Most Secret letter from the AOC-in-C, signed by Air Commodore S C Strafford, who was chairman of the Combined Planning Staff for *Starkey*.[19] For each target there was a serial number, determined by the number of the list, for example 9(A)/37 – 9 because the target was in List 9, and 37 its unique number on that list; a geographical location, in this instance Boulogne/Le Portel; a pinpoint, 49/653525, the first two digits corresponding to the sheet number in War Office map series GSGS 4040, the remaining six digits providing the means to pinpoint the position of the target on that sheet; and lastly a description: 3 x about 21 cm guns in turrets on open concrete platforms with a range of about 35,000 yards. The bracketed letter A in the serial number perpetuated the alphabetical sequence of the Appendices to a GHQ Home Forces letter a month earlier initiating proposed *Starkey* air targets for the consideration of the Combined Planning Staff at RAF Fighter Command – the long range coastal guns forming Appendix A while lesser enemy fire power was grouped as Appendix H, a listing of artillery likely to be able to fire on the beaches. GHQ Home Forces acknowledged the restraints imposed by conflicting requirements when taking that first crack at selecting *Starkey* targets. Specifically, the need to avoid giving away what was already known about enemy dispositions and equipment for fear that this might compromise the real invasion intended the following year; preventing the enemy from learning useful lessons about the efficiency or otherwise of his different types of defences and equipment; and having – in their words – to avoid 'the politically undesirable step of unnecessarily bombing French civilians'. And all this while nonetheless convincing the Germans that *Starkey* was meant as a serious threat.[20] Although the phrase 'politically undesirable' seemed to lack the human touch, those who drafted this document were at least registering early recognition of the prerequisite to safeguard the French population in inevitable aerial attacks during the course of *Starkey*.

The pinpoint in the target lists that Air Commodore Strafford sent forward to Air

Ministry for clearance was a grid reference in line with military custom. Each sheet was squared off with numbered vertical and horizontal lines. The first three digits determined the position on the vertical axis (the 'north–south' line), the last three the position on the horizontal axis (the 'east–west' line). If looking for pinpoint 650512, 650 put the target on the vertical line numbered 65, and 512 put it between the horizontal lines numbered 51 and 52. The third and sixth digits indicated the decimal place, a subdivision of the squares printed on the map. In 650512 the target was two-tenths of the distance northwards from line 51.

War Office maps in the GSGS 4040 series were scaled 1:50,000, so all targets marked in this manner on these maps were individually pinpointed within a 100 metre square. It followed that in *Starkey* the locations of all the gun batteries selected for air attack were map-referenced within an accuracy of 100 metres, precise to, say, 110 yards.

List 1 identified airfields in four main areas (Pas de Calais, Somme/Seine, Le Havre/Caen and Ghent/Antwerp), corresponding to the main areas of attack planned for escorted medium bombers, and all seventeen were given specific clearance.* List 2 identified marshalling yards and canal centres in those same areas plus an 'outer circle' of marshalling yards. Twenty were cleared, but not so one at Arras, one at Namur and an area within the Creil marshalling yards. List 3 identified selected industrial targets. All eleven were cleared – power stations, coke ovens and by-product plant. List 4 identified ammunition dumps. All fifteen were cleared, including one in the Forêt de Raismes, regarded as being among the most important in the whole of France, and one in the Forêt de Mormal. List 5 identified fuel oil stores. Twelve were cleared, including locations in the Forêt d'Hesdin and the Forêt de Mormal, but not so one at Lumbres. List 6 identified military HQ. Twelve were cleared, but there was one exception: an SS Division HQ in Hazebrouck, located in a street near the south-east end of the town. List 7 identified military camps and barracks. Clearance was given for attacks on sixteen of them but refused for two apiece in Lille, St Omer and La Panne.

List 8 identified enemy beach defences in selected localities which were intended to come under attack from RAF light and medium bombers plus USAAF medium bombers in the final phase. Of those listed, five locations were cleared at Plage Ste-Cécile, seven at Mont Duchemin, nine at Hardelot, two at Ecault, three at Equihen, one at Le Touquet, two at Étaples, two at Camiers, three at Dannes, two at Neufchatel, two at St Etienne, one at Boulogne and one at Le Portel. Four more at Boulogne, one more at Le Portel and one more at Le Touquet were cleared only for daytime attack.

List 9 identified coastal and railway artillery for attack by US heavy bombers by day and by RAF heavy bombers by night in the final phase. Some thirty-six locations were cleared. Ten were fixed gun batteries at Calais, Cap Blanc-Nez, Cap Gris-Nez, Boulogne/La Trésorerie and Boulogne/Fort de la Crèche and Sangatte; eleven were railway battery positions at Calais, Cap Gris-Nez and Pointe aux Oies;

---

* In respect of all 200 targets specified on lists 1 to 9, clearance (or otherwise) came from Air Ministry to the AOC-in-C Fighter Command the same day.[21] It was from these lists of objectives that particular targets would be selected for attack during *Starkey*.

and the other fifteen were gun emplacements at Pointe de St Quentin, Fort Mahon, Berck, Plage Ste-Cécile, Hardelot, Equihen, Cap d'Alprech, Mont Soleil, Le Chemin Vert, Le Portel, Moulin Bleu, Marlborough, Marquise and Cap Gris-Nez. Two gun emplacements at Calais, one at Le Touquet and one at Etaples were cleared only for daytime attack. Guns at La Trésorerie, Fort de la Crèche, Pointe aux Oies, Hardelot, Cap d'Alprech and Le Portel were among the thirteen meriting a triple-star annotation as 'Most Important' targets by virtue of their firepower capability against shipping between Dungeness and Le Touquet.

List 10 comprised roads for reconnaissance purposes, rather than listed at this time as targets considered for attack. List 11 was intended to be issued separately, covering objectives on which special attacks might be arranged by the Air Force Commander during the course of the operation. Additional to those lists of prearranged targets would be 'targets of opportunity' arising during *Starkey*, for example troop concentrations, mobile HQ, shipping and airfields brought into emergency use, for which any specific clearance regarded as necessary could be sought at the appropriate time.

Consideration of such targets and the procedures to assure rigid adherence to War Cabinet policy in respect of bombing occupied territories ran concurrently with both the planning and the carrying out of a mixture of activities, significant and less so, obvious and less so, which together made *Starkey* the most comprehensive deception campaign so far undertaken in the Second World War.

Combined Operations had begun its series of small-scale raids in expectation of gaining prisoners and information. Some 14 raids were planned, 8 were put into operation and on 4 occasions troops landed on enemy soil.[22] Success was minimal – some would say non-existent – because only once did the raiders, slipping in from the sea in darkness, see or hear any Germans. During one foray, a party of two officers and eight men failed to penetrate the wire at the clifftop. In another, a group the same size stayed ashore for 20 minutes without finding anyone or provoking any reaction. The contribution to Morgan's deception plan was zero, but no doubt points were scored for trying!

Clandestine operations of another sort were the focus of teams within the PWE and the SOE, which were jointly involved in countering the repercussions of *Starkey* on the patriot armies in Europe and overcoming the effects of the enemy's propaganda in presenting the outcome as a failure by the Allies to invade.

The situation in the occupied countries was such that the deception plan would be unfolding when the expectation of early liberation was the main sustaining factor in the resistance of the population to their oppressors. Anticipation of an Allied landing would heighten the flashpoint expectations of relief on the eve of the most desperate winter of the war, only to bring disappointment when it became obvious that their friends across the Channel would not be coming – at least not for the time being.

So the idea was to broadcast strict orders that members of the underground must 'stay their hand' until receiving from London a direct injunction to rise. Meanwhile there would be leaflets and propaganda to explain that the forthcoming activity was only a rehearsal. This would have the double advantage of misleading the enemy at the time and of maintaining the confidence of the patriots in the accuracy of

London's instructions, and so persuading them to pay strict regard to any future instructions.

The enemy would be looking for underground activity as a natural preliminary of a real invasion, so the PWE and SOE must come up with schemes which would disturb and confuse the enemy without provoking uprisings, or squandering any stratagems or devices needed at the time of the 'real' invasion. Coded phrases would be broadcast in increasing volume, because the enemy would regard this as further proof that this was the prelude to a large-scale landing. The substance of the PWE/SOE message was: Be careful of German persecution . . . be disciplined and discreet . . . maintain order . . . we'll tell you when the time comes for action.

And when the 'landing' was seen not to have happened? People had to be made aware not only that this was a dress rehearsal but also that their negative cooperation and obedience to the injunctions of London had advanced the day of liberation. Also they needed to know that their work, in forcing the Germans to maintain considerable numbers of troops in Europe, continued to play a most useful part in the general dispersion of the enemy forces.[23]

While the proposals from the PWE and SOE appeared practical and acceptable within the framework of *Starkey*, there were two areas of concern which still needed to be addressed. One was the possibility that some resistance groups might take premature action; the other was the possibility that the enemy might be precipitated into taking reprisals, not only against those in the resistance movement but also among the civilian population at large. Notwithstanding, the PWE and SOE considered that the objectives of the deception plan could be pursued 'with every reasonable hope of success' through their combined activities.[24]

Meanwhile, preparations of a more visible nature were taking place throughout south-east England in the countdown to the day that *Starkey* was intended to reach its climax: Wednesday 8 September 1943. The date was 'written in stone' now, unless, of course, circumstances arose that required the plans to be halted, or they go ahead and then something happened that forced a postponement.

Chapter Four

Troops in Transit

Around the global war theatres there was much more happening that summer of 1943 than those behind-the-scenes moves in London to trick the enemy that the Allies were about to take to their landing craft and swarm ashore to do battle in the most jealously defended part of north-west Europe. In the Mediterranean there was a real invasion going on – the island of Sicily was the scene; the Russians were into a new offensive in the Ukraine; Japan was in the process of losing some of its earlier won strongholds; and in the air war against Germany's military, industrial and economic system, 'Bomber' Harris was systematically hammering Hamburg.

The swing of the bombing-offensive pendulum was seen to have reversed dramatically when Air Ministry published a 'balance sheet' showing that whereas the tonnage of bombs dropped by the *Luftwaffe* on Britain decreased in the three years from 1940 to 1943, the tonnage dropped by the RAF on Germany increased. The first- and last-quarter totals revealed a reduction from 18,900 tons by the *Luftwaffe* in the third quarter of 1940 to 700 tons in the second quarter of 1943 compared with the RAF's rise from 2,750 to 36,700 tons.[1]

Apart from *Operation Starkey* of course, the British public knew all of this and took heart from it. The deception plan being unfolded progressively within the armed forces in Britain, with the knowledge of the American leadership (but not, yet, revealed to the Russians), meant that more and more people with a need to know did see a little of the overall picture. As the days and the weeks passed, the preparations gained greater visibility – the movement of landing craft from their production centres and between the ports was intentionally obvious.

Despite the scale of the activities backstage, COSSAC had to accept that no longer could he contemplate the inclusion of battleships, or USAAF heavy bombers other than for 'a number of instructional sorties'. As he told the Chiefs of Staff, it was nevertheless hoped that the operation in its modified form might achieve the result desired. Detailed planning was now in progress and 'the first steps have been taken'.[2]

Signed-off by Air Marshal Sir Trafford Leigh-Mallory at a conference at the COSSAC HQ in London on the afternoon of 22 July 1943, to be issued 'for the information and guidance of authorities concerned', the Combined Plan for *Operation Starkey* called for the force commanders in charge of the land, sea and air activities to draft their operation orders for final coordination and approval by the C-in-Cs. True to form, the document began with succinct statements as to the object, the intention and the plan. D-Day for the culmination of the operation would be 8 September 1943, although weather conditions might necessitate postponement 'to any date up to 14 September [i.e., D plus 6]'.[3]

The object was now defined in the following terms:

to mount a major amphibious operation against the Pas de Calais in such a manner as to convince the enemy that a large scale landing is imminent; and so designed, without actually committing our land forces to an assault, as to compel the German Fighter Force to engage in air battles of attrition at times and places most advantageous to us.

The intention was:

to mount an operation, including the assembly of landing craft, the marshalling of major military formations and the concentration of air forces in an area threatening the Pas de Calais. The threat to be intensified by actual naval and air operations.

The successive phases were then defined, the plan covering all stages of the operation from the date of issue of this document until completion of the operation: reinforcement of fighter squadrons and of anti-aircraft (AA) defences and balloon barrages in the south-eastern counties; a gradually increasing air offensive directed on targets in and related to the Pas de Calais area; concentration and marshalling at points of embarkation of a substantial assault force and the embarkation of some vehicles and AA; assembly of landing craft (including dummies) at ports of departure for the assault; minesweeping operations towards the French coast; and sailing of ships and craft for the assault.

The Prime Minister had been brought into the picture by means of a short account which the Chiefs of Staff put together from material supplied by COSSAC. Churchill was not entirely happy with what he read: 'I cannot feel there is enough substance in this,' he noted in a minute that he initialled [WSC], explaining that, 'even at some inconvenience, a much larger mass of shipping should be assembled'.[4]

A problem emerging when investigating those prospects at an earlier stage was that one of the consequences of withdrawing further coastal shipping would be the effect on the coal position on the south coast. Still, with the Prime Minister now suggesting that Lord Leathers, Minister of War Transport, 'would very likely help' if he was shown that minute, it was worth pursuing again.

Churchill's weight did the trick. Twenty additional ocean-going vessels were released to form a special convoy to assemble in the Solent and sail eastwards in order to be off Beachy Head during the critical period of the operation. Morgan considered that this would materially increase substance to his plan, and this new mini-armada would sail up to the limits of effective enemy artillery fire to simulate the approach of an additional division in the assault force.[5]

Meanwhile, on Britain's airfields, fighter squadrons could be moved around without exciting much attention. Troop movements and the landing craft to await them were a different matter. To preserve secrecy for the intentions of the deception plan, the military involvement was brought together as a training exercise and given a codename of its own: *Harlequin*. There was need for particular caution in the assembly and embarkation areas, when the soldiers began arriving, so that those who were 'in the know' about *Starkey* would remember to stay tight-lipped on the subject. *Starkey* was known to very few military officers, so, if names were used, this was *Exercise Harlequin* and nothing else. The story was that this was an exercise to test the arrangements in the ports for operating large numbers of landing craft.[6]

Some of the craft in position for apparent loading would have proved incapable of receiving either armoured vehicles or assault troops. After initial hiccups in delays from the manufacturers, delivery and erection of these so-called Bigbobs (dummy tank-carriers) and Wetbobs (dummy troop-carriers) was proving satisfactory, though the combination of real craft and lookalikes was falling short of anticipation. The more the better: that was Gen. Morgan's philosophy.

The size of the gathering army could be judged from the preparation made for its arrival in key locations from Portsmouth to Dover: tented camps were to be provided for, or increased to, 11,800 in the Portsmouth area, 11,000 at Southampton, 5,850 at Newhaven, 3,850 at Hastings and 8,190 at Dover – potential accommodation for more than 40,000 in all.[7]

The first landing craft were at Portsmouth, Shoreham and Newhaven; more assembled at Richborough; and then others gathered at Rye and Dover. All leave was stopped for Army personnel taking part in *Exercise Harlequin*, which involved the First Canadian Army moving into deployment areas in the Portsmouth/Southampton sector (as if to embark up to 21,000 personnel and 2,700 vehicles), and the British Second Army in the Dover/Folkestone/Newhaven sector (17,200 personnel with 2,425 vehicles), the troop-carrying craft holding as many as 200 men apiece. Anticipating shot-down pilots 'ditching' in the sea or taking to their parachutes, RAF air-sea rescue units were increased at focal points on or close to the Channel coast, among them Shoreham and Hawkinge. Arrangements were made to reinforce existing balloon barrages at Dover, Portsmouth and Southampton, and to install new ones at Shoreham and Newhaven.

'Second Front' fever increased when abroad the war news was encouraging and at home the general public found increased restrictions in some areas. Mid-August saw the authorities imposing a ban on visitors to some parts of southern England, with notices posted in London railway stations, and hotels and boarding houses in affected resorts having to cancel existing bookings. It was a disruptive move: staff in railway booking offices and travel agencies 'will not be able to answer questions and the issue of a ticket implies no guarantee that a traveller will be allowed to enter his destination'. And this was the height of the summer holiday period! Roads were closed and the carrying of cameras, telescopes and binoculars forbidden without a special permit, all of which hinted at an intensification of military activities. Where entry was curtailed, approval had to be sought from the police for visits for business and family occasions: for example, weddings, funerals, hospital visits and seeing aged near relatives.[8]

In Kent, where the military authorities defined the regulated area apparently without reference to their colleagues in navy blue, the public were left with a grandstand view of assembling vessels. Two large concentrations of landing craft at Richborough and Rye, plus one of the bases for the escort ships, Ramsgate, remained for all to see, sight over them being unhindered through this oversight when restricting the movement of civilians.[9] At one stage, evacuation of the civilian population here and elsewhere was on the cards, to protect them from anticipated enemy bombing and to enhance realism.[10]

From the start, Morgan had demanded realism, and realism he was going to get so long as the resources existed and training was not jeopardized for the 'real thing'. Without delay the armed forces, American as well as British, introduced their own censorship methods covering letters and the monitoring of phone calls. Dover Command personnel, whether seagoing or ashore, came under full postal censorship of all correspondence. This was considered necessary as the crews of coastal and minor landing craft were accommodated together ashore with the base staff, and to censor just some of the letters was regarded as presenting difficulties while achieving nothing. Security of this sort was not confined to those in uniform; instructions went out for snap censorship of civilian mail and there were mobile telephone censorship units at Canterbury and Brighton.[11] Careless talk costs lives.

Communication facilities among the participants in *Starkey* were necessary so that everyone knew what was going on. Equally, communication in certain forms had to be seen to be taking place in order to achieve credibility in the enemy's eyes, or rather in the enemy's ears. Simulation of wireless traffic appropriate to the build-up for large-scale landings was pertinent to give the effect of final training and assembly of a real assault force. The Admiralty's Signal Department recognized that there were two aspects to be taken into account in faking messages across the air waves. Obviously such training and assembly would give rise to a considerable volume of wireless traffic into, out of and within the assembly areas; conversely, the absence of such traffic would immediately make the enemy sceptical of any intelligence that might come their way, even if it did point in the direction of such a build-up.

In conjunction with the Army, practical interservice wireless linkages were established both to draw attention to the presence of supposed HQ and to the toing and froing of landing craft. New wireless telegraphy stations were mocked up until more than fifty of these were in use. Exercise, test and tuning traffic added to the illusion, along with some 1,000 messages that were contrived solely for the purpose of heightening the deception.[12]

There was another component of any invasion plan that the enemy would expect to find as a result of air reconnaissance over Britain during this time. Besides the landing craft to carry troops by sea, the enemy would anticipate seeing glider fleets being assembled ready to transport troops to their objective by air. The deception plan would see to this with the inclusion of arrangements to withdraw gliders from storage until these were visible on the airfields of RAF Fighter and Bomber Commands across eastern and southern England. At least twelve Horsas were to be produced for show on each of three airfields of No. 2 Group, eight of No. 3 Group, five of No. 5 Group and one of No. 92 Group.

In a week that saw the commencement of the Preliminary Phase of *Starkey*, 16 to 24 August 1943, German planes carried out 6 daylight reconnaissance sorties to within 10 miles of the coast: 4 in the Isle of Wight/Portsmouth/Southampton area, 1 to Portland Bill and 1 to Brixham/Exeter/Exmouth. Bombers were busy too with raids on Plymouth, Bournemouth, Portsmouth, East Anglia, the coastal areas of East Kent, South Essex and Sussex, and the area from the Humber to Norfolk.[13]

However, the following week, which saw the deception programme move into the Preparatory Phase, 25 August to 8 September, no enemy air activity was reported which could be put down to *Starkey*.[14]

On the other hand, Allied formations were taking to the air as often as weather conditions would allow. The sorties flown were disappointingly few compared with the planned schedule for the Preliminary Phase (28 attacks in all, all but 7 on airfields), and enemy reaction was on the whole cautious.

Opposition was greatest when the US 8th Air Force's Fortress heavy bombers were employed; and even when they were not, enemy fighters were frequently positioned well to the rear as if to meet a potential threat of deep penetration by heavy bombers. The Air Force Commander's team reckoned that the enemy fighters appeared reluctant to 'mix it' with the bombers' escorts. Nevertheless, the records showed 45 enemy planes destroyed for the loss of 23 Allied aircraft: 6 Fortresses were lost, 4 in an attack on Le Bourget airfield, a target beyond the effective range of fighter escort, and 2 to AA fire; the medium bomber formations, comprising Marauders under escort, lost only 1 of their number to enemy fighters throughout 741 sorties. In the nine days of the Preliminary Phase, 4,518 fighter and fighter-bomber sorties and 1,597 bomber sorties were reportedly flown, a daily average of 680 daytime sorties, with a further 439 by fighters and fighter-bombers at night.[15]

The Preparatory Phase envisaged a considerable increase in the tempo of operations, with attacks concentrated on enemy airfields, certain industrial targets and selected military targets in, and related to, the Pas de Calais area. There were four main areas for these attacks: the Pas de Calais; between the Seine and the Somme; south of the Seine; and southern Holland and Belgium.

Again, unsuitable weather reduced the effort that was both intended and available. Of 42 major operations planned, 14 were cancelled entirely, 11 abandoned and 3 curtailed. It was possible to increase the rate of operations, but the effort fell 'far below' what it would otherwise have been. Bad weather generally placed a 'serious' restriction on the scale of operations which had been planned. As a consequence the Air Plan was frequently adjusted and amended at short notice to take full advantage of those parts of the Continent which promised the best chance of reasonable weather and suitable cloud conditions.[16]

The fifteen days of the Preparatory Phase took *Starkey* right up to the eve of sailing, assuming that the pseudo-assault force would still leave the south and south-east ports and head for France.

In the first period of the Preparatory Phase, covering the ten days from 25 August to 3 September, besides 20 attacks on airfields there were attacks by small forces of bombers led by RAF Pathfinder Force on targets hidden deep within the French forests. As anticipated in the commitment which 'Bomber' Harris accepted, each of those 4 night raids relied on crews from his operational training units – crews completing their period of instruction before qualifying to join the front-line squadrons. The first was on the night of 30 August, when the target was armament and fuel dumps in the Forêt d'Eperlecques; the following night it was an ammunition dump in the Forêt d'Hesdin, when there was a blaze that lasted for 24 hours; and on the nights of 3 and 4 September the targets were ammunition dumps in the Forêt de Mormal and the Forêt de Raismes respectively. A total of 171 aircraft were detailed for these 4 attacks (122 OTU aircraft among them), which constituted a new outlet for the activity of the OTUs whose pupil crews in their Wellington bombers were earmarked to make a further and considerably more substantial contribution to *Starkey*. In the second period of bombing activity within the Preparatory Phase, comprising the five days from 4 to 8 September, the offensive turned away from the ammunition dumps and fuel stores to railway marshalling yards, anti-shipping sorties and saw a return to attacks on airfields. It was a break for Bomber Command before the Culminating Phase of the plan, which had Harris's crews standing by for a knock-out blow against the guns that threatened the amphibious operation.

In the meantime, building up credibility in the Channel, minesweeping was in progress, which drew forth immediate air reconnaissance over Deal/Dover (the first over land since 16 August) and also brought a spirited response from some of the long-range guns on the French coast. On 1 September, heavy and accurate shelling appeared to be directed at the *Hydra*, which was straddled repeatedly with several near misses. This minesweeper was not alone, however – *Hound* and *Ready* both received splinters which fell on their decks when shells exploded close by.

One of the shells targeting *Hydra* came so close that those aboard thought at first that the ship had suffered a direct hit. Two ratings were wounded, the gyro compass was put out of action and other damage was sustained that made it impossible for the vessel to carry on its minesweeping duties. It was decided to return to Dover to effect necessary repairs. *Hydra*'s ordeal was not over, however, for the enemy's firing remained both accurate and persistent, and it was being straddled continually under a hailstorm of shells.

Everyone on board who was in an exposed position stayed flat and under whatever cover was available as protection against the deadly flying splinters. A further two-gun salvo caused further damage, perforating the ship's side, putting the 4 inch gun out of action and destroying the wireless aerial. The enemy had their range 'to a nicety', and staying in that vicinity 'was to court disaster and endanger the town and citizens of Dover'.[17] Prepared to sacrifice itself to avoid increasing such risk to the port, *Hydra* changed course to the Small Downs anchorage to survey the damage and await instructions, which saw her ultimately secured to No. 1 buoy at Sheerness, the ordeal by gunfire happily long since ended.

Hydra was not the only victim during the minesweeping operations. *Qualicum*, one of the attendant ships, which was making a prompt effort to screen the minesweeping flotilla from enemy gunfire, suffered six casualties when one round exploded close astern. A steward was killed, and the captain and two of his officers were among those who were injured. Before this, *Qualicum* began making smoke when the port look-out reported evidence of gunfire coming from the French coast. Within 3 minutes the first salvo arrived, a mile or so short, but the next one exploded immediately astern and shell splinters showered the ship from bow to bow, nose to stern. An inspection indicated that there was no damage below the waterline – fortunate considering the proximity of the shelling, two shells having landed apparently within a few yards of each other, a mere 10 yards astern of *Qualicum*.[18]

Those shells came from the Cap Gris-Nez/Framzelle battery; the ones which straddled *Hydra* and damaged her hull came from Cap Blanc-Nez/Noires Mottes, one of the four in concrete casemates which Harris's specialists described as being invulnerable to bombing attacks; while earlier firing on the minesweepers, in which *Sidmouth* was straddled, was attributed to Boulogne/Fort de la Crèche.

Intelligence reports put the size of the German heavy gun batteries between Calais and Boulogne at 9.1 inch to 16 inch calibre, the range of the 15 and 16 inch guns being 45,000 yards – as much as 26 miles.* Medium coastal batteries were at varying intervals along this coast too: the calibre 6 inch and 8.1 inch, which could reach 26,000 yards – more than 14 miles. Adding to this formidable offensive coastal armoury there were the dual-purpose guns for beach defence and use against aircraft.

In the closing stages of *Starkey*, however, the focus was going to be on specific gun installations: long-range batteries down to beach defence positions, which attracted the interest of the planners because by now their thoughts were crystallized on where to head the assault vessels.

* Guns at Calais, Cap Blanc-Nez and Cap Gris-Nez were all considered capable of bringing effective fire to bear on the English Channel ports of Deal, Dover and Folkestone.[19]

Chapter Five

Good Luck to *Starkey*

Operation Starkey was devised both to deceive the enemy about landings in prospect and to encourage air battles in which they would suffer badly at Allied hands; it was certainly not the intention to put the ships at risk from the gun batteries along the coast from Calais to Le Touquet. The plan required heavy and medium bombers of the British and American air forces to behave as if trying to neutralize those guns. The Germans would expect this to happen if a large-scale landing was to take place, and the Allies had to make this happen in order to safeguard their ships while in the Channel.

However, much had occurred since the plan was first raised. It was not to become a real assault on the Continent: there were no battleships to pound the coastal guns able to fire on whatever ships were mustered to form the pseudo-armada. The biggest of those batteries had been judged invulnerable to air attack, and in any case there were now far fewer bombers available. On top of all this, from the start the weather had weakened the impact of the deception plan, and so far the efforts to stimulate the interest of the enemy fighters were proving disappointing. So, carry on or call it off?

Unfavourable conditions of impenetrable cloud, gusty winds and frequent showers proved to be a double-edged sword: the Allies missed opportunities to attack; the Germans missed opportunities to reconnoitre Britain and thus pick up signs of the landing craft, gliders, men and machines that were gathering as if for the big day. Gen. Morgan had to admit that this was so. He reported to the Chiefs of Staff that the bombing effort was being impeded on account of the weather and that this had also reduced enemy reconnaissance to very small limits, which meant that the Germans had not learned as much about the Allies' activities as the scheme had envisaged. He did not stop there either: it was possible, he conceded, that a further appreciation of the situation 'would lead him to recommend that the operation should be cancelled'.[1]

Morgan's view was that with no clear indication of the assembly of enemy fighters there was no justification for completing the operation. However, it was agreed to wait until the morning of Monday, 6 September 1943 to decide whether or not *Starkey* should continue to its conclusion as planned. By now the minesweeping activities were over, with 'very small' reaction from the enemy; the extent of aerial reconnaissance was disappointing – it had been very much greater ahead of the Dieppe raid; and, Leigh-Mallory opined, perhaps the Germans were taking the view that the Allies were fully committed in the Mediterranean so there were insufficient resources in the UK for invasion.[2]

Not all was 'doom and gloom', however. The Naval and Air commanders were very anxious for *Starkey* to be carried through, if only for the valuable operational experience which would be gained. Also, thought had to be given to the USAAF which, having put a big effort into its bombing operations for *Starkey*, would be very disappointed if the operation were not completed. Additionally, evidence had emerged that the German intelligence service had reported to the General Staff that in its view an operation was about to be launched from the UK, probably against the Channel ports. This welcome news came from the London Controlling Section, through Col. Bevan, who had been asked to make himself available for this particular meeting.[3]

Various options faced the Germans: in the wind could be a raid considerably greater than Dieppe; a series of three or four raids of the Dieppe order; a large-scale bluff; or a foolhardy attempt at a 'semi-invasion' drawing on the small forces available. A COSSAC intelligence team, arguing the inclusion of the last of those four possibilities, reckoned that the enemy would hold the view that, when dealing with the English, one must always be prepared to anticipate both the unexpected and the unsound.[4]

The decision was made: carry on with the final phase and complete according to plan. A message was drafted, agreed and despatched to the Prime Minister, setting out the reasons for this decision 'after careful examination of prospects of success of *Starkey*', that, while German reactions to the preparatory moves in the operation were insignificant, the latest information from 'most secret sources' established about seventy bombers having laid mines off Boulogne the previous night – 'doing so by air indicates considerable anxiety'; that the German secret service considered a cross-Channel operation imminent; that in this last phase it was hoped to gain valuable experience for *Overlord* (the name already chosen for the landings targeted for 1 May 1944); that the Americans were showing much enthusiasm and their medium bombers were putting out maximum effort against the coastal defence batteries; that the most important phase was still to come – concentrating the ships and sailing them; that although bringing on a big air battle was problematical, there was no reason to anticipate the failure to do so; and that even if the Germans failed to react to the culminating phase, 'which we think unlikely', *Starkey* might well be preventing the diversion of their forces towards *Avalanche* (Allied landings near Salerno in southern Italy on 9 September 1943); that abandoning *Starkey* at this stage would give the Germans as good an opportunity to claim an expedition was mounted ending in failure as if going right on with it.

The Chiefs of Staff 'feel strongly' that *Starkey* should proceed as planned and had issued instructions accordingly. The Foreign Secretary had been consulted and, 'balancing military advantages against failure to stage cross-Channel operation', endorsed their action.[5]

The reasons must have satisfied the Prime Minister; he sent back this brief yet rewarding message to them: 'Good luck to *Starkey*'.[6]

In Morgan's original scheme, the projected landing beaches were both north and south of Boulogne. Commensurate with the reductions in scale that followed, the final stage would ignore the area to the north, requiring all attention to be directed to the stretch of coastline to the south of Boulogne, between the port and Le Touquet. This being the focus and the long-range guns at Cap Gris-Nez and northwards therefore removed from the equation, seven battery positions were considered by the Naval Force Commander to be those most likely to engage the assault convoy during its sea passage towards and away from the French coast.[7] There was, of course, no intention to land. The executive order Spectacle would initiate the sailing; Backchat would prompt the retirement, at 0900 hours, unless previously ordered, on the final day of *Starkey*. Backchat would be what the senior officers in charge of the various groups of vessels would be awaiting – the instruction to turnabout 180 degrees without further orders and head home.[8]

The seven battery positions were these:

Three at Pointe aux Oies, north of Wimereux: four 8 inch guns at Pointe aux Oies/Les Garennes, two railway guns at Pointe aux Oies/Les Oies and one railway gun at Pointe aux Oies/Wacquinghen. They occupied rising ground in a 4,000 yard stretch of virtually open countryside running inland due east from the coast below the Pointe aux Oies. To clarify and simplify for those planning and carrying out Allied operations against them, these three batteries were brought together under a single codename: *Millstone.*

Two nearer to Boulogne: the three 15 inch guns at Boulogne/La Trésorerie, inland from Wimereux, on open high ground and known as *Pomeranian* – one of the four that Bomber Command's experts described as invulnerable to air attack; and the four 10 inch guns at Boulogne/Fort de la Crèche, on the clifftop midway between Wimereux and Boulogne, a battery known as *Pumicestone*. Both were outside a built-up area.

Two at Le Portel, the seaside resort 2 miles south of Boulogne. One of the batteries was just to the north of the resort, Fort de Couppes, with three guns of about 21 cm [8 inch] in turrets on open concrete platforms and a range of about 35,000 yards (20 miles). The other was a little further beyond the resort and to the south, Cap d'Alprech, with four guns of about 15 cm [6 inch] in open concrete circular emplacements and a range of about 25,000 yards (14 miles). These two positions had codenames too: Fort de Couppes was known as *Religion*, Cap d'Alprech as *Andante*.

The batteries at Pointe aux Oies were the most northerly of the seven positions, which spanned a stretch of about 8 miles. Pointe aux Oies was some 5 miles from the centre of Boulogne. Cap d'Alprech, the most southerly, was some 3 miles from the centre of Boulogne. All were on list 9, which identified coastal and railway artillery for attack by US heavy bombers by day and by RAF heavy bombers by night. Air Ministry cleared all seven battery positions when the target lists were submitted. All seven carried the triple star annotation, signifying a 'Most Important' target.

In common with other prospective targets, whether or not related to *Starkey*, aerial photography presented comparatively up-to-date pictures from which much intelligence could be deduced. For instance, they offered continuing confirmation of their existence and their purpose, as well as revealing any build-up or reduction in their size and importance. With *Starkey*, for example, when considering *Religion*, planners judging its importance and its location had the benefit of details visible in photographs taken earlier in the year – on 17 January and 18 May. With *Andante* there were similar opportunities as photographs taken on 5 April were on file.[9]

Gun batteries were seldom, if ever, constructed without subsidiary armament. When critical to the enemy's defence organization, as those in the Pas de Calais, guns with this capability would necessarily require some form of defence themselves. It didn't require specialist intelligence skills to reach that conclusion. Built for firing long-range, such armament was neither needed nor able to cope with closer targets if faced with an assault by land or by sea. Besides, the guns and their crews needed protection against attack, particularly from the air, so it was reasonable to expect the presence of smaller, dual-purpose (AA/Coastal Defence) weaponry on the same site or close by, as was the case with the *Religion* and *Andante* installations.

As well as the principal target, therefore, serial number 9(A)/37 on list 9, with its GSGS 4040 grid reference 49/653525, *Religion* included a battery of smaller guns on the identical map reference and, located at Moulin Bleu half a mile northwards, six 8.8 cm dual-purpose guns mounted on the roofs of concrete shelters. With *Andante*, besides target 9(A)/34 (49/650512) there were a further three gun positions in this target grouping. Two were six-gun emplacements at Mont Soleil, the highest open ground in the area, one of them with 8.8 cm dual-purpose guns – guns capable of firing a distance of 10 miles. The third was at a location more than a mile to the south-east, which the planners called Boulogne (S), where there was another six-gun position.* Subsidiary gun positions were on list 8, showing enemy beach defences intended to come under attack from RAF light and medium bombers and US medium bombers in the final phase of *Starkey*. However, Air Ministry made an unusual distinction when clearing two of the locations near Le Portel: the lesser guns with the grid reference identical to that of Fort de Couppes in the *Religion* target grouping and the six-gun position Boulogne (S) in *Andante* 'should be attacked by day only'.[10]

Back in the spring, when *Starkey* was conceived, Gen. Morgan had high hopes that the weather was going to be supportive for the naval and air activities fundamental to the operation's success. In the event, the commanders responsible for running the operation on a day-to-day basis were having to vary their plans daily, even hourly, to cope with changing meteorological conditions.

Despite the setbacks, *Starkey* would proceed. There was the determination to make the most of the remaining opportunities and there was the commitment to Churchill himself which prompted the 'good luck' telegram he sent to the team via the War Cabinet Office. Seizing its chances, with just four days to go before the sailing scheduled for daylight on 8 September, Fighter Command had already taken the thrust of the operation to the very doorstep by carrying out a series of attacks on the docks and shipping in the Boulogne area, the targets including German E-boats which would be expected soon to do battle with the *Starkey* expedition.

---

* At La Tour du Renard, a battery known to the Germans as *Veilchen* (it translates as Violet, following the practice of naming many military installations in this area after flowers).

E-boat flotillas, torpedo boats and mine-laying vessels had been active in that area within the past few days, particularly during darkness, with movement into and out of a number of ports along the Belgian/French coast.[11] A 75-strong force of medium bombers from No. 2 Group of RAF Fighter Command was assembled on the airfields at Dunsfold and Hartford Bridge to attack the one most relevant to the deception operation, Boulogne Harbour, on 4 September. Dropping 100 tons of bombs, those twin-engined Venturas, Mitchells and Bostons enjoyed escort and support from Spitfires and Typhoon fighters which destroyed one FW 190 and damaged another, without loss. Although well-intentioned, these attacks in daylight ranged the breadth of the waterfront towards Wimereux to the north and included Le Portel to the south, causing civilian casualties as well as damage to prespecified objectives. Bomb bursts were seen on and near buildings, by railway tracks in the port areas and among construction activity in open countryside. The same night, in the Channel south of Boulogne, in a skirmish between German naval vessels and HM gunboats, one of the enemy was hit by torpedo and two others were seriously damaged by gunfire. Then, on 6 September, came more attacks on Boulogne Harbour with thirty medium bombers dropping a further 46 tons of high explosives, one Mitchell and one Ventura crash-landing on their return home, the crews safe but the aircraft flak-damaged. As on the previous occasion, an array of enemy vessels was present: R-boats alongside the Quai Chanzy, E-boats in the Avant-Port and some small auxiliaries. Port installations were hit again, but the nine E-boats that were seen two days earlier were no longer present. By departing, they had escaped once more the bombs intended for them. Close on 3,000 sorties were flown that day, and eleven enemy planes were destroyed for the loss of six Allied aircraft.[12]

Still to come was the heaviest effort, largely by night and from Bomber Command, the direction changing so that for the first time the emphasis was to be on the big guns with their field of fire capable of wreaking havoc on the 'invasion' force.

However, the weather continued to put a question mark over the operation. The key day, 8 September, the day fixed for the sailing and the day which therefore triggered the effort against the gun batteries and the beach defences, appeared not to be able to bring the appropriate conditions: for the naval forces, wind of force 3 or less, sea slight and visibility of not less than 3 miles; for the air forces, ideally, a completely clear sky, although clouds up to four-tenths at 5,000/7,000 feet or eight-tenths above 10,000 feet were acceptable. On the forecasters' reckoning, a 24 hour postponement was ordered.[13] The forecasters were optimistic that 9 September would offer conditions suitable from both the naval and the air force points of view, so there was every chance that this would be the only deferment, though the planners were prepared to keep putting off the big day until, but not beyond, 14 September.

With the decision made to proceed with *Starkey*, thoughts among the British and the Americans necessarily turned to acquainting the third of the big powers. At a meeting of the British War Cabinet, when the Chief of Air Staff gave members a briefing on *Starkey* and they took note of the position 'with approval', it was minuted that the Russian Government be informed 'forthwith, in outline, of our intentions in regard to this operation before it took place, in order to avoid any misunderstanding with the Russian Government'.[14] The message went out via the Air Ministry's mission in Moscow, which relayed the purpose of the deception operation and advised not falling for the Germans' anticipated comment about a failed landing.[15]

It was recalled that at the Casablanca Conference (when Churchill and Roosevelt met with their chiefs of staff in January 1943) it had been decided to carry out a deception scheme to pin the enemy in the west and keep alive expectations of large-scale cross-Channel operations in 1943. This feint would come to a head 'in the very near future' – the date of the message to Moscow was 6 September 1943 – and it was hoped to learn valuable lessons for *Operation Overlord*. The Germans would doubtless put out that they had thrown back an attempted invasion, or that, when it came to the point, the Allies could not face the landing. The cypher telegram from Air Ministry concluded by indicating that the Moscow mission 'should tell the Russians of our intentions and warn them against being hoodwinked by German propaganda'.

For Bomber Command crews earmarked for *Starkey*, the final days were particularly tense. Operational training units and some operational squadrons were committed to providing planes for both the penultimate and the ultimate nights, so these aircrew members faced the mental as well as the physical turmoil of an on-off operation on successive nights, 6/7 and 7/8 September. Typically, at Allerton Park near Knaresborough, Yorkshire, where the HQ of No. 6 (Royal Canadian Air Force) Group was situated, instructions had been received by teleprinter from HQ Bomber Command on 6 September to provide ten aircraft that evening to attack 'a special target' in north-western France. Accordingly, ten Wellingtons and their crews were detailed from one of the squadrons, only to find that the operation was subsequently cancelled. It was the same the next day with planes and crews detailed and the operation called off.[16] Typically, too, No. 82 Operational Training Unit, based at Ossington, Nottinghamshire, received its orders via No. 93 Group HQ on 6 September to have four aircraft and crews ready that evening to carry out what was described as 'a special operation'. At 1800 hours it was cancelled, while the crews were assembled for briefing. The following day the same operation was ordered, this time with an additional aircraft and crew detailed, and again there came the cancellation – at 1800 hours, just as on the previous evening.[17] On both days there were showers and a cloud base as low as 3,000 feet, so the decisions to 'scrub' the operation were not entirely surprising to these pupil crews.

On each occasion there was a pre-operation routine to follow, with planes to be inspected and flight tested, and the supplies of fuel and armaments to be brought out of store – the bombs that were to be dropped and belts of machine-gun bullets to be fired should the need for defensive action arise. As it happened, Bomber Command units with other 'targets for tonight' on the first of those two nights were able to escape any cancellation. Deeper into the Continent the weather was less restrictive on their operations. Formations comprising 257 Lancasters and 147 Halifaxes were detailed for a raid on Munich in which all but 29 attacked their primary target with a total of 579.8 tons of bombs.

A signal from HQ No. 11 Group to the main participants on the afternoon of 8 September confirmed the *Starkey* 'D-Day' for the next day, Thursday 9

September 1943.[18] Thus there was no 'penultimate night' opportunity to soften up the coastal artillery ahead of the pseudo-landings. Thanks to bad weather, therefore, Harris's squadrons had not been obliged to honour their commitment for the first of the two *Starkey* nights and their potential targets were spared. In tandem with a major attack planned against Berlin, Bomber Command undertook to supply 250 sorties for what was now the ultimate night (8 September) before the ships were to sail. Arguably, Harris was being over-generous: *Starkey* called for this night's effort to come from OTU resources, Wellington squadrons and Stirling squadrons 'up to the limit which the AOC-in-C Bomber Command finds possible and not less than 200 sorties'. He was offering 250 sorties: 250 planes, twin-engined Wellingtons and four-engined Stirlings in the main, each of these bombers to make one 'sortie' (a single flight) against the big guns south of Boulogne.

Precisely which of those tempting targets would be chosen so as to make the most of the available resources became the prerogative of the service commanders who, between them, would make the decision.

The seven long-range batteries from Pointe aux Oies, north of Boulogne, down to Cap d'Alprech were considered by the Naval Force Commander to be those 'most likely' to engage the assault convoy during its sea passage to and from the French coast during the daylight hours of 9 September. The service commanders agreed that the effort should be concentrated on those positions. Of the seven, *Religion* (Fort de Couppes, north of Le Portel) and *Andante* (Cap d'Alprech, south of Le Portel) were considered to be 'the most dangerous'. Accordingly, Bomber Command was requested 'to put their entire allocated night effort on to the area bombing of these targets'.[19]

The other five long-range batteries – the 8 inch guns and railway guns at Pointe aux Oies (*Millstone*), the 15 inch guns at La Trésorerie (*Pomeranian*) and the 10 inch guns at Fort de la Crèche (*Pumicestone*) – would be bombed in daylight by medium bombers. *Religion* and *Andante* would be bombed in daylight by medium bombers too, as well as being the targets for night attack by heavy bombers on 8 September, the eve of the sailing. As events would show, the effect of this target selection by the upper echelon of *Starkey* commanders would have far-reaching consequences on the town and people of Le Portel. For this was the civilian cluster closest to the most critical, the most threatening of all seven gun positions that, in the force commanders' eyes, challenged the very presence of the assault vessels now visibly gathering in sheltered home waters.

Thus the stage was set for the Culminating Phase of *Starkey*. The troops were assembled, though not for embarkation; vehicles and AA guns were ready to go on board waiting craft, with the necessary manpower which included gun crews from AA Command brigades and RAF Regiment squadrons; there was a sizeable force of ships about to get under steam – twenty more than expected, thanks to Churchill's intervention; the warships to protect them were under orders; and there was plenty to occupy the air forces, with escort duties, holding up a defensive aerial umbrella for the armada, ground strafing and bombing on their strict timetable.

How would it go though, this so-real threat against the men and machines in occupation across the Channel? Time would tell – and that time had almost come.

PART TWO

Decimation

Chapter Six

The Early Days

As *Operation Starkey* entered its final phase, air attacks on Le Portel caused a greater number of deaths in a single day than had occurred in total throughout three years and four months of German occupation. That said, the toll was mercifully small. Given the proximity of this seaside resort to the important port of Boulogne, the civilian casualties that Le Portel suffered in this manner between 25 May 1940 and 4 September 1943 were so slight as to be insignificant overall for northern France.

Some six dead, seven hurt and fifteen homes destroyed was the total during that period;[1] adding the seven who lost their lives on Saturday 4 September 1943 was sufficient to more than double the death toll to date from aerial bombardment. These seven, together with a further six townspeople injured that day, fell victim to high explosives loosed by RAF planes whose targets were the E-boat shelters in the Bassin Loubet and port installations elsewhere in the harbour area of Boulogne.[2] As a *Starkey* operation it was all part of the scene-setting activities intended to make the Germans think that the Allies were coming – and coming soon.

At that stage, of course, the people of northern France generally and Le Portel particularly had no reason to suppose that the focus of war was in the process of moving to this coastal area; no reason, naturally, to imagine that when the weather was favourable, heading in their direction would be waves of heavy bombers by night and waves of medium bombers with fighter escort by day. This unexpected onslaught by American-built twin-engined medium bombers of RAF Fighter Command gave away nothing to those on the ground. Protected by Spitfire and Typhoon fighters, formations of 19 Bostons, 18 Mitchells and 15 Venturas, followed in the early evening by a further 16 Mitchells, carried out separate attacks, dropping 100 tons of high explosives, none of which caused any harm to the E-boats. The Bostons came from RAF Station Hartford Bridge in Hampshire (No. 88 Squadron and No. 107 Squadron, whose R-Roger carried an all-USAAF crew), as did the Venturas (No. 21 Squadron), while the Mitchells that figured in both attacks (Nos 98 and 180 Squadrons jointly on both occasions) were from RAF Station Dunsfold in Surrey. The first attack at 1422 hours produced burning offshore and immediately west of the railway, those fires still being in evidence during the next attack some 4 hours later, at 1832 hours. The fighters, providing escort and support for these raids in a proportion of between two and three fighters for each bomber, claimed to have destroyed one FW 190 and damaged another in the day's activities, without loss.[3] Anti-aircraft fire was intense in the target area, particularly in the evening when it took the form of a barrage with coloured marker bursts[4], sufficient to require the bombers to take violent evasive action and to hole several of them with shell splinters.

Alerted by AA fire coming from the batteries at Mont Soleil and the sound of bombing comparatively close by, the people of Le Portel stayed in their shelters until it seemed safe to resume everyday life. Many, curious to see the effect on their neighbourhood, took to the streets that warm summer afternoon to enquire about relatives and friends, and to view any damaged property in their vicinity. For most, the news was good – people unharmed, homes untouched. For a few, though, there was the immediacy of personal tragedy to be borne. Le Portel, it appeared, took the brunt of the civilian casualties in a series of wave attacks that day which burned out one ship and damaged some others. As an operation of war the achievements were neither rewarding nor spectacular, but for those on the receiving end this was like lighting the touchpaper to human tragedy, like crossing the threshold to destruction and lasting grief.

The people of Le Portel – the Portelois, for this is the collective noun in the French tongue – know how to carry their grief. Originally a hamlet administered by Boulogne's neighbour to the south, Outreau, Le Portel existed at least as far back as the fourteenth century. It is in a region where fishing has been the dominant occupation for even longer, with much rivalry down the centuries between the fisherfolk of Le Portel and those of Boulogne. On occasion, however, both communities have had to share their grief when faced with disasters of one sort or another.[5]

One of the earliest recorded was a huge fire in Le Portel on 19 April 1755, which destroyed twenty-eight houses and with them much of the 'tools of the trade' of the fishermen occupants. The people of Boulogne rallied round, as did those of far-off Calais, to help the Portelois in the coming mackerel season. Cholera was next to take its toll, wiping out 462 Portelois, split 'straight down the middle' between male and female, in a series of epidemics. These occurred in the years of 1832 (lasting six months, this was the longest), 1849 (with 138 victims, about one in five of the population, the worst), 1854, 1866 and 1892.

Tragedy at sea also punctuates the history books. Franciscan priest Père Césaire Duval recorded just how much this community had suffered at the hands of the cruel sea: 54 lost in the first half of the nineteenth century, 162 in the second half and 111 between 1900 and the outbreak of the Second World War. A number of these were multiple tragedies. For example, as many as 16 on the *Bon Pasteur* alone on 14 October 1881, a day on which a total of 71 fishermen from Le Portel (and a further 44 from Boulogne) failed to return home. The storm that took this appalling toll left 96 orphans in Le Portel alone. It was a marine catastrophe without equal, before or since.

Hardly a year passed without the town mourning one or more fishermen lost to the perils of the sea: 12 in separate incidents over a period of nine days as recently as January 1937. The war years saw fishing continuing, as did the losses. Père Césaire's list, which he acknowledged as unlikely to be complete, includes 5 Portelois lost aboard the *Seigneur conduisez-nous* on 30 January 1943, in the last winter prior to *Operation Starkey*. In a sense, all were tragedies within the same family. In some cases this was literally so; in every case, beyond all doubt, this was communal grief that was felt within the wider family of the Portelois.

In England, country houses love to boast that 'Queen Elizabeth slept here'; in France, Napoleon's movements are similarly revered, and Le Portel is not without its fond memories of him. It was he who ordered the construction of the familiar Fort de l'Heurt.* It stands on rocks that remain from a former promontory close to the shore, the name being an eventual contraction from d'Heustrière (Oyster Island). Napoleon had this twelve-cannon fort with forty to fifty men started in 1803, fearing that the English were coming. It stood there, part of what the English called 'Côte de fer' (literally the Iron Coast), ready to repel any invading forces, in conjunction with other batteries between Ambleteuse to the north and Ningles to the south. Among those defensive positions were coastal emplacements at Mont de Couppes and Cap d'Alprech, north and south of Le Portel respectively, whose successor firepower would threaten the *Starkey* 'invaders' 140 years on.

There are other links with Napoleon.[6] In the cemetery at Le Portel is a tomb commemorating a recipient of the Cross of the Legion of Honour, presented to him by Napoleon when he held a mass investiture in 1804 on a campsite just outside Boulogne. In the following year, visiting Fort de l'Heurt in doubtful weather conditions, Napoleon suffered the indignity of being tipped into the water along with others in his entourage. Soaked, he made his uncertain way ashore where he was pleased to accept the hospitality (and the best clothes) of a resident of Le Portel. The story goes that this saviour's descendants thoughtfully preserved, most carefully, the very cup from which Napoleon drank what he graciously called an 'excellent' coffee.

In his *Histoire du Portel et des Portelois*, André Verley recounted yet another anecdote about Napoleon. It appears that when visiting the Boulogne campsite in 1804, a Le Portel resident named Marianne Renard told him that her home suffered in a bombardment by the English and, 'as you are the cause of it', it was Napoleon who had to pay for the damage.

He asked how much it cost to put it right, learned that it was 1,500 francs and promised the sum to the lady. But she demanded to know who was going to give her the money. Napoleon indicated one of his marshals and told the lady to return in the evening to receive the 1,500 francs, which is exactly what happened!

Père Césaire,[7] besides assembling the facts and figures of tragedies befalling the Portelois at sea, even documented that particular bombardment. In voluminous files built up so meticulously over the years in his own hand or using a typewriter, he had the date 23 August 1803 recorded for this incident. He referred to three victims

---

* The *Association de Sauvegarde de Fort de l'Heurt* actively seeks to sustain public interest in this landmark. It welcomes new members within and beyond Le Portel, produces an annual bulletin for them and from time to time updates its illustrated history of the fort, offered free to tourists.

petitioning the *Sous-Préfet* with a claim for damage to their property. Marianne Renard would seem to have been one of the first three casualties of English high explosives unleashed against the town of Le Portel, the inhabitants on this occasion being regarded as the enemy and therefore 'fair game'.

Of course Le Portel was hardly a town in those days; it was no more than a hamlet within Outreau, though its population of less than 1,800 was nevertheless just over half that of Outreau (which also included Capécure and Equihen), and it covered 253 hectares (about 625 acres). Soon there would be murmurings that it was high time that Le Portel was given its 'independence', set free from Outreau to become a self-administering community in its own right. It nearly happened early in the 1840s, but Outreau's governing body put its feet down firmly and managed to win the day, after Le Portel's plea had gone 'through channels' and surfaced with no lesser a government dignitary than the Minister of the Interior.[8]

Refusing to give in, the Portelois battled on into the next decade, when a deputation staged a peaceful demonstration and halted Emperor Napoleon III on a visit to the region. He was going to see construction work at Equihen. A petition with 204 signatures was handed to him, asking for Le Portel to be granted its independence, and once again the matter came before the Minister of the Interior. Outreau's opposition was overruled on this occasion, and on 13 June 1856 Le Portel became self-governing with Gabriel Fourcroy its first mayor, a position he held for fourteen years. Later, encouraged by his many friends, Monsieur Fourcroy accepted a regional office, though he returned to Le Portel in the closing years of his life. He died on New Year's Eve in the year 1905, remembered still, for, like de Gaulle, Foch, Leclerc and others, a street was named after him.

In the latter years of the nineteenth century, Le Portel began to blossom as a seaside resort and its picturesque setting attracted celebrities from Paris. The late 1890s saw the number of bathers increasing and almost doubling year on year. There was talk of Le Portel becoming 'L'English Boulogne', with plans to build a major hotel, private accommodation facing the sea and facilities for tennis, football and even cricket. Alas, with finance hard to come by and the development of Le Touquet forging ahead, Le Portel didn't quite make it – either as an English Boulogne or even as a French Riviera.

In the First World War, Le Portel escaped aerial bombardment until the final year, when the early weeks saw one comparatively harmless – and certainly amusing – incident on 25 January, and another, though unfortunately more serious, on 23 March. In the first, one of a number of bombs hit the town hall, penetrating the roof and coming to rest on the mayor's chair. His worship was away from his office at the time, and in any case the bomb failed to explode. It was a different story in the second incident, with a woman in her mid-thirties and her two children, one aged four and the other just seven months old, losing their lives in this bombing.[9]

Between the wars, along with hotel development to support efforts to bring more visitors to the region, there were even plans for an aerodrome – not just a landing strip but also with plenty of space for a well equipped airport worthy of this district. The idea was sound: to create important new communications opportunities in the Boulogne area and, with those facilities sited at Le Portel, further improve the amenities in this popular resort.

Although the concept was aired as far back as the late 1920s, government approval for the project came only in the autumn of 1931 with the go-ahead for construction to begin.[10] Like many ambitious building schemes, however, there would be a world of difference between the powers-that-be signifying their agreement and those with control of the purse strings obtaining the signatures necessary to assure funding.

Some two-and-a-half years elapsed before sufficient backing became available, and a further period, twice as long this time, elapsed before the big day came for the formal opening of what was to be known as the Boulogne-Alprech airport. The subsidiary part of its name came from Cap d'Alprech, this being its location on a 'greenfield' site within the civic boundaries of Le Portel. All was ready that last weekend of July 1939, with everyone doing their best to ignore the war clouds that were gathering across Europe, to invite people and planes for a showpiece opening ceremony. It had been quite long enough in embryo.

Boulogne's flying club soared into action to make this a day to remember. Invitations winged their way to colleagues in clubs near and far: as near as those at Saint Omer and Dunkirk; as far as Le Bourget in Paris, and clubs in Belgium, Holland and England. There were invitations, too, to civil and military organizations internationally to bring representative aircraft to the new airport. Imperial Airways was among them, with a proposal that this was surely an occasion to welcome some of that company's biggest and finest passenger planes (no doubt the unspoken motive being to try to set up a cross-Channel service of mutual benefit for communications and trade between the two countries).

The precise number of planes that turned out for the grand opening of Boulogne-Alprech airport seems not to have been recorded, though the estimates ranged from more than 80 to about 100. In the event, participants, spectators and particularly observers from the press were to have their attention diverted from such statistics as their eyes turned to the skies to watch a thrilling aerobatics display.

A number of military units had agreed to take part in the inauguration, one of them being a French naval air squadron whose aircraft were to perform team manoeuvres. These began faultlessly, their airborne antics delighting the crowd, but moments later one of the planes found itself far too low to recover properly from its aerobatics. Intent on avoiding spectators at all costs, it struck the ground in an area set aside for vehicles, fortunately without causing injury to others. Inevitably, in a crash as severe as this one, the pilot, aged twenty-seven and a father of two children, lost his life. The tragedy took a while to sink in: some of the planes which were airborne continued with their displays, and one of them, high-flying and steady as a rock, dropped a parachutist as scheduled. On the ground, however, the authorities ordered the crowds to disperse, and that was the end of the inauguration programme.

The euphoria having been dissipated by the shock accident on the very day that was meant to be a glorious climax to so many years of waiting, Boulogne-Alprech airport was destined to make little impact in the few weeks that remained to the start of the Second World War. The armed forces had their eyes on these brand new facilities, and with war declared it became a French naval air base, only to fall an early victim to the *Luftwaffe* on that fateful day, 10 May 1940.

A pair of low-flying planes with the distinctive identification marks of the German air force approached and overflew Le Portel. One dropped a high-explosive bomb, which burst in the middle of the roadway in rue Gilles, and incendiary bombs, which set fire to buildings between rue Saint-Michel and rue du Pont-Hamel. With the airport in their vision and presumably following their original orders, both planes carried on to Boulogne-Alprech and turned their attention to the French warplanes. Some were tanked-up for take-off and others were being made ready in their hanger. Their job done, the dozen or so planes and the buildings left burning, the enemy bombers headed for home. Visibly, the war had come to Le Portel.

This attack on Boulogne-Alprech airport coincided with the Germans invading Holland, Belgium and Luxembourg, the main armoured thrust being through the Ardennes. It was a prompt, if one was needed, that this was 'decision time' among the people of Le Portel, which had a pre-war population of about 8,500.[11] Well aware that the Germans' sights were clearly set on occupying the whole of north-west Europe, fisherfolk families with access to boats capable of crossing to England had already begun weighing up the possibilities of leaving ahead of the invading forces. Unpleasant experiences inflicted by the Germans on the French in overrun territory in the First World War were remembered – and abhorred.[12]

These were decisions that could not be taken lightly. If not everyone could go, what would happen to family members staying behind? If the cross-Channel journey was undertaken, what would be the risk – from conditions at sea and from enemy action? And what about when the fleeing fisherfolk arrived in England – would the respite merely be temporary with the Germans overrunning Britain too?

The distant shores of England were not the only haven to tempt the worried Portelois. Getting away somewhere, anywhere, was the objective for those with their minds made up. Brittany was also a prospect because this was a fishing area too. They just wanted to get away, anywhere, before the Germans came goose-stepping down rue Carnot.

Surprise and concern were the governing factors: surprise that the enemy was advancing so rapidly; concern that atrocities and reprisals committed during the First World War would be repeated. Conditions worsened and fears increased as the Germans swept towards and along the coast, a pincer enclosing the retreating British Army. At 0800 hours on the morning of 25 May 1940, the blood-red and black flag bearing the swastika was unfurled from the belfry in the high town at Boulogne.[13] Most of France remained free, but this part had fallen, a valuable prize, its population now well and truly 'under the jackboot'.

By then, in increasing numbers, those residents of Le Portel who had made the choice to leave had seized their opportunity and taken to the boats.[14] For example, the *Saint-Joseph* carried 200 refugees and the *Sainte-Rosalie* another 60, and sailed together under cover of darkness, one towing the other (which lacked vital parts), with the sounds of gunfire ringing in the ears of their passengers and crew. Hit by shells from a British AA position at the harbour entrance when caught in the beam of a searchlight, a Ju 52 transport plane came down close to the smaller vessel and burned fiercely for several minutes. The situation became aggravated when the plane's fuel tanks ignited, the wind forcing the flames and the intense heat nearer and nearer to the tiny boat while it struggled desperately to pull away from the threat of being engulfed in the conflagration. It must have seemed like the end for the helpless refugees, for at one time the menacing wall of flame raged 60 feet high.

Although both vessels made it together to Ouistreham in Normandy, their fuel almost gone, neither was able to achieve a Channel crossing. The *Sainte-Rosalie* tied up in the Caen Canal, at the end of its voyage, while the *Saint-Joseph* (damaged when a mine blew up in the harbour at Cherbourg) sprang a leak mid-Channel, passengers and crew being rescued by a ship from Brittany which put everyone ashore at Belle Isle.

By now, ahead of occupation, Le Portel had suffered its first casualties: a youth of seventeen and a man in his sixties were killed in rue Carnot on 21 May, with six more killed in other parts of the town over the next four days, their ages ranging from fifteen to seventy-five, all of these deaths the result of bombing or shelling.[15] The exodus beginning in earnest, others left their homes by rail and by road, heading for the south, many indeed making for Brittany, either as a staging post or as their ultimate destination. Their flight was largely in the expectation that there would be the chance to delay their confrontation with the advancing troops, a number of them seeking refuge as far away as La Rochelle and even Bordeaux. Once there, the alternatives increased: besides choosing between staying put in their new locations or trying to get to England, there was now another prospect facing them, which was to see how things were going and maybe consider returning to Le Portel – soon to be designated an entry-regulated area (the '*zone rouge*') – and a future beyond anyone's comprehension.

Every possible means of transport was brought into play in the evacuation: cars, lorries, trucks, horse-drawn vehicles, motorbikes and pushbikes. Everyone, it seemed, wanted to go. Many, anxious to quit, couldn't do so: there were the sick to be looked after, as well as the elderly who had not the strength to try, and there were those without transport who were incapable of attempting many miles on foot. Journeys that began in hope often ended in desperation. Military roadblocks and highways choked by traffic forced some to turn back. Others had a rethink on their original intentions and chose to retrace their steps.

Whatever the reason for returning, this journey was liable to turn into a nightmare beneath the frightful screaming sirens of the dive-bombing Ju 87s, and the roar of explosions from a mixture of bombs from passing aircraft and shells from distant guns. Even then, once back home, what fresh horrors were in store? It was a life that the British, except for those in the soon-to-be-occupied Channel Islands, would fortunately escape.

Chapter Seven

Le Portel – the Fatal Flaw

In the period between the occupation of the Boulogne region and the surrender of the French nation, families from Le Portel which had already chosen to leave their homes were caught in the uncertainty of not knowing whether they should stay where they were, move on if the chance came or return.

It was a dilemma facing many Portelois who were now in temporary homes on the Brittany coast, among them families which had left Boulogne aboard the *Sauveur du Monde* on the afternoon of 21 May.[1] Carrying just over 100 people, many of them Portelois, the vessel had made its way towards Dieppe, which proved to be under bombardment, and so then continued to Fécamp for the night. At Granville, with the families sleeping on shore, the *Sauveur du Monde* was requisitioned in readiness for the evacuation of the British forces beleaguered at Dunkirk, a rescue operation in which a number of Le Portel vessels would be taking part.

With the arrival of the Germans, this boat returned to Granville, picked up some of its original passengers and carried on to Paimpol, from where it crossed to Newlyn, Cornwall, on 18 June. It made the voyage in the company of another boat, then a few miles along the coast, the *Notre Dame de Montligeon*.[2] Slipping away beneath the noses of the occupying forces, together they carried about sixty people to freedom. For those on the *Montligeon* it had been particularly eventful, the passengers being woken by an urgent knocking on their door ashore around midnight. Those wanting to risk it to England had to hurry because there was no time to be lost – the boat was waiting. Down at the sea there was initial anxiety because the only transportation seemed to be a lifeboat, and no way would it cross the Channel with all those people!

In fact, this was not a problem – this was merely the means to reach the bigger vessel waiting offshore. As silently as possible the *Montligeon* began its journey, its refugees spanning a remarkable extreme of ages, from a baby whose first sights and sounds were Cherbourg Harbour under bombardment, to a grandmother aged eighty-five. Problems related to age – all problems, come to that – vanished as the people of England opened their doors and welcomed new-found friends.

Another refugee ship was *l'Espérance*,[3] which made the journey to Newlyn via Roscoff with more Portelois families on board. It too left Le Portel on 21 May and resumed the journey when night fell on 26 May, reaching England the following afternoon. The closing stages of this final leg were completed in real style: the ship was given an escort of two Royal Navy destroyers and watched over from the air by a Sunderland flying boat and even some RAF fighters, their appearance always a comforting sight as they twisted and turned in the sky.

In the Dunkirk evacuation, which saw the survivors of the British expeditionary force and their brothers-in-arms in the uniforms of other national armies plucked off the beaches to live to fight another day, the trawler *La P'tite Marie* was one of the heroines.[4] It had sailed out of Boulogne on 21 May, heading for Cherbourg, where it joined a convoy of a dozen similar ships, ten of which failed to make it – sunk under merciless German attack. In the drama of 'The Little Ships', *La P'tite Marie* was never far from the action, scuttling to and fro between the cross-Channel ports and picking up even more soldiers out of the sea on the way to England. Battle-scarred but still afloat, unlike others less fortunate which had gone to do their bit in this memorable evacuation, the brave *P'tite Marie* stayed in France. The number of ships and crews from the Boulogne area lost in this operation was impossible to document with any real hope of being an accurate reckoning.

Certainly the *Denis Papin* and the *Vénus* were among them, victims of a daylight attack by German bombers when in the company of the *Briand* and the *Moussaillon*, the latter having already carried out two rescue trips with more than 200 Allied soldiers on each occasion. Hauling the survivors of the *Denis Papin* and the *Vénus* on board, the *Moussaillon* succumbed itself in a follow-up attack and sank within seconds of the captain's order to abandon the stricken ship. Beneath machine-gun fire, the rescuers were in turn rescued, completing the journey to England on an English boat. One crew member was lost and two others injured.

Daily life contrasted sharply between those who evacuated Le Portel and those who remained during the occupation. Those who settled in London were there for much of the Blitz, yet those who stayed saw little of the horrors of intense aerial attack for more than three years. Food rationing was the norm on both sides of the Channel. So was the 'call-up' for young men and women, though if you were in Le Portel it was to do forced labour for the Germans instead of the forces or the factories for those living in England.

Marie-Jo Duval, who was a child refugee aboard the *Notre Dame de Montligeon*, which crossed from Paimpol to Newlyn, spent the first six months in Tottenham, north London, before moving to the south Devon port of Brixham.[5] She reckoned that the Blitz was less frightening to the children than it was to adults, but nonetheless it was a relief to be out of the capital and into 'an enchanting region' which was similar in many respects to the small seaside town she had left with her mother and others in her family. Marie-Jo's father was not among them; he was serving at sea and many months elapsed before, by chance, the family learned that he was safe and sound in England. By one of those strange coincidences, a relative, familiar with the appearance of his ship, surprisingly saw it riding at anchor at Devonport, as he was glancing out of a railway carriage while going up to London!

Joining new classmates in the garden of her Devon school, Marie-Jo was first introduced to the English language by means of translations of the names of flowers and plants. Each was identified by a card bearing the English subtitle – daffodil, for *la jonquille*, being the first flower she came to recognize and one of the first English words she learned. Committing the alphabet to memory, she became aware of the surprising fact that with English there were no accents on the 'e', 'a' and other letters, nor the need to struggle with '*le*' or '*la*' to differentiate the gender of nouns. Money was a different matter: twelve pennies to a shilling, twenty shillings to a pound – where was the logic in a system like that? Oh, for the decimalization of francs and centimes!

A move to Falmouth in Cornwall followed because this promised a better livelihood for this family of fisherfolk, and there were contrasts here between these two areas of south-west England: the French Riviera appearance of Torbay giving way to the craggy coastline of Cornwall, beloved of writers and painters. England was, Marie-Jo wrote to friends still in France, an opportunity to learn a second 'maternal' language and to make new and lasting friendships.

Michèle Bourgain made the Channel crossing on *l'Espérance*, via Roscoff, as a five-year-old, settling like so many Portelois in the West Country.[6] Three ports were her successive homes – Penzance, Brixham and Mevagissey – because her father, too, knew only the sea as a means of earning a living. The similarities between Brittany and Cornwall were further strengthened one day with the arrival of a film company to make *Johnny Frenchman*. It brought its own costumes, which were distributed among the 'extras'. Wearing a communicant's snowy-white robe with a lace veil, Michèle faced the cameras with others from Le Portel, both of her parents among them, and also in Breton costume. Not surprisingly their thoughts that day were not far from their homeland, the borrowed gear accenting the link because prior to the war the Portelois had worn traditional costumes of their own 'on high days and holidays', and very similar they were to those of the Bretons.

She remembered the star of the film, the strict-looking Françoise Rosay, as being a kind and gentle person who must have found Mevagissey a home from home with so many French people living in the district. Equally popular, though more so with the children, was the English actress Patricia Roc – 'so young, so pretty,' noted Michèle. Watch out for *Johnny Frenchman* on television, and pay particular attention to scenes with Françoise Rosay aboard a fishing boat and the preparations for a banquet. Then you may catch a fleeting glimpse of young Michèle, a child of Le Portel, in exile yet among her own people.

For those that the Duvals, the Bourgains and the like had left behind, Le Portel faced its first days of occupation, a fate that was first brought home in an odd manner when notices went up everywhere that it was time to change the clocks to '*L'heure allemande*' – German time, 2 hours ahead. Rather more pointedly, a curfew was introduced which barred civilians from the streets between 1900 hours and 0700 hours (which made the evenings seem endless). Yet even without the curfew there would not have been much movement in the streets, an estimated 2,000 Portelois of all ages having left out of a working population of some 3,000 at the beginning of the war. Of these, 2,000 were fishermen, the rest breadwinners in a range of occupations among the farms, shops, offices, transportation and in the few factories which operated in the district.[7]

In Le Portel, 23 May had seen a number of shells falling in the vicinity, whether by accident or design was immaterial, and the following day saw the first of the occupying troops marching through the town,[8] their fingers not far removed from the trigger of their guns because no one quite knew what to expect. The Portelois regarded them more with curiosity than fear, and their arrival was without incident.

As if to make their presence felt, a series of instructions required the Portelois first to ensure that the gutters were kept clear and clean 'for the sake of hygiene', and then to stick to the pavements and leave the roads to the vehicles 'to avoid accidents – and because the regulations require it'. There were blackout enforcements and there were restrictions on the civilian use of cars and motorcycles.[9]

Authoritarian as ever, the Germans seemed to some to have invoked an attitude of being more anti-British than perhaps they were anti-French. It turned out that some found it impossible to hide their feelings, even to the point of refusing to use anything marked 'Made in England'; and others were openly hostile when in houses left empty by families that they suspected of having gone to England.[10]

Administrative services continued, albeit on a limited scale because of the reduced personnel available; bread was rationed; there was little meat to be had; passes were required to leave and enter the area – and all this even before Marshal Pétain put his signature to the armistice document in the railway carriage at Compeigne where the Germans' surrender had ended the First World War. Later, the occupying forces' grip tightened visibly with measures such as the threat of imprisonment for being out at night, homes requisitioned for the military, access to the beach and the cliffs blocked, and mines laid on the shore.

Communiqués issued by the local commandant indicated a progressive strengthening of the movement regulations in the district. One of the first prevented people in a 7 mile deep coastal strip from going beyond a 3 mile radius of their home; then came a bar on entering the area between Le Portel and *le bassin* Loubet, unspecified punishment to be inflicted on anyone found in this forbidden zone, which was a port area.

Thus parts of the town were empty of civilians while others became suddenly crowded, for instance around the butchers', the bakers' and the grocers' when queues lengthened as a hungry population sought to make use of newly valid coupons. Some augmented the system by buying at source in country areas, but with a 3 mile limit imposed on travel, plus transport problems, this was difficult and risky. Others opted for homegrown supplies and sought to protect their sources by putting up notices in their gardens warning that the ground was booby-trapped.[11] It is not hard to imagine those with a wry sense of humour, even in such troubled times, proclaiming in the familiar phrase of the occupying forces: '*Achtung, minen!*'

As well as food rationing, controls covered other essentials and there were coupons needed for clothes and textiles, and even for shoes essential for work. In the wartime equivalent of latter-day recycling, women carefully unpicked their cast-offs and made this wool go round more people by knitting pullovers, scarves and socks with it.

In time, some semblance of recreation and entertainment returned. For instance, the town's cinema reopened (with a Fernandel comedy for the first performance), and concerts took place in schools and public halls. These were arranged not only to divert people's minds from the war, but also to provide cash for parcels of 'goodies' for prisoners of war. The occupying forces had a go at an open-air band concert, which promised a choice of music both judiciously selected and competently performed, taking into account their nation's capabilities in this area of the arts. Unfortunately for the waiting musicians, however, the expected audience chose to be elsewhere – in a gesture that must have quickly sunk home, the Portelois opted to stay away in their droves!

The sadness of war was never far away though, with aircraft in deadly combat overhead, repeated attacks on Boulogne's docks by the RAF, arrests, deportations – and worse. The loss of so many Canadian lives at Dieppe, down the coast, revealed itself in tragic manner when some of their dead were swept ashore on the tide at Le Portel. Taken first to a makeshift mortuary at the town hall, the Canadian soldiers were laid to rest in a cemetery in the heart of the town, remembered for eternity in the hearts of its people. This costly raid in August 1942 had manifested itself initially to the Portelois with distant explosions in the early hours, their source unknown, which were so severe as to shake the ground and rattle doors and windows.

Air-raid shelters began to take on a role as meeting grounds, privileged places providing somewhere to swap reminiscences and, perhaps more importantly, to exchange the war news that passed by word of mouth. Generally this emanated mainly from the BBC and was picked up on radios that were tuned in only when some trusted soul had agreed to mount guard against the risk of discovery by the Germans. Under occupation, radios were not meant to have been retained by civilians – the regulations required them to be handed in to the local authorities, but many 'forgot' to do so, and these clandestine sets came to be regarded as the only reputable source of national and international information.

There was always much to talk about: criticizing the meagre amounts of food, clothing and footwear obtainable, and suggesting new ways around these deficiencies – beetroot juice as jam, grass instead of tobacco and clay as a form of soap for washing and shaving.*

The Battle of Britain offered a grandstand view for the people of Le Portel, as it did for those along the Kent coast, the difference being that in England one could cheer openly when enemy planes were shot out of the skies. Then, with all ideas of invading Britain set aside on Hitler's orders, Germany turned its attention to improving its defences in the Pas de Calais by erecting massive concrete blockhouses, laying down new roads, and building naval bases and airfields. The Todt Organisation was in charge of this work, and to secure its workforce it was necessary both to recruit local labour – even by rounding up likely candidates off the streets – and to import foreign labour. The possibility of being 'requisitioned' for this purpose was another threat, another fear, that faced the Portelois.

Around Le Portel the defences began to take shape, including fresh hangars at the eastern end of Boulogne-Alprech airport to accommodate a squadron of reconnaissance biplanes; while later this airfield, built in better times for better times, would assume an air-sea rescue role. Clearly a key vantage point, this whole clifftop area was to become increasingly important with two huge Wurzburg radar dishes dominating the skyline and a varied selection of armaments, for both offensive and defensive purposes. Seeing the site develop in this manner came as no surprise to the Portelois: there had been a French gun battery there since 1877, and in the early days of the Second World War, with the British active in the town, the 'Tommies' had set up an AA battery there for airfield defence, leaving this firepower intact when the troops moved out in May 1940.

---

* By the autumn of 1943, French people were down to a quarter of the meat, half the sugar, a third of the butter and a third of the cheese in the British rations, according to an exhibition that was organized by the French Committee of Liberation and held at Selfridges, the big London store.

Cap d'Alprech was just one of a number of French coastal batteries in this area which the Germans seized, among them Fort de la Crèche (just north of Boulogne) and Fort de Couppes, the latter position being developed progressively to increase the firepower substantially beyond what had been available when the French were obliged to abandon the site. Less than a mile behind the seafront at Le Portel, Mont Soleil was turned into a third defensive position, its 88 mm guns being among the most deadly of all AA weapons, and this site the highest and the most commanding in the immediate area. Apart from the beach, Le Portel was enclosed by high ground: Mont Soleil to the rear, and Mont de Couppes and Cap d'Alprech the cliffs on either side. The most populated area was contained within this 'horseshoe', some of the streets stretching up to meet the higher ground which virtually surrounded the town.

There were other AA positions coming into use at Cap d'Alprech, Fort de Couppes and at the Fort de l'Heurt, the latter forts evoking memories of the Napoleonic influence on Le Portel and its environs. The Germans were probably not best pleased at the length of time it took for the construction work at Fort de l'Heurt: the tiny 'workhorse' train, carrying the cement across when the tide was out, becoming derailed more times than they cared to remember. And as the wheels left the track, the waggons overturned with the loss of their valuable loads spilled over the wet sand.[12] Sabotage? Who could tell, who *would* tell!

Sabotage was one means by which a Portelois with the distinctly non-Portelois name of Ernest MacKenna chose to continue his personal struggle against the Germans who had overrun his country. A soldier at the age of twenty, he was also the son of a soldier – a British soldier – a Scot who was gassed on the battlefields near Ypres in the First World War, stayed on in France where he married a French girl and settled in Boulogne-sur-Mer in the 1920s. Ernest was brought up by his maternal grandmother after the death of both parents; first his father, a delayed-action victim of that terrible 'war to end wars', when the boy was ten years old, and then his mother, two years later, in childbirth.

Ernest served first with the 5th Infantry Regiment on the Maginot Line from March 1940, then with the 1st Infantry Regiment on the demarcation line when the armistice came, and finally with the French Navy in North Africa before capture and eventual repatriation through Italy to the Pas de Calais in December 1942.

It was a condition of repatriation that while administratively still in the French Navy he would work in France for the Germans. Orders came through for Ernest to take up a job at a locomotive repair centre in the Rhône – but only after a spell of home leave which changed the course of his life. He learned that the family was now evacuated to Bernieulles, near Montreuil-sur-Mer, where his grandmother was able to recuperate after being severely injured in an air raid. While he was staying there the grandmother was instrumental in getting a German officer, billeted in the same house, to arrange for Ernest to work instead on the construction of the Atlantic Wall.

This he did, taking up residence in the family home in Le Portel, though uppermost in his mind was the intention to carry on the fight against the Germans, either in the French Resistance or by finding a small boat capable of taking him to England where he could enlist in one of the Free French organizations. Finding that escape by sea was virtually impossible, Ernest located and joined the *Front National* resistance group in Le Portel led by Louis Fourrier. Meanwhile he had been laying barbed wire defences close to the beaches, and then earned promotion to take charge of one of the shift-working round-the-clock teams building a network of underground passages connecting the guns, the ammunition stores and the living quarters at Fort de Couppes.

Soon came orders from the Resistance cell to slow down this work as much as possible, by whatever means, and he opted to absent the whole team for an entire 8 hour shift on the grounds that the Catholic Church forbade its members to work this particular day – the Feast of the Assumption. This 'strike', which the German security services called 'an act of sabotage', cost Ernest some 48 hours under fierce but humane interrogation, and a move to a job that was more menial for him and less critical for them.

Being branded as a potential troublemaker was a disturbing experience: it made Ernest more cautious and it made others in the Resistance more prudent. Activity against the Germans continued, naturally, but precautions were introduced to limit the number of fellow members that any individual could identify, thus protecting the majority if anyone fell into enemy hands.

Organized disruptive measures against the occupying forces included ambushing French women who were known to be fraternizing with German soldiers – the woman's hair was shorn, and the man's gun and ammunition were incorporated into the Resistance group's secret stores; cutting telephone links; keeping guard for other groups carrying out sabotage missions; stealing explosives; distributing clandestine publications; and recirculating food and other ration cards.

Tackling some of the more dramatic operations could mean travelling as much as 20 miles by bike, often over fields and criss-crossing the '*zone rouge*' boundary line (prohibited-entry region) in which Le Portel was situated. Nevertheless, Resistance activities in an area as tightly controlled as the Pas de Calais were limited by the availability of supplies, for example munitions, which were more easily delivered by parachute elsewhere in France.*

Early in 1943 came the creation of the STO (*Le Service du Travail Obligatoire*), which conscripted young people to work in Germany. Initially, Portelois aged twenty and twenty-one were those caught in this sinister net, which some sought to avoid by going to live 'underground' and accepting the consequential risks. Action of this sort

---

* It transpires that the bombardment of Le Portel on 8/9 September 1943 widened substantially Ernest MacKenna's own opportunities to serve as an effective member of the French Resistance. In the subsequent evacuation he chose the more remote Amplepuis in the Rhône, where he had relatives, rather than Arras, moving on to St Armand Montrond in the Cher in the opening weeks of 1944. Documents made available to the author testify to an increasing number of activities while serving as a *caporal* in the post-armistice resistance organization of the former 1st Infantry Regiment – activities which included concealing an injured member of the *Maquis* in hospital; organizing the collection and distribution of arms; assisting at parachute drops; and a range of individual and group acts of sabotage against the enemy, such as ambushing lorry convoys. A member of the British Legion, 'and proud of it', Ernest MacKenna would like to see due recognition accorded to other '*fils de britannique en France*' who carried out a similar struggle against the common enemy, 'risking their lives while doing their best with limited means to make the occupation as unpleasant and as ineffective as possible for the Germans'.[13]

called for a new identity, a change of residence and foregoing ration cards, but a number considered all of this worthwhile. There were exceptions to this form of call-up, among them those working in local government, the police, the fire service and so on.

Resistance organizations throughout France were quick to respond to the introduction of STO by circulating leaflets calling on the youth of France to gain time first by ignoring the summons, then by missing the medical examination and, if all else failed, by making themselves unavailable when the moment came to report for the journey (a one-way ticket?) to Germany. The message was that France would need these young people as 'soldiers for the liberation'. In the meantime they should hinder the Germans, sabotage their activities and stay in France, undercover. They were urged to enlist with the Resistance, not with the STO.[14]

Meanwhile, what were the consequences of Allied bombing attacks to which Le Portel and the Portelois fell victim? There were 14 occasions when high-explosive bombs dropped on the town between the summers of 1940 and 1943; 6 when incendiary bombs accompanied them; and 1 when incendiary bombs alone fell.[15] In the first incident, in September 1940, three high-explosive bombs wiped out one dwelling place, without causing personal injury. The first deaths occurred on 7 December 1940: three children (aged seventeen, thirteen and seven), whose mother was seriously hurt and in hospital for several months when their home in rue Auguste Comte was destroyed. The following year saw the most raids, the most high-explosive bombs dropped in any one raid, the most incendiaries, the most homes wiped out and the most casualties.

During February, in four separate incidents, thirteen high-explosive and twenty incendiary bombs fell on Le Portel, destroying two homes, making four uninhabitable and damaging a further nine, rue Auguste Huguet suffering the greatest destruction. One person died in rue de Chemin Vert – a lady whose husband and son were in another part of the town at the time – while a woman from St Martin, visiting her parents in Le Portel, suffered injuries in the same incident. A two-year-old girl belonging to the same family was also hurt in this bombing.

On an occasion when the largest number of high-explosive bombs fell on Le Portel, the population escaped without injury, although there was some damage to property. It was 7 September, around midnight, and reportedly people defied the curfew to venture into the streets and watch the proceedings, apparently taking comfort from the fact that the Germans were otherwise engaged, Fort de Couppes and the airfield having been hit.[16] With just four civilians dead and three injured up to this point, it also seems possible that there was a vestige of hope – a belief, even – that the French population was immune to British bombs.

Two months would pass before this was shown not to be the case, with two dead and four hurt when twenty high-explosive and fifty incendiary bombs fell on the town in a single raid, destroying five homes, making four uninhabitable and damaging a further fifteen. A husband and wife, both in their fifties, died in rue Jean Bart. Their daughter was seriously hurt. The other three suffering injuries were all men: one in rue Pasteur, one in rue Monseigneur Bourgain and the other in rue St Michel. In another part of the town, living accommodation burned down despite the efforts of German soldiers who were reinforcing the work of the fire brigade. In terms of numbers of bombs, casualties and the extent of damage to property, this bombardment on 7 November 1941 was the most severe of all those suffered by the town and the people of Le Portel ahead of *Operation Starkey*.[17]

Ironically, in this period of 'calm before the storm', more Portelois were killed away from the town than while in their own homes. On 5 March 1941, a day when Le Portel escaped totally, three men were killed in Boulogne. One left a widow and seven children and another was a member of a family which was forced to move when their home in rue Auguste Huguet was severely damaged only the previous month. There was another death of a Portelois in Boulogne on 14 August 1941, again when there was no incident in Le Portel. Then, on 12 October 1941, a whole month when no bombs fell on Le Portel, as many as five Portelois died in a raid on Boulogne. Two of them, men killed on the quayside, left between them a total of six children. The others were a youth aged sixteen and two sisters – one a war widow since June 1940 whose seven-year-old son was himself severely injured at her side. Such deaths were not confined to those with their feet on dry land: in an attack at sea on 5 December 1941, a fisherman from Le Portel was killed by machine-gun fire from an unidentified aircraft. He left a widow with four young children.[18]

Bombing aside, the Portelois also found themselves suffering at the hands of the AA gun crews, whose role it was to beat off all would-be attackers. From time to time a shell failed to carry out its proper task and crash-landed in the town. In such an incident, one of these missiles sliced through the wall of a house and missed a woman occupant by a hair's breadth, confirming in a bizarre manner that 'what goes up must come down'. Less fortunate were two women walking down rue Carnot one day when an AA shell fell on empty houses nearby. One was seriously hurt and taken to hospital, the other less so and was able to go home after first-aid treatment. There were other, more tragic, incidents, when fate appeared to deal an unkind hand. In one, a mother of six was caught in the path of machine-gun fire in the course of a training exercise, hit and fatally injured.[19] Death could strike from all directions in wartime Le Portel.

For how much longer could this seaside town remain, as it certainly must have appeared to be, a 'safe' place to live? Although in the front line so far as the German defences were concerned, Le Portel was not in itself a target, prime or otherwise. Within the town there was nothing that was militarily attractive – it had no industry beyond fishing and its communications value was minimal – but there were, for all to see, military objectives ringing the town. However, the airport was not sufficiently operational to warrant particular attention and the heavy guns at Cap d'Alprech and Fort de Couppes were not in themselves interesting enough to call for bombing.* As for the other gun positions, these were comparatively small fry, even if troublesome to Allied planes as undoubtedly were the AA batteries at Mont Soleil. It was not that Le Portel bore a charmed life, it was simply that prior to *Operation Starkey* there were many more worthwhile objectives for the Allies' bombs and bullets.

Starkey was about to change all of that. By definition, Le Portel was not the

---

*The airport served as an emergency landing ground for German planes damaged in action and as a link in the air-sea rescue chain, as well as receiving VIPs from time to time.

objective for those planning and carrying out the missions of 4, 8 and 9 September 1943 which quite literally decimated the town by killing one in ten of its inhabitants and destroyed upwards of 90 per cent of its buildings, not one left habitable.[20] The objective was to pound the gun batteries at Cap d'Alprech and Fort de Couppes so heavily that the enemy would be persuaded that there was an invasion looming. This had to be done because *Operation Starkey* demanded it. Those big guns were judged to pose a threat, and the plan required that threat to be minimized, if not removed entirely. It mattered not one iota that the whole thing was a ploy.

There was nothing secretive about these emplacements. Their locations were known and recorded, they showed up in aerial photographs and their positions were marked on the planners' maps with the customary grid-referencing using conventional six-figure identification on standard issue War Office maps. Individually, both gun batteries could be regarded as justifiable targets, and both had been approved by the Air Ministry for bombing attacks within *Starkey*, despite the proximity of a built-up area.[21] Jointly, however, the risk to civilian life was compounded because of a fatal flaw: the fact that the town of Le Portel lay equidistant between the two targets, and the safety margin, if one existed, would be infinitesimal by any standards.

Chapter Eight

The Pathfinders go in . . .

It was a devastating prospect: Bomber Command's entire allocated effort for the eve of *Operation Starkey*'s D-Day was to be launched against those two big-gun installations reckoned to pose the greatest threat to the pseudo-armada that was about to sail towards France.

To the north of the coastal resort of Le Portel was the battery codenamed *Religion*, and to the south the one with the code-name *Andante*. The quiet of the night would soon be torn apart by the mighty roar of Air Chief Marshal Sir Arthur Harris's massive bomber force crossing the Channel.

Compelled to give way to the 'top brass' running *Starkey*, he was obliged to promise no less than 200 of his planes for this twin-pronged attack on those guns. In the event he had found 258 without drawing on those he needed for Germany.[1]

While the crews which would be doing the bombing were by and large the less experienced pilots, navigators, bomb-aimers, flight engineers and air gunners in Bomber Command, those in the spearhead would be among his most skilled men.

Try to imagine what this raid was going to be like. It would be night-time. Even in the most favourable moonlight conditions the targets were so small as to be impossible to pick out from planes 3 or 4 miles up.

So the plan was to use the most accurate methods so far available to locate, pinpoint and bomb those long-range gun positions: the planes, the crews and the distinctive Target Indicators (TIs) of Pathfinder Force, together with the use of a device that the 'boffins' had invented, called Oboe.[2]

Whatever the performance during training and in intersquadron competitions, results achieved on actual bombing raids were generally much less impressive, which was hardly surprising given the conditions of a real mission. There were the psychological pressures to be overcome (Are we going to get to the target? Are we going to get back home?); there was natural exuberance when all seemed to be going well; and there was fear when under enemy attack.

It was far from generally known that, just a couple of years previously, Bomber Command's ORS team considered then that only 15 per cent of all sorties bombed within 5 miles of their target.[3]

Not only were crews missing their targets with their bombs, but there were those who ought to have known better who dropped their bombs many minutes of flying time short of their target, yet came back home convinced, until photos proved otherwise, that their bombs had scored bull's-eyes.

In those past two years, fortunately, much progress had been made which improved significantly both the opportunity and the prospect for bombing by night with increased accuracy. Greater experience and better equipment did much to reduce the overall error rate by 'Main Force' bombers, no single contributor arguably doing as much to help as Oboe.

The routine was now to send a small number of Pathfinders some minutes ahead of the Main Force of bombers. Pilots, navigators and bomb-aimers in this vanguard were individually experienced and belonged to specialist squadrons in a dedicated Pathfinder Force, trained and equipped for the purpose. It was their role to find the target so that the Main Force crews streaming along behind them would know where to go and where to bomb. Constantly improving methods and devices could thus be concentrated, tested and proven in the most capable hands. Though this practice 'de-skilled' the job of Main Force crews, compared with that of their Pathfinder colleagues, it made best use of the available manpower and the limited resources of planes and equipment. It also got results.

Operational research studies into specific raids in the opening months of 1943 showed that with Oboe to ground-mark the target, the average success of the Main Force increased threefold. It was a tremendous morale booster, though tempered by the knowledge that in one in two of those raids, on industrial targets in Germany, less than 50 per cent of the bombing was estimated to have occurred within 3 miles of the AP.[4]

Oboe enabled a Pathfinder crew to follow signals received in their radio headsets, the first set of dot-dashes to guide them towards their target and the second to tell them when to release their TIs to mark the target.

Scientists at the Telecommunications Research Establishment (TRE) came up with Oboe while working on various systems using radio beams for directional purposes. It was neither particularly clever nor a capability that was confined to Britain to plot a course by radio waves using a transmitter on the ground and a receiver in the plane.

There were obvious problems with 'flying the beam' – an aerial corridor directly between the source of the beam and the target. The most glaring was that radio beams could be traced and, once the direction of the beam was known, the target was revealed. Assuming that the warning was sufficient, the attacking force could find reinforced defences waiting for it.

Where Oboe was unique was that it did away with the direct line of flight from the beam source to the target. Think of a ground station transmitting a signal which the pilot hears while flying along the circumference of a circle whose centre is the ground station and which passes over the target. On that arc he will be maintaining a constant range from the ground station as measured by the secondary radar link between the ground station and the aircraft. He is automatically made aware of any deviation by 'dots' when edging towards the ground station and 'dashes' when edging away from it, the beam's width scarcely the wing span of a small plane.

The intricacies of the system meant that the aircraft only needed to maintain something approaching straight and level flight for a short time – a period of some 10 minutes while following the arc in the final run-up to the target.

The name for this transmitting station was the 'Cat', which was responsible for tracking to the target. Another ground station, 'Mouse', the releasing station, sent a signal into the navigator/bomb-aimer's headset, again as dots and dashes but now as a time sequence forming a countdown to indicate the release point.

An early use of a primitive form of Oboe was during the Trinity operations against the German warships *Scharnhorst* and *Gneisenau* in the French port of Brest. The tracking signal was a Baillie beam, a narrow radio beam developed by No. 80 Wing in the first year of the Second World War.[5] This provided a direct line to be followed as distinct from the arc in the much more sophisticated Oboe. The role of Oboe here was solely to signal when to let go of the bombs.

The name Oboe did not come from any conventional storeplace of military code words (as did *Starkey*, which was a not uncommon surname*). John Hooper, one of the scientists developing the system at Swanage, Dorset, before TRE moved to its better-known home at Malvern, recalled one of his colleagues, a music-lover called Tony Bates, remarking that the sound in the headsets was 'just like someone playing the oboe'.[6]

In this matter-of-fact way, rather than observing convention and having someone take the next available codename from a list conceived in the depths of Whitehall, Oboe stuck for what was to this team the primary guidance system on which all of them were pinning their hopes.

Those December 1941/January 1942 attacks on the 'Salmon and Gluckstein', as these twin prides of the German navy were often known, made history as being the RAF's first use of radio-directional equipment to locate and bomb a target.

Trials with Oboe proper, with both 'Cat' and 'Mouse' stations operating, proceeded with increasing optimism during 1942. An aircraft from the former Wireless Intelligence Development Unit (WIDU) at Boscombe Down, Salisbury, carried the equivalent of a giant photographic flashgun in the bomb bay. On receiving the release signal the bulb would go off to register the instant the bombs – if there had been any – left the aircraft. The 'flash' would be seen on a camera obscura and used to prove the accuracy of Oboe.

Subsequently there were bombing trials on a range, first only when the skies were clear and then, as the system proved itself, even in cloud. The range operators could scarcely believe their eyes when the bomb explosion splashes continued to appear in exactly the same area as when the sky was clear.[7]

The early Oboe at the ground stations and in the aircraft was little more than 'string and sealing wax' manufacture, yet the system was working at the leading edge of guidance communication performance. Nevertheless, its initial successes were well up to the expectations of the development team at TRE. Not everyone 'in the know' was as confident, though, and from time to time there were the inevitable complaints about crank ideas, money-wasting and so on.

For bomb release, a built-in interval of a fraction of a second allowed for hesitation or nervousness when the countdown radio signal cut to silence, and this was the moment to trigger bombs-away. Technically there was nothing to prevent the ground station from automatically sending a radio signal that would release the bombs. However, this idea, from the civilians, did not go down too well with their

* UK telephone directories contain a sprinkling of Starkeys and coincidentally there was at least one with that name among the active participants in *Operation Starkey*. An RAF aircrew NCO, he was not engaged in any attack on the Le Portel batteries.

colleagues in uniform.[8] It met with opposition from what might be described as the bomb-aimers' 'trade union', the argument among the aircrews being that the possibility of there being any last-minute hitch, known only to them, required on-the-spot human control.

While regarded from the outset as promising to be the ultimate in precision bombing aids, it was accepted that Oboe could never be entirely without its limitations. For example, there was the result of the curvature of the earth, which limited its effectiveness to some 250 miles from the ground stations, even with aircraft flying as high as 30,000 feet, without some form of airborne 'repeater' stations. There was also a restriction on the number of aircraft able to operate with Oboe, because a pair of Oboe ground stations could only handle one at a time. Additionally there was the deterioration that came with the sharpness of the angle between the two ground stations at the point of release – the 'angle of cut' was the term. In real terms this meant that if the target on the Continent was due east of two ground stations on, say, the Norfolk and Kent coasts, there was no problem; but move the target due south and the reduced angle of cut would make Oboe less efficient.

However, with the bulk of the more obvious targets for the RAF bombers being to the north-east, east and south-east rather than north and south, this potential deficiency did not pose an immediate problem – improvements in this respect could take their course and follow in good time.

Operationally, Oboe was introduced in December 1942 with a number of 'calibration raids' to cross-check the absolutely critical longitude, latitude and distance data – 'geodetic data' – because of variations which had become apparent when studying published maps.

For one such raid the Belgian resistance movement was given advance notice so as to feed back to Britain precise information on where the bombs had fallen on this important enemy communications base. The first major attack with the benefit of Oboe was then still to come. This was against Essen on 5 March 1943 and signalled the opening of the Battle of the Ruhr.

Early on, Oboe was considered by the powers-that-be as offering target-marking opportunities comparable with its advantages as the blind-bombing device which was its original purpose. Studying the performance of RAF Bomber Command over a period of 38 raids – 20 led by Pathfinders using Oboe for ground-marking (as distinct from 'sky-marking' when cloud obscured the target area) – prompted specialists in operational research to hail this technique as Oboe's greatest success. Those raids included the heaviest and most successful that Bomber Command had ever mounted, and the damage caused was on a scale never previously achieved by night bombing.[9]

Operational research showed that not only was Oboe enabling very successful attacks to be made against targets which had previously proved almost impossible to locate, but also it was accurate enough for Main Force bombers to aim at individual markers, instead of having to settle for the centre of a number of scattered TIs.

With the failure of the high-flying Wellington Mk VI during its trials, the timely availability of the new, faster and higher-flying Mosquito 'wooden wonder' enabled the Oboe system to be more fully realized. Oboe efficiency improved with height, and the Mosquito's speed would be a help when fighters were around. Indeed, Mosquitoes went on to enjoy a very great measure of immunity from enemy action. In six months, though two of these planes went missing, there was just one reported interception by enemy fighters and only nineteen instances (less than 6 per cent) where Mosquitoes were hit by AA fire, none of this causing serious damage.[10]

Certainly there were problems with Oboe during that time: roughly one in three sorties failed for one reason or another. There were failures in the air – problems with the equipment, aircraft being out of position and manipulative errors – and there were failures on the ground – generally interference or weak signals – but Oboe was regarded as sound in design, very highly serviceable and excellently maintained in the planes and at ground stations.[11]

Coincidentally, two brothers were a dominant force in the development, introduction and use of Oboe as a specialist device for pathfinding among the RAF's bomber crews. Sid Bufton was an operational bomber pilot, squadron commander and strong advocate of pathfinding techniques long before there was a Pathfinder Force. Moving on to senior positions at Air Ministry, he was by now directing bomber operations as an air commodore. Hal Bufton was a trials pilot helping to develop Oboe and, once WIDU became 109 Squadron in December 1940, he flew operationally including the first Oboe-led bomber missions over occupied and enemy territory. The squadron was one of the original units in Pathfinder Force and the first with Mosquitoes, which was the only operational aircraft type then being equipped with Oboe. The Mosquito's role was to spearhead Bomber Command attacks against targets as far as Germany's industrial heart in the Ruhr and to drop target markers on the AP so as to pinpoint precisely where the Main Force aircraft must bomb.

The summer of 1943 disclosed increasing activity on the V-weapon front, with fresh launching sites under construction in the Pas de Calais and Cherbourg areas, which prompted discussion about Oboe taking on the target-marking responsibility here too – a 'vital and new commitment' for the system. It was decided to go ahead, first with one pair of ground stations where an accuracy of plus or minus 100 yards was guaranteed, dropping markers at the rate of one every 10 minutes.[12]

It was not surprising, then, that 109 Squadron with Gp Capt. Bufton, its Officer Commanding, found itself playing a pivotal role in the Culminating Phase of *Starkey*. This was to provide ten Oboe-equipped Mosquitoes to mark the APs north and south of Le Portel.[13] A further two from 105 Squadron, new to pathfinding responsibilities (operational on 1 August 1943), and neighbours on the same airfield at Marham, Norfolk, joined the marking force, half of each squadron's aircraft detailed for each AP. It would be a further step in the initial testing of the 'blind marking' technique in its new territory – a perfectly valid proving ground, even though the targets were unrelated either to the V1 flying bomb or to the V2 rocket.

As the plans were being finalized it must have appeared that success was 'in the bag' for this component of the *Starkey* strategy: there was no bombing aid as precise as Oboe; pilots and navigator/bomb-aimers highly experienced in Oboe-led target marking were on call; and excitement was understandably running high on results from the last few nights.

Against a target in the Forêt d'Hesdin, estimated impact points gave an average error of 114 yards among the five Mosquitoes spearheading the attack; against the Forêt de Raismes, an average 76 yards off-target, also by five Mosquitoes; and, better still, against the Forêt de Mormal (this time with one of the four Mosquitoes marking this target judged to have come within 10 yards of the AP), the average error being just 66¼ yards.[14] All three were ammunition dumps and prime targets in *Starkey*, though each time Bomber Command limited the size of the attacking force to some thirty Wellingtons in keeping with its 'hit Germany first' policy.

In the Culminating Phase of *Starkey*, 109 Squadron joined by 105 Squadron, the very squadrons whose crews had carried out those three operations, would be dropping their TIs on APs to the north and south of Le Portel – those two 'most dangerous' big-gun sites.

For technical reasons – the location of these sites relative to Oboe ground stations – the full Oboe system was able to operate only with Worth Matravers, the 'Cat' station at Swanage in Dorset, tracking the target-marking aircraft, paired with Trimingham, near Cromer in Norfolk, the 'Mouse', to give the release signal. So to cope with the number of aircraft mustered for these twin operations, each compressed into just 15 minutes, a supplementary aircraft-handling system was mooted.*

Recognizing the problem of 'angle of cut', which could reduce Oboe's effectiveness depending on the geographical location of ground stations and targets, Air Ministry specialists had begun looking into arrangements to enable Oboe-controlled aircraft to attack coastal and inland targets (the V-weapon sites) between the French ports of Calais and Cherbourg.[15]

For example, it was pointed out that only one pair of Oboe ground stations was available for attacking targets in the Calais area. It was proposed, therefore, that this limitation might be overcome by using Oboe stations in combination with the 'straight line' Baillie radio beams. There was a qualification: 'very short range targets only', the reason being that the greater the distance from the transmitter the less accurate it became as a tracking aid.

This created a problem in itself in that pilots might not have time to 'settle down' on the beam before reaching the target. In effect this suggested that with short-range targets there could be insufficient time to track positively, and the point of intersection between tracking and releasing might come so quickly that the moment for accurate release would have passed by.

More work had to be done, and it was made clear within the appropriate hierarchy responsible for directing the course of radar and bombing activities that too much reliance should not be placed on this Oboe alternative at this time.[16] It had only been considered theoretically when Air Ministry began focusing on its own detailed planning to contribute to *Operation Starkey*.

Thus, to spearhead the attack on the two gun sites, instead of Oboe tracking all of the aircraft to their APs, some would make use of a Baillie beam to provide a

*The number of paired ground stations available determined how many Pathfinder Mosquitoes could function with full Oboe, each pair being able to handle only one aircraft at a time in the several minutes' run-up to the moment of release, just one aircraft being passed over the target approximately every 10 minutes.

straight-line invisible pathway through the night skies, directly between ground station and target. There was no shortage of Baillie beam sites – these were already at Oldstairs (Hawkshill Down), Caistor (Trimingham area), Constantine (Sennen area) and St Alban's Head (near Worth Matravers), with more to come – but choosing the most suitably located needed some care.

With full Oboe promising the greater accuracy, Mosquito crews responsible for dropping the more critical of the two kinds of target-markers, those burning a fierce flame-red, would tune-in to track on Oboe. Those with the back-up greens would 'fly the Baillie beam' to the target and then take the release signal from an Oboe ground station.

It is interesting to note that by combining Baillie and Oboe in this manner, the crews were reviving the procedure followed for the 'Salmon and Gluckstein' bombing raids when Oboe was still very much in its experimental stages. All the more evocative for those crews of 109 Squadron was the knowledge that their squadron had provided second pilots and wireless operators for those missions.

At Marham, crews were briefed to mark the two targets: Gp Capt. Bufton, with Sqn/Ldr 'Ding' Ifould as navigator/bomb-aimer, flying J-Johnny and carrying four 250 lb red TIs, would initiate the night's attack, marking the exact AP by dropping these long-burning, incendiary-based marker flares over the northern target at 2158 hours, 2 minutes before zero hour for the aerial onslaught on the gun emplacement named *Religion*.[17]

Experience certainly showed in this crew: Hal Bufton and 'Ding' Ifould, an Australian, had secured themselves a place in aviation history[18] as being respectively the first pilot and the first navigator to drop Oboe-aimed bombs against an enemy target – a power station at Lutterade, Holland – during the night of 20/21 December 1942.

A further five Mosquitoes – four from 109 Squadron, the other from 105 – would follow at predetermined intervals to mark the same AP at later stages of the attack, one more with red TIs and three with greens, the fifth in reserve and carrying more of the all-important reds in case of problems. The other five from 109 Squadron and the other one from 105 would similarly mark the second AP, *Andante*, commencing at 2243 hours – 2 minutes before zero hour. As in Phase I, a reserve aircraft would be taking an additional salvo of reds.

Minute by minute, though, those best-laid plans began to fall apart – zero hour came but the Mosquitoes didn't . . .

TIs were first used in a raid on Berlin at the beginning of 1943.[19] The red the more dominant, the green ones to reinforce them, they fell slowly and cascaded, on this occasion from 6,000 feet, continuing to blaze on the ground. Fierce-burning, brilliantly illuminating, TIs had to be dropped to a carefully timed sequence to keep the AP visible for the bomb-aimers throughout the entire bombing operation – even through cloud. Their brilliance came from sixty 12 inch pyrotechnic candles that were packed inside a 250 lb bomb casing.

The Mosquitoes were carrying four 250 lb TIs apiece for release as a single salvo, the idea being that they would land 30 yards apart and appear as a positive and entirely unmistakable marking point to the bombers way above them.

The pattern for each phase of the Le Portel attack was to begin with a red, back it up with greens, drop a second red at the halfway stage and back that up with more greens. The reds and some of the greens would be released 'blind' on Oboe signals, the remainder visually by other well experienced crews in Pathfinder Force flying the much bigger Halifax bombers. The Halifaxes would watch for the red TIs burning on the ground and aim their own TIs on top of them, together with the high explosives which (unlike the Mosquitoes) they were also carrying in their bomb bays.

At 28,000 feet, Gp Capt. Bufton was flying under the guidance of the Oboe ground station at Worth Matravers.[20] With 20 minutes before Sqn/Ldr Ifould was scheduled to let go the opening salvo of four reds, all seemed to be fine.

Relying on the dots and dashes in his headset to follow the arc at his 160 mile range from Worth Matravers, this first of some 240 raiders to be heard over Le Portel that night sped closer and closer towards *Religion*.

There were now 10 minutes to go . . . now 5 minutes . . . now 3 . . . now 2 . . . just 10 seconds, and he knew this was to be an unsuccessful run. The tracking signals were faulty and, in an operation like this, where total reliance must be placed on the combination of equipment in the aircraft and on the ground, that meant abort. Phase I would have to proceed without his reds.*

The first green TIs were scheduled 2 minutes later, coinciding with zero hour, the aircraft carrying them being W-William, a Mosquito from Bufton's squadron, following the Baillie beam and waiting for Oboe ground station Hawkshill Down I to signal the release.

Station personnel were given the rare opportunity to see with their own eyes whether or not the aircraft under their control would be carrying out its mission – in this case dropping TIs – because from the grounds of their camp the descending green flares were clearly visible – brighter than the finest pre-war fireworks and starting more than a mile high.

It made a more comforting sight than the menacing aerial display of close on a year previously when formations of FW 190 fighters, streaking low over the water, swept across the Channel in a raid on Deal and fired their cannon against Hawkshill Down,[21] its Oboe not yet fully installed.

Due to go down at 2200 hours and 2 minutes behind schedule with their release, W-William's green TIs were a welcoming sign for the Halifax crews whose job was to back up with their own greens. Expecting first the all-important red, which did not appear, then a green that was late, a Halifax from 405 (RCAF) Squadron, K-King, joined the marking team and also loosed some of the first high explosives of the night (the first, quick-off-the-mark Main Force crews having already shared that distinction).

---

* It was an inauspicious climax for the Hal Bufton/'Ding' Ifould partnership, this mission turning out to be their last operational sortie together. Before the month was out, Ifould (with the DSO now added to his DFC) was posted to RAF Station Warboys after a brief attachment in the USA; Bufton (who held the AFC as well as the DFC) stayed in command of 109 Squadron until a posting to RAF Station Bourn. In the interim Bufton added seven more operational sorties which he crowned on 1 March 1944 with an Oboe bombing at 25,600 feet against an enemy airfield in Holland when his was the only one in a quartet of Mosquitoes to escape technical failures which forced one after the other to abort the mission.[22]

By now, though, another of the Mosquitoes, J-Johnny from 105 Squadron, should have dropped its greens. As with all of the Mosquitoes carrying green TIs, it was tracking along the Baillie beam towards its source and awaiting the release signal from an Oboe ground station, in this instance Winterton II in Norfolk. This station had become operational a fortnight or so earlier and made its debut as a 'Cat', tracking for aircraft ground-marking at Leverkusen, Germany.

It was a time of feverish construction activity: Winterton I was begun only in May, yet by the time Winterton II was contributing to *Starkey* a third station was completed, a fourth was near-finished and a fifth was four-fifths towards completion. Oboe was definitely an ongoing commitment.

Following the bombing-run procedure, J-Johnny's navigator/bomb-aimer was just about on schedule when he heard first the morse for A at 2155 hours and then, very loud and clear, the signal for B at some 35 seconds past 2157. At this point the signal from Winterton II was 'swinging badly'. It missed the C altogether and the D, transmitted 15 seconds after 2201 hours, came through the headset more as a V.

Up there, flying at 26,000 feet and making a ground speed of 235 mph, the navigator was desperately trying to concentrate on this series of dots and dashes. Last to come would be five 'dots' over 5 seconds and then a dash. When the dash cut and gave way to silence, that would be the moment to squeeze the TIs' release-button. He reckoned that he probably had got release – and about on time – but could not be certain.[23]

With a split-second decision, because of this lack of confidence the navigator followed procedure and abandoned the mission. Thus, out of three target-markers from Marham so far that night, only one had released while the other two had aborted because the ground signals gave the aircrew cause for doubt.

The first successful release of a red TI, the one scheduled for the midway point in Phase I, the attack on *Religion* north of Le Portel, came from H-Harry. Like the others carrying reds, this was under full Oboe – both tracking (Worth Matravers) and releasing (Trimingham) – and, more fortunately also than A-Apple in reserve, it was proving to be a textbook mission.

A further green from V-Vic completed the Mosquitoes' marking in Phase I to leave the score standing at one successful red out of three and two greens out of three – a 50 per cent success rate which, accuracy of marking apart, meant that only half of the markers carried were dropped, the red-carrying reserve aircraft also not having contributed to the marking schedule due to Oboe failure.

It was now up to the Halifaxes, colleagues in Pathfinder Force whose task was to 'stoke up' the Mosquitoes' flares with their own, dropped visually. Then all that remained was to hope for a better showing in Phase II against the second gun position.

There was early promise when E-Edward, a full Oboe marker carrying red to mark the exact AP, released marginally late but still about 2 minutes before zero hour for Phase II. S-Sugar, tracking by Baillie and releasing on Oboe, loosed its green fractionally earlier, in this instance 'jumping the gun' by 114 seconds.

The next with a green, 105 Squadron's C-Charlie, experienced a problem unrelated to either the Baillie beam it was using for tracking to the target or to Oboe, on which the bomb-aimer would have relied for the release. Failure of another directional aid, the Gee system, caused him to opt for an early return.

G-George, with red for the halfway stage, experienced Oboe failure and aborted, as did 109 Squadron's C-Charlie, also with red and flying reserve, the releasing station losing contact. However, R-Roger achieved a successful green release to equal the score in Phase I: one red dropped out of three, and two greens dropped out of three. In each of the four successful green releases, Hawkshill Down I was the controlling Oboe ground station.

In all, ten Mosquitoes from 109 Squadron and two from 105 had taken off; only six marked the two APs – one with red and two with green on each occasion. Crews returned with mixed feelings as to their releases, with confirmation of their accuracy yet to come.

It was not the right time to determine the respective merits of Oboe and the Baillie beam for tracking. Under the circumstances, given the limited availability of ground stations brought about by the geographical location of the chosen targets and the number of target marker aircraft to be handled, a supplementary system was imperative.

With the Halifaxes, each of the seven from 35 Squadron at Graveley, Huntingdonshire, and the three from 405 Squadron at Gransden Lodge, Bedfordshire, were required to make a double drop in this operation, half of their TIs and half of their bombs dedicated to each of the two phases. In the event, 35 Squadron's G-George aborted Phase I for fear of the TIs visible being inaccurate (the bomb-aimer dropped the total load during Phase II), and in each phase other Halifaxes dropped only their bombs.

Originating during the First World War, 35 (Madras Presidency) Squadron had been re-formed on 5 November 1940 for the express purpose of introducing the new Handley Page Halifax into operational service.[24] Its first Halifax sorties were in March 1941 when six aircraft were sent to attack Le Havre dockyard. Incidentally, Boulogne was its alternative target on that debut mission; no one chose it.

The squadron was one of the five selected to form the nucleus of Pathfinder Force at its creation in August 1942. It was pleased to be in the new group's first operation, but saddened that one of its aircraft was the Pathfinders' first loss in action. In its first year, 35 Squadron had performed target-marking duties in its own right, and more recently (on the night of 17/18 August 1943) against Peenemünde, the Germans' research establishment on the Baltic coast, and also backed up the Oboe-equipped Mosquitoes from their debut.

Now in the midst of re-equipping with Lancasters to replace their Halifaxes, the other Halifax squadron marking and bombing *Religion* and *Andante* was No. 405, which enjoyed the distinction of carrying out the Royal Canadian Air Force's first bombing mission (on the night of 12/13 June 1941). While in No. 6 (RCAF) Group, 405 Squadron was selected for Pathfinder Force and moved down from Leeming, Yorkshire, in April 1943. Its squadron commander, Johnny Fauquier, had an odd yet unique personal distinction in the RCAF's history: he was the first to drop a 4,000 lb 'blockbuster'.[25]

Hailed as one of the RCAF's 'greatest bombing leaders', Fauquier's actions during the Peenemünde raid earned him a DSO to add to his earlier DFC. He had further enhanced his reputation by circling the target for 45 minutes, exhorting his crews to more accurate bombing and closer concentration. A major raid,

Peenemünde involved close to 600 bombers. The citation for his DSO, announced soon after this attack, described him as a first-class officer with 'bounding energy and great drive' who 'contributed in a large measure to the high standard of operational efficiency of the squadron he commands'.

Without the Mosquitoes' radio directional and location equipment, the Halifax crews of 35 and 405 squadrons had to rely that night on their own skills and considerable operational experience to find the twin targets at Le Portel and to drop both their high explosives and their markers on those of the Mosquitoes. The priority was to 'stoke' the red TIs so that Main Force was in no doubt about where to bomb.

Bomber Command instructions issued down through the groups which were providing the Pathfinders and Main Force crews were that the Halifaxes would back up the TIs already burning and the bombers in Main Force would bomb only on the TIs – on the reds, otherwise at the centre of the greens. There were 'Special Instructions' that bombs were to be dropped on TIs only, and that if no TIs were seen, bombs were to be brought back[26] (a clear indication, if any was needed, that Bomber Command did not want to kill, maim or harm French people or property unnecessarily).

The onus was quite clearly on the Mosquito crews, with the benefit of their proven 'blind-bombing' equipment and the marking capabilities of the Halifax crews. If the reds and greens of the Oboe-equipped Mosquitoes were in place and backed up visually by the Halifaxes, then the massive maximum bomb loads of successive waves of Main Force bombers were cleared for release. Crews would open the bomb doors, see that the TIs were in their sights, then let go.

First-arrival Halifaxes held back as no TIs had been released – the first Mosquito aborted, the next one delayed. The crew in Z-Zebra of 35 Squadron was rather anxious on the run-up to the first drop because no markers were visible – 'nothing to go at', their captain remarked.[27] It seemed almost the last minute when one did appear. Failure to see any markers meant either 'going round again' or aborting the mission.

The crew called this operation a 'pongo' – an easy trip because there was little time over enemy-occupied territory and apparently a target that was none too heavily defended. There was a set number of trips to a tour of operations – generally about thirty – which earned either a rest or an end altogether to bombing. So a pongo was much sought after as it improved the chances of completing a tour, and made survival a better prospect.

Although the Halifaxes had to mark twice, the operation was not so much troublesome as bewildering. The two zero hours were three-quarters of an hour apart and the Halifaxes had to spend the bulk of those 45 minutes circling in mid-Channel doing rate one turns to waste time. It became more and more confusing as there were searchlights criss-crossing the skies and AA guns blazing away on both sides of the Channel. Considerately, those on the English coast confined their activities to German raiders and left the RAF bombers well alone.

Each side was doing its stuff, at least one Halifax pilot admitting to being in a general state of disorientation, tending to lose track of which coast was which while going round and round.[28]

Keeping the markers topped up meant following as closely as possible the timetable set in the orders for the operation: generally one plane every minute, two Mosquitoes with red TIs, three with greens and ten Halifaxes with greens – fifteen aircraft in 16 minutes in each phase, Main Force with an intended 123 bombers streaming in to bomb between 2200 and 2215 hours in Phase I and a further 114 between 2245 and 2300 hours in Phase II.

Rounding off the entire operation was a twist – back came the Mosquitoes, four from 105 Squadron that had not been mustered for a marking role, all carrying out a bombing mission armed with three 500 lb and one 250 lb bomb apiece. It was small compared with the Halifax markers, the individual loads of which were five 1,000 lb and six 500 lb, but nonetheless effective in swelling the overall tonnage.

Unlike the Halifaxes, the Mosquitoes had the facility of direction and release under radio control from ground stations. Winterton II was their 'Mouse' for Oboe release and all four crews noted its signal transmission as 'very good' or 'good'.

At 26,000 feet, the bomb-carrying Mosquitoes raced to their target, *Andante*, at roughly 10 minute intervals, D-Dog, K-King, H-Harry and B-Beer releasing successively between 2309 and 2339 hours to end the night's operations in which the first high explosives had been dropped precisely 1 hour 35 minutes earlier at 2204.

The bombs loosed by the Halifaxes and Mosquitoes of Pathfinder Force together exceeded a formidable 38 tons – as much high explosive as carried on some of the bombing missions against enemy territory earlier in the war.

Yet even this paled beside the combined tonnage of the huge numbers of bombs that had been trundled out of secure armament stores and into the waiting Stirlings and Wellingtons on airfields across England in readiness for Bomber Command's unique contribution to *Operation Starkey*.

No one intended it, no one guessed it – the outcome that no one foresaw was the tragedy of Le Portel, a seaside resort just south of Boulogne – 'the town that had to die'.

. . . and the Bombs go Down

Before Pathfinder Force's nifty little Mosquitoes and the bigger, much heavier Halifaxes were poised for take-off to spearhead Bomber Command's onslaught against the gun batteries, W-William, a comparatively ancient Wellington bomber based at Finningley, Nottinghamshire, beat them all to it!

At a couple of minutes before 2000 hours on that evening of 8 September 1943, the crew of this aircraft were gaining one distinction in their own right together with a second as members of one of Bomber Command's training units.

No. 18 OTU's W-William was the first into the air among the 258 aircraft in Bomber Command that were mustered for this raid. Indeed, the raid would be employing more aircraft from the OTUs than at any time since the showpiece 'Thousand Bomber Raid' against Cologne on the night of 30/31 May 1942. On that memorable occasion, even planes from Flying Training Command contributed to the 1,047 massed for this history-making event,[1] though probably it achieved more in propaganda value around the world than in effective attack on the selected targets.

Apart from isolated occasions – for example, when thirty or so joined in each of the *Operation Starkey* raids on the ammunition dumps and other targets in the forests of Northern France during the last week of August and the first in September – OTU crews were never sent on bombing missions. It was not the practice to expose these trainees so early to such hazards.

For Bomber Command, *Starkey* was the time to pull out all the stops. It was no use recriminating now that the 'man at the top', the AOC-in-C, Air Chief Marshal Sir Arthur Harris, had made his views perfectly clear in the most forceful of terms, that this operation was at best simply 'play-acting' and he really must be allowed to get on with the proper job of bombing Germany.

At this time 'Bomber' Harris had the benefit of the newer Halifaxes and the still more recent Lancasters for the raids against enemy territory. The pre-war Wellingtons were coming to the end of their operational days and the Stirlings, the first of the four-engined bombers, carried smaller loads slower and less high than their successors.

Against Germany he was relying more and more on the Halifax and Lancaster squadrons. That very night, until weather conditions caused it to be cancelled,* some six waves of bombers from five groups with target markers from five squadrons in

---

* Codenamed *Whitebait*, this Berlin raid was timed to begin at 0010 hours but was cancelled by HQ Bomber Command at 1810 hours, which then issued orders delaying zero hour for the *Starkey* attack by 30 minutes to 2200 hours.[2]

Pathfinder Force were all set to continue a new series of raids on Berlin. There were 334 bombers ready to go – the 198 Lancasters each with a 4,000 lb bomb and the 136 Halifaxes with a mixed load of 1,000 lb and 2,000 lb bombs.[3]

Now, having promised no less than 200 bombers for this final stage of *Starkey*, Harris called up all that were left in the cupboard: Stirling squadrons whose crews were nonetheless no strangers to operational duties and Wellingtons from a combination of operational squadrons and training units – pupil crews yet to be tested in action.

OTU instructors were drawn principally from aircrew who had completed one or more operational tours; and the pupils under training were generally teamed up to form complete crews that would then stay together, going first to a conversion unit if a change of aircraft became necessary, then to a squadron in Britain or to an overseas command.

With the 'Thousand Bomber Raid', Bomber Command called on OTU crews to help make up that magic number. For *Starkey* the situation was much the same in that this too became a numbers game . . . the choice was to include the OTUs or reduce the size of the force committed for what Harris regarded as his far more worthwhile targets.

No. 93 (Operational Training) Group was required to put up thirty-nine Wellingtons, the greatest number among the three OTU groups involved in the Le Portel attack. It had just completed its first year, passing out 218 fully trained crews the month before, well over four times the initial intake.

Formed in September 1942, No. 93 Group began with Nos 28, 30 and 81 OTUs, subsequently increasing to a total of seven with the creation of No. 83 at Peplow in July 1943. A total of 1,123 fully trained crews had already gone through the system in No. 93 Group, August having seen both the highest output and the most flying hours in any single month so far.

At No. 18 OTU, which had moved from Bramcote earlier in the year, sixteen British and eight Polish crews completed their training during August, the British crews being posted to conversion units, mostly in No. 1 Group, the Poles mainly joining their fellow nationals in this and other groups.

The closest that OTU crews usually came to operating against the enemy was in what the RAF called 'Nickelling': dropping leaflets over enemy-occupied territory. These were 8½ by 5 inch sheets assembled for dropping in bundles 4 inches thick and held together by a rubber band about the waist, one third the distance from the end, and by a light string lengthwise round the bundle.[4]

The rubber band would hold the leaflets together long enough to prevent them from blowing back into the tail of the aircraft; the string was to stop bundles blowing apart when loading. Each bundle of 1,500 leaflets was released at 5 second intervals. For the record, the estimated rate of fall was 220 feet per minute. Awareness of wind direction at all times was vital: where a message was intended for a particular town, having the leaflets fluttering down on open countryside was a waste of everyone's time, and, maybe, a waste of life because not all Nickelling planes came back.

OTU crews had their misfortunes in such missions. No. 18 lost a plane in a crash soon after taking off on the night of 1/2 August; another, the same night, returned showing the wounds of war – damaged by enemy action during the mission.

Losses were not necessarily confined to flights over defended territory. On the day of the Le Portel mission, a Lancaster visiting from another airfield crashed within 3 minutes of taking off from Wymeswold, Leicestershire, on a routine flight, and all nine people – the crew of six and their passengers, three lads in the Air Training Corps – lost their lives.[5]

No. 91 Group was the other operational training group involved in Phase I of the twin attacks on the long-range guns. Its newly published summary of events noted that 'on the last two nights of the month [August 1943] aircraft from the Group, manned by pupil crews, took part in bombing operations for the first time since the 'Thousand Bomber' series of last year'.

Commenting on photographs taken automatically from three of its aircraft which were subsequently plotted as showing the AP, the publication noted that those results were 'convincing evidence of the readiness with which our crews are able to adapt themselves to modern operational conditions and reflect favourably upon the standard of our training'.

It is sad to relate that the standard of dress did not always result in similar praise. The AOC, writing to his station commanders at Abingdon, Harwell, Kinloss, Lossiemouth, Moreton, Wellesbourne, Pershore and Honeybourne, called their attention to 'a marked deterioration which I have observed in the general smartness and turn-out of RAF personnel, particularly aircrew, both on and off their stations'.[6]

He was precise in his criticism: laxity in the giving and acknowledging of salutes, bad deportment, irregularities in uniform and, in particular, the growing habit of aircrew to slouch about with a hand or hands in their pockets. Those, the AOC demanded, required immediate attention.

Station commanders were instructed to take 'energetic steps' to put those matters right, including, he proposed, 'placing a restriction on leave and passes to offenders'. In the services, this was the 1940s version of the ultimate weapon.

Harwell-based crews had enjoyed a brief absence from such disciplines when ferrying bombers from the UK to the generally relaxing environment of 'behind the lines' bases in the Middle East. A total of twenty-nine bombers were despatched and all arrived safely at their first overseas destinations in Gibraltar, Ras Elma and Port Lyautey.

Coincidentally, almost the same number of aircraft made brief visits to Harwell in that same month of August 1943, though these were all planes which, for one reason or another, landed at Harwell instead of their own bases when homeward bound from operational sorties as far afield as Nuremburg, St Nazaire and Milan, the target area in the latter having been left 'a concentrated mass of flames'.[7]

As with the operational squadrons, not all of the OTU crews made it safely back home, either to their own bases or when having to get down quickly at the nearest airfield in the event of trouble. On the night of 3/4 September, one of No. 22 OTU's Wellingtons back from France just failed to reach Harwell and came down near Wantage, a number of the crew taking to their parachutes in the final moments.

The planes from Nos 91 and 93 Groups detailed for Phase I comprised respectively 22 (from 4 airfields) and 39 (from 7 airfields), a combined total of 61, with W-William from Finningley the first of these pupil crews to become airborne and the first of the grand total of 263 intended for the targets north and south of Le Portel.

When W-William, a Wellington Mk X, lifted off from the runway at Finningley, it was followed by eight more from No. 18 OTU, all of these crews destined to reach their target and drop up to eight 500 lb bombs apiece from maximum height during Phase I of the operation. This particular OTU and four others in the group combined to contribute a greater number of planes than any other of the OTU groups.

Compared with the sixty-one pupil crews flying the twin-engined Wellingtons, No. 3 Group's effort had considerably more muscle: it put five squadrons into both phases of the twin attack, another two squadrons into Phase I and four more squadrons into Phase II, a total of 112 of this group's four-engined Stirlings taking part.

Inevitably there would be aircraft which would not reach and bomb their target. One OTU in Phase I lost the benefit of two of its number, which brought back their bombs for entirely different reasons. One had hydraulic trouble, which made the rear gunner's turret unserviceable – 'Tail-end Charlies' were indispensable for the safety of the bombers when under fighter attack; the other experienced a fire in the port engine on the home side of the English Channel.[8]

Much worse was the tragedy that befell one of the Stirling crews in No. 3 Group, a group well used to the dangers that came with bombing missions, though what happened on this occasion was something that was a risk every time any aircrew climbed aboard, switched on the engines and made ready for take-off, whether for a training flight or a mission.

It happened to 75 (New Zealand) Squadron, the first New Zealand squadron in the RAF and the first Commonwealth squadron in Bomber Command. Based at Mepal, 6 miles west of Ely, Cambridgeshire, it had carried out its first bombing attack of the war on the night of 17/18 April 1940 when two planes attacked the airfield at Stavanger in Norway. Historically it must be noted too that on a subsequent raid, against the German town of Munster on the night of 7/8 July 1941, Sgt J.A. Ward, one of the squadron's second pilots, gained the VC, only to lose his life, in action, within six weeks of colleagues and the world learning that he had won this highest of awards.

Considerable gallantry was displayed that night at Mepal when, with 75 Squadron's bombers carrying maximum loads for this unusually short-range target, one of them swung off the runway and crashed into two houses on the far side of the perimeter track. It caught fire almost immediately, and in the fire various bombs exploded, the aircraft becoming a total wreck. A petrol tanker and a petrol bowser were also damaged beyond repair.[9]

The first civilian deaths in this stage of *Starkey* occurred at this time – two plus a number of injured – as well as the captain of the aircraft, who was a New Zealander, the navigator/bomb-aimer and the flight engineer. The toll in this tragic incident rose higher still with deaths among people going to the assistance at this grim scene. One was a member of another aircrew and the other an officer in the Women's Auxiliary Air Force.

The station personnel at Mepal were accustomed to losing comrades and friends in operational sorties. Just the previous month, four planes went missing when laying mines, three others in a single raid on Berlin, two in raids elsewhere and there were three crash landings: one plane with its rear gunner dead when heavy flak struck the aircraft over the target, causing the bomb-aimer and wireless operator to bale out inadvertently owing to an intercom failure.[10]

The unit providing the most aircraft for both this first phase of the Le Portel attack and the second was 90 Squadron at Wratting Common, with ten planes for each. This was a squadron which originated in the First World War and re-formed in November 1942 as a heavy-bomber squadron, equipped with Stirlings from the start.

Longer-established was 218 (Gold Coast) Squadron, which flew its earliest missions with single-engined Battles. It gave up these for Stirlings towards the end of 1941, three months after the Governor of the Gold Coast and the peoples of the Gold Coast territories officially adopted the squadron.

It, too, included a VC holder among its former aircrew: Acting Fl./Sgt Arthur Aaron, whose operational skills and dedication had already earned the DFM. No. 3 Group's third aircrew VC, and the first to a former member of the Air Training Corps, the award was granted posthumously for his role during an attack on Turin on the night of 12/13 August, in a month which turned out to be Bomber Command's most active of the year to date.

Despite being severely wounded and his navigator dead, he landed the plane safely in North Africa, only to die from his injuries within a few hours.* For much of the flight, while he was too badly hurt to stay at the controls, the wireless operator and the flight engineer together shared this onerous task – a stirring example of devotion to duty which gained for both of them the DFM.

Of the remaining squadrons in Phase I, 15 Squadron had carried out its first bombing attack on the day the Germans invaded Holland, Belgium and Luxembourg, on an airfield near Rotterdam that had been seized by their paratroopers; 196 had six months' operations under its belt; 620 had formed out of C Flight in another squadron (214) as recently as 17 June 1943 at Chedburgh, starting operations just two days later; and 199 was an even more recent arrival on the bombing scene, only now into its second month flying Stirlings.

Besides the operationally qualified and pupil crews in Bomber Command, No. 3 Group had some noteworthy 'guests' on the roster – planes and crews not merely 'going along for the ride' but playing an active role in the proceedings: five Boeing B-17f Flying Fortresses with the Stars and Stripes to the fore, for these planes were dressed in the colours of the United States 8th Air Force.

For night training and operations, 422 Squadron of No. 305 Bombardment Group was affiliated to No. 3 Group, being based at Chelveston, which was one of the group's several airfields in Northamptonshire and elsewhere in the Midlands. History was certainly being made that night, for this was to be the USAAF's first experience of night bombing off British soil.[11] The high-flying 'Forts' were more accustomed to daylight operations when, generally in big formations and bristling with guns for mutual protection against fighters, they were the 'day shift' to Bomber Command's 'night shift'.

---

* All the more tragic is that Aaron was hit by gunfire from another bomber; the crew mistook his plane for an enemy fighter. However, if the culprits were ever aware of their error, it was a cross that they did not have to bear for very long. They lost their own lives on a subsequent operation.[12]

Due to commence with the critical red marker burning on the ground by zero hour, 2200 hours, Phase I suffered a delayed start on account of the Oboe failure, so the first visual indication of the AP came when the Mosquitoes' green markers dropped at 2202 hours. Within 2 minutes the Stirling squadrons and the OTU Wellingtons were loosing their bombs onto the northern gun emplacement – 1,000 and 500 lb from the Stirlings, 500 lb from the smaller, older Wellingtons. Four experienced crews and two pupil crews shared the distinction of releasing the first high explosives, all aiming on the first green of the night, at 2204 hours.[13]

Visibility was good with no cloud and bright moonlight. Defensive action varied during the course of the attack, but a common assessment was that while the searchlights were very active – a dozen or more at a time in a comparatively small area – the AA fire was moderately light.

Among the first into the attack was 15 Squadron's G-George when, flying at 13,500 feet, the TIs came into the bomb-aimer's sights and it was 'Bombs away! Let's go home!' H-Harry reckoned that the TIs were short of the target, but the instructions were to bomb only them so that was what they did. Coming in a minute later and seeing where the greens were burning in relation to the breakwater, W-William also thought they were short of the AP and decided to try to remedy the situation by aiming their bombs to overshoot. C-Charlie did two orbits before the bomb-aimer saw the TIs. When they were in his sights he considered that while half of the bomb load was placed centrally, the other half had overshot the markers on which he had aimed.

By now, 620 Squadron's bombing strength was cut by two Stirlings: one crashed on take-off, though no casualties were reported, and one jettisoned its high explosives in the sea when engine failure prompted a return to base. Pupil crews in the OTU Wellingtons, having reached and bombed the target without encountering those sorts of hazards, expressed surprise at what seemed to them to be an almost tedious routine in this first taste of a bombing mission: 'We didn't expect such a quiet one,' remarked one of the crew of No. 27 OTU's R-Roger.

Not all of the crews would have agreed. No. 23 OTU had two planes in trouble: one returned with three of its 500 lb bombs still in the bomb bay, hung up because of an electrical failure; the other was unable to bomb through a bizarre set of circumstances – it headed for home owing to starboard engine failure following pursuit by an unidentified plane.[14]

On average, a plane was bombing every 8 seconds, each one dropping eight (sometimes nine) bombs as a single consignment. Down below, though, this rate would have seemed far more intense because the bulk of the attack was concentrated within the 5 minutes before the only red TI arrived. The skies were alive with the sounds of aero-engines and explosions, the night seemingly turned into day with the split-second flashes of exploding bombs and the penetrating brilliance of the target markers.

In the space of 60 seconds, No. 22 OTU alone had five planes all bombing on the first two green markers to go down, those of the first Mosquito and the first backing-up Halifax, K-King from 405 Squadron, whose joint effort ahead of the only red TI in Phase I appeared to be drawing the attention of more than half of the Main Force bombers.

Bombing on the greens, 90 Squadron's K-King saw large fires increasing on leaving the target area. One of 199 Squadron's planes, while seeing nothing of the results of its own bombing, reported one fire visible even when passing the Thames Estuary, 60 miles away.[15]

The first two backers-up from 35 Squadron, Z-Zebra and M-Mother, refrained from releasing their markers because the expected red was not present, so they bombed on green. There was a further green at about the same time as the single mid-stage red – 35 Squadron's first. Both of the Halifax squadrons followed up with two aircraft apiece, dropping more greens. The final Mosquito green came when all of the action was just about over. The only other Halifax from 35 Squadron to play any part in Phase I decided that it was best to hold back from further marking and just to bomb.

What about No. 18 OTU's W-William, first of the Wellingtons, indeed first of all the planes into the air that night, even before the Pathfinders and ahead of the operational-experienced Stirlings? Early take-off was necessary because of the Wellingtons' slower speed: they needed longer to reach the target area than the Stirlings, longer still than the Halifaxes and considerably longer than the Mosquitoes, which fairly raced through the sky.

W-William bombed 5 minutes after zero hour, the first of its unit to do so, and headed home without incident. However, one of the others saw a single-engined Messerschmidt fighter in the target area and another an enemy aircraft which it could not identify. One brought back a 500 lb bomb because of a mechanical failure and three diverted to other airfields when the weather deteriorated.

Inevitably there were those which missed their slot in the timetable: A-Apple from 15 Squadron bombed on the apparently still-burning red TI at 2228 hours, almost a quarter of an hour after the Phase I bombing was due to have been completed, confidently reporting 'several good explosions seen on the run-in'.

The Americans, over the target 6 minutes earlier, flying at 28,000 feet, far higher than any of the RAF bombers, loosed a total of forty-three of their 500 lb bombs on what the briefing officers said would be ammunition and fuel dumps. This description was as inaccurate as the terms used by their opposite numbers in air force blue were vague.

In some aircrew briefings, Boulogne was named as the target area. Within No. 3 Group, more used to bombing enemy territory than an enemy-occupied country, the reason for a heavy attack on targets near Boulogne caused considerable conjecture.[16] Elsewhere, phrases such as 'special targets' were used, although obviously the map reference showed precisely where, if not what, was coming under attack.

It was not unusual for the nature of the attack to be withheld, although sometimes it was obvious: for example, the submarine bases on the French coast and industrial centres in Germany. The name *Starkey* was not mentioned: few were privy to its existence, and there was no disclosure that there were long-range gun emplacements to be knocked out. Le Portel was scarcely mentioned – the town was not a target – though Cap d'Alprech, the geographical location for Phase II, would have rated a mention in a number of those briefings.

By chance rather than by design, this was a night when No. 3 Group was to host a top-level visitor representing none other than the Russian leader, Joseph Stalin:

Maj.-Gen. Skiliarov, Soviet Military and Air Attaché, with members of the Soviet Military Mission in London, who were keen to observe procedures at an operational bomber station.[17] However, it seems unlikely that the VIPs would have learned much more about the targets and the intentions of the *Starkey* missions that night than the crew members who were about to perform them.

The precise number of aircraft allocated to this first part of Bomber Command's role in the Culminating Phase of *Starkey* would have been known to its HQ via an interchange of teleprinter signals, the method of communication employed to transmit an outline of the operational orders passed down first from Bomber Command HQ to the various group HQ and ultimately to the airfields.

In time the final statistics would be collated at Bomber Command HQ, and then inside Air Ministry and among those running *Starkey*. For Phase I, 9 aircraft having dropped their target markers and 116 their bombs; 665 of those bombs were 500 lb – a total weight of some 148.4 tons; and 409 of the bombs were 1,000 lb, which added a further 182.6 tons to produce a Phase I total of some 331 tons, to which must be added the 9.6 tons (43 x 500 lb) dropped by the 5 Fortresses of the US bombing group whose numbers were not included in Bomber Command's tallies.[18]

There were 2 men in each of the 3 Mosquitoes, and generally 6 in each of the 54 Wellingtons, 7 in each of the 9 Halifaxes, 7 in each of the 53 Stirlings and 9 in each of the 5 Fortresses. Thus some 800-plus officers and non-commissioned officers were over this target at some time or other between 2202 hours, when the TIs dropped by 109 Squadron's W-William in Pathfinder Force began burning, and 2230 hours, when the camera in 90 Squadron's B-Beer at the tail end of Main Force 'clicked' to provide film evidence back at base to plot its position when the bombs were released.

In Phase I the multinational force included individuals from the Dominions and occupied territories such as Poland, besides the Canadian and New Zealand squadrons and the American unit. In Phase II an entire Polish squadron joined forces – 300 Squadron, which was in another of Bomber Command's operational groups, No. 1 Group.

The first Polish-manned bomber squadron to form in the RAF, 300 (Masovian) Squadron, began its career at Bramcote, Warwickshire, on 1 July 1940 when personnel from its 10 flying crews and 180 in maintenance and other sections saw the Polish Air Force flag hoisted for the first time in Britain. The first operational mission came on the night of 14/15 September 1940 when three of its Battle bombers attacked barges and shipping in Boulogne harbour, 'on the doorstep', so to speak, of its present target.

The Polish squadron introduced a new dimension into the attack: while generally the fifteen Wellington crews from Ingham, Lincolnshire, were each to carry nine of the more usual 500 lb general purpose bombs, two were to be loaded with a single 4,000 lb high-capacity bomb, familiarly known as a 'blockbuster'. This was not particularly unusual as a bomb – the RAF had been using it for two-and-a-half years, though not extensively. However, to give the Wellington the carrying capability it was necessary to use a modified Mk X available within this squadron. For the raids on the gun batteries, Bomber Command's orders authorized its squadrons to make discretionary use of such planes with such a load.[19]

Among crews of 300 Squadron, E-Edward missed the raid: the pilot abandoned the task on take-off when both engines were found to be unserviceable – they were over-revving. This meant facing up to the problem of bringing down the plane safely while fully loaded with bombs and the tanks full, but for the fuel so far used.

In the language of understatement favoured by aircrew, here was 'a very difficult situation' where two attempts at landing with the bombs were unsuccessful. The power coming from the port engine was beyond control and the pilot had to overshoot on both occasions rather than risk landing.[20]

The wireless operator fired a red cartridge to alert airfield personnel to the emergency and in doing so the fabric and soundproofing material inside the cabin caught alight. With this further potential hazard and the fact that by now the port engine was still playing up, E-Edward jettisoned its entire load of nine 500 lb bombs and the photoflash about 3 miles east of the airfield. Despite the precautions taken to make them all safe, one of the bombs and the photoflash exploded on the ground, though no damage or casualties were subsequently reported.

Around 6 minutes later, E-Edward landed at its third attempt, successfully but 'with considerable difficulty', in the pilot's words (another understatement?), and he cut both engines just after touchdown to avoid running out of runway. Meanwhile the fire caused by the warning cartridge had flared up and become a serious menace, only being put out when ground crews could get at it with chemicals.

The Polish pilot, a flight lieutenant, brought his plane and crew home to fight another day. This was 32 minutes of drama unknown at the time to the thirteen (lucky thirteen?) Wellingtons of 300 Squadron who did make it to France.

One crew, however – G-George's – got cold feet soon after leaving Ingham. This was no reflection on their courage, but the effect of a problem related to the aircraft: the pilot's escape hatch stayed open during the entire flight,[21] and as a consequence everyone aboard virtually froze – they bombed from a height in excess of 3 miles where the night air is enough 'to freeze the private parts off a brass monkey'.

Red and green markers released about on time and almost simultaneously by the first two Mosquitoes gave 300 Squadron's C-Charlie and A-Apple an early and positive identification of the AP. The target area had been evident long before, however, because the glow of what one crew considered to be a fairly large fire could be seen from as far away as 25 miles. At 2244 hours 30 seconds, therefore jumping the gun by precisely half a minute, A-Apple estimated the centre of the green salvo as its AP, and B-Beer chose the centre of the reds, which had reached the ground in a 'set of three' rather than as a single pinpoint.

Both of the 4,000 lb 'blockbusters' were released without problem: J-Johnny's from 18,500 feet at 2246 hours, a minute after zero hour for Phase II, and judged to have exploded in the centre of the markers; likewise W-William's 4 minutes later, exploding in the centre of the reds.

No. 1 Group provided one more squadron, No. 166, formed like others during the First World War and re-formed at Kirmington, Lincolnshire, as recently as January 1943. The hazards of bombing became quickly evident when one of its Wellingtons failed to return from the squadron's first operational mission on the night of 29/30 January, one of a series of raids on the German U-boat pens at Lorient.

About to re-equip with Lancasters and against what their briefing team described as 'a special target', 166 Squadron put up ten Wellingtons, each with nine 500 lb bombs. The consensus was that the enemy opposition was slight, consisting chiefly of the AA defences at Boulogne. Although their attacks spanned the period between a minute after the scheduled commencement time and a minute before its intended conclusion, none of these crews had any hint of the enemy night fighters which others saw looking for likely victims.

The mission went 'entirely according to plan – very uneventful,' according to W-William, whose pilot was the highest ranking commissioned officer among the crews in 166 Squadron; 'a very quiet and uneventful sortie,' according to R-Roger's pilot, a warrant officer with the DFM; and 'a very easy sortie – uneventful,' in the words of one of their lowest ranking non-commissioned officers, flying M-Mother.[22]

No. 3 Group was back in again with more Stirlings: five of these squadrons – 15, 75, 90, 196 and 218 – providing further aircraft in succession to their contribution to Phase I. An additional four squadrons – 149, 214, 622 and 623 – came on the scene for the first time.

The three aircraft from 623 Squadron, which had been formed for less than a month, stemming from a 'spare' flight of Stirlings belonging to 218 (Gold Coast) Squadron at Downham Market, Norfolk, experienced no trouble with the searchlights ineffectively probing the night skies.

However, 4 minutes after E-Edward loosed its bombs from 15,800 feet on red TIs in the bomb sight, a twin-engined aircraft gave cause for concern among the crew. Some thought it was a 'friendly' – one of the OTU Wellingtons – while others suggested that it was perhaps an enemy fighter.

Although suspicions were increasing, machine-gun fire was withheld pending confirmation. This came soon enough when the suspect dropped to the rear and into position for a stern attack. E-Edward began to 'corkscrew' on a warning signal from the rear gunner and there was an exchange of rounds, the Stirling's tracers seen tracking towards the enemy fighter which was now identified as being a Ju 88. Four of E-Edward's crew saw the bullets hit but the plane disappeared out of sight before anyone could reach a conclusion as to whether it had been damaged or destroyed.[23]

For Phase II, 622 Squadron, born the same day as 623 and formed as a two-flight squadron from the third flight of 15 Squadron at Mildenhall, Suffolk, produced five bombers, all of them dropping their nine 1,000 lb bombs on the red TIs. It was a 'special target' designated 'Boulogne (South)', according to the briefing teams.

For the nine crews in 149 (East India) Squadron, whose first mission of the Second World War took place on day one, the location given was rather more precise: Cap d'Alprech. The first to attack, A-Apple, found the coastline clearly visible and easily recognizable. Crew members saw the green TIs going down, followed by the reds, while making the run-in to the target and bombed within 4 minutes. The arrival time was such that the crews in several of the planes saw the green TIs cascading while the reds were burning on the ground.

Of those from No. 3 Group which were operating only against the southern target, 214 Squadron was potentially the most powerful, with ten Stirlings loaded with a total of sixty 1,000 lb and eighty 500 lb bombs. The effectiveness diminished when Q-Queen crashed on take-off and M-Mother failed to attack – it was too late arriving in the target area and had to waste the bomb load. Four of the 500 lb bombs were jettisoned in the sea, while two more together and a 1,000 lb bomb were made safe and dropped at Rushford Range. The remainder, still in excess of 2½ tons of high explosive materials, stayed on board.[24]

The first of 15 Squadron's aircraft to attack in Phase II ran into a problem with faulty action of the distributor arm. O-Orange was on the run-in to the target, following a course of 120 degrees and making 200 mph. Choosing his moment with the skills born of practical experience, the bomb-aimer triggered release, but while the photo flash worked, the bombs didn't.

The distributor arm, associated with the bomb release mechanism, decided not to move over, which meant that the bombs could not be freed from their racks. Those nine 1,000 lb bombs were clearly not destined for the gun batteries; instead, two were jettisoned on the journey back home but the remainder simply would not budge.

It was an anxious but safe landing with those seven lethal missiles still in the bay. This tended to happen from time to time, and there was a familiar routine to be followed by members of the squadron's armament team to ensure that there was no risk of an explosion when removing the bombs and returning them into store for checking and possible reuse.

The seven aircraft from 75 (New Zealand) Squadron, all of them taking off in the wake of the tragedy which cost civilian as well as service lives, bombed on the markers, undeterred by the searchlights and the predicted AA fire, and free from combat with the fighters.

The ten Stirlings from 90 Squadron, the four from 218 (Gold Coast) and the three from 196 were similarly unaffected. In all, eleven of No. 3 Group's squadrons participated in these two attacks. This was only one less than the number amassed for the German cities of Munchen-Gladbach and Berlin on the last two nights of the previous month. By comparison, the objective at Le Portel was a short-range target which senior officers on the headquarters staff regarded as 'an opportunity to carry out a model operation'.[25]

There were still two further components in the second phase: a contribution from another of Bomber Command's operational groups and additional support from pupil crews.

Canadian crews in Pathfinder Force's 405 Squadron had already carried that country's Maple Leaf emblem on the Halifaxes marking and bombing the gun batteries. Now twelve Wellingtons from 432 Squadron, the twelfth Royal Canadian Air Force squadron to be formed overseas during the Second World War, would extend the Canadians' involvement. It was the most northerly based unit in action that night, being located at Skipton-on-Swale, 4 miles west of Thirsk, in Yorkshire, and a member of No. 6 Group.

Evenly spreading themselves throughout the attack, Z-Zebra led 432 Squadron on a due east course, at an indicated air speed of 170 mph, when the red markers were seen cascading and in the bombsight at the moment of releasing the nine 500 lb bombs some 30 seconds after zero hour for Phase II.

Within a few seconds, H-Harry had also released; then there were V-Vic and U-Uncle together at 2248 hours; L-Love at 2250 hours; D-Dog, whose pilot was on his twenty-second mission, released at 2252 hours, sharing this moment with Y-Yoke and K-King; B-Beer following at 2256 hours; and finally G-George, bombing from 17,400 feet on the centre of the green markers at 2301 hours and 30 seconds, by which time the raid was due to have been over for 90 seconds. Oddly enough, but quoting the pilot's words, by now all of the defences 'seemed to have closed down'.[26]

No. 92 (Operational Training) Group had five of its units in Phase II – 'Special Operations against targets in the Boulogne area' – all flying Wellingtons: No. 12 OTU at Chipping Warden, Oxfordshire; No. 16 at Upper Heyford, Oxfordshire; No. 17 at Upwood, Huntingdonshire; No. 26 at Wing, Buckinghamshire; and No. 29 at Bruntingthorpe, Leicestershire.

Where the pupil crews were concerned, a number were to be tested to the limit that night, and more sharply than many with considerable operational experience to look back on.

The maximum OTU involvement was down to No. 12 OTU with six Wellingtons detailed for the mission. Exceptional for these briefings, there was a touch of melodrama in the terms used: that the objective pure and simple was 'to attack and destroy a military target in the Boulogne area'.[27]

An incident during the day cast a heavy cloud over the preparations, one of the unit's aircraft having crashed near Bridgnorth, Shropshire, while on a cross-country flight. It was totally wrecked and there were no survivors among the crew: pupil pilot, navigator, bomb-aimer, wireless operator/gunner and mid-upper gunner – friends of so many.

This unit was particularly unfortunate. Just the previous month another of its Wellingtons had crashed near Snitterfield, Stratford-upon-Avon (the crew baling out and the pilot dying the following day as the result of injuries sustained). Twice there were instances of engine trouble forcing bale-outs while the pilot made an emergency landing.[28]

Apart from one of the six planes failing to take off, No. 12 OTU's 'attack-and-destroy' mission proved routine with all five crews satisfactorily pressing home the attack. However, whether the 'destroy' element was equally satisfactorily accomplished had to await efforts at confirmation.

No. 17 OTU had five crews taking part, and all of them bombed. No. 26 had four crews taking part and again all of them dropped their bombs. No. 29, also with four crews involved, dropped all but a solitary 500 lb bomb, which preferred to stay put in the bomb bay and return to base.

It was Z-Zebra which suffered this minor setback, its five bursts being claimed as seen in the centre of the green target markers at 2249 hours, a release time shared with N-Nuts and X-X-ray. The fourth plane, B-Beer, also bombing on the centre of the greens, though 9 minutes later, joined in a brief skirmish with a Ju 88 which moved in to attack from below in the port quarter. B-Beer made a diving turn to port and lost the fighter before any damage was sustained.

No. 16 OTU, seeing red and green markers beckoning even before crossing the English coast in the area of Dungeness, missed any excitement with enemy night fighters. However, engine trouble heightened the tension for two of its number – B-Beer and W-William – both crews wondering whether this night was going to be their last.

Bombing within 5 minutes of each other, B-Beer was the first in trouble when, shortly afterwards, the starboard engine failed and the pupil pilot correctly applied single-engine procedure. It was something that pilots under training were naturally required to follow as these mishaps easily happened. Eventually the engine picked up again but, with the revolutions alternating between 1,200 and 3,000 and then fire breaking out, the decision was made to set course for the closest, most suitable friendly airfield, which was Manston in Kent.

Manston, just about the first airfield visible when crossing the coast, proved the salvation for many an RAF plane in trouble on the way home from operations over the Continent. B-Beer crossed the coast at 1,000 feet, spotted Manston and made a successful forced landing without casualties. In this crew there were two Australians – the wireless operator and the bomb-aimer – so this further increased the number of nationals of countries besides Britain who were participating in these two bombing raids.

W-William experienced a similar problem, though it was the other engine which failed on this occasion. The pilot set course for Manston, as the other plane from the same unit had done, but this time the pilot ordered the crew to use their parachutes from 5,000 feet while he prepared for a single-engine landing, which he completed successfully. It was 'happy landings' all round: the crew suffered no injuries through baling out and the pilot gained a commendation from No. 92 Group's AOC.[29]

The same AOC was already on record as saying, in respect of these operational training units joining in the bombing of ammunition dumps in the forests of Northern France, that the quality of their crews had been tested 'in the fire of war'. This quality was high, he declared, and air photos showed that on each occasion the right target had been attacked by a high proportion of crews.[30]

What about those gun batteries to the north and south of Le Portel? Had 'a high proportion of crews' attacked 'the right target' there?

It would be some time before anyone knew the answer to that question, which would require all of the available photographic evidence to be collated, examined and assessed. Given that there were some 19 Pathfinder bombers and 215 Main Force bombers (plus the 5 Fortresses) effective in the two phases of this attack, the magnitude of the operational research teams' job was abundantly clear.

Phase II saw 17 more Pathfinders and 108 more Main Force bombers brought into the attack. Some 11 dropped target markers and 122 dropped bombs. Four of those were 250 lb bombs – a total weight of some 0.5 tons; 746 were 500 lb – 166.5 tons; 374 were 1,000 lb – 166.9 tons; and when adding the two 4,000 lb bombs there was a Phase II total of some 337.5 tons. Phase I and Phase II saw a combined force of 234 aircraft dropping 2,243 bombs containing 678.1 tons of high explosives, plus some 5.9 tons of incendiaries. Strictly speaking the TIs were so categorized because of their capability as fire-raising projectiles when burning on the ground. Some 1,500-plus men were in the air during those 90 or so minutes. The two attacks absorbed the bulk of the planes that 'Bomber' Harris could call on: virtually 90 per cent of all of the Stirlings that No. 3 Group had available for operations at 1800 hours that night, all but one of No. 1 Group's Wellingtons and all but three of those in No. 6 Group, together with 20 per cent of Pathfinder Group's combined force of twin- and four-engined aircraft, 40 per cent of its Halifaxes and a slightly greater percentage of its Mosquitoes.[31] Statistically, it is interesting to note that if the Berlin operation that night had not been cancelled, a total of 103 Pathfinders and 571 Main Force bombers would have been assembled for take-off – one of the largest forces amassed for a single night's operations since Harris took charge of Bomber Command on 22 February 1942, and exceeded less than a dozen times in raids on the Ruhr (6), Hamburg (4) and Berlin (on 23/24 August 1943). A 'reciprocal' effort on the *Luftwaffe*'s part saw some 8 German bombers over East Anglia and the southern counties of England between 2118 and 2240, dropping no more than 7 bombs without causing damage or casualties; 2 of the raiders were destroyed and 1 damaged.[32]

In the air that night, four RAF planes were hit by German AA fire, which an interceptions/tactics report would later assess as generally having been 'moderate' in intensity and accuracy.[33] This came not only from the fixed defences of the areas attacked, but also from ships in port and off the coast, as well as from other points along the route. Although there was little evidence of activity by controlled night fighters, enemy aircraft were seen by a number of crews besides those of 623 Squadron's E-Edward and No. 29 OTU's B-Beer. Sightings included what were said to be an Me 210 and Do 217s in addition to Ju 88s and single-engined aircraft. Most did not open fire and broke away when fired on by the bombers' gunners – six Stirlings and two Wellingtons among the operational squadrons, and five Wellingtons from the OTUs all having directed bursts lasting from 2 to 5 seconds at enemy fighters that night. It was otherwise uneventful: no significant damage to the RAF or USAAF planes and no claims of *Luftwaffe* planes being destroyed or damaged.

On the ground, French families in the vicinity of the twin attacks saw their homes crumbling around them – the population was decimated and hardly a building was left standing. While the survivors picked themselves up, the accuracy of those pinpointing markers and the bombs aimed at them became apparent in the RAF's photographic darkrooms.

Chapter Ten

Life in the Cellars . . . and Death

It was Wednesday 8 September 1943, and in Le Portel there were no indications as to what lay ahead, either in the immediate future or in the longer term. It was true that the uncanny period of calm had been disturbed by the daylight bombing four days previously when seven Portelois had lost their lives, and just this day their families had laid them to rest. However, there was no pattern emerging: Sunday, Monday and Tuesday had passed without incident and now, Wednesday, daylight had come and was nearly gone with nothing untoward happening. Could this be a further respite? What was the purpose of the previous bombing and what was now in prospect? These were fair questions. Nothing had changed in Le Portel to make this seaside resort any the more interesting to their friends across the water, and nothing had changed to make Le Portel any the more useful to the occupying forces.

In the Pas de Calais, people knew that some areas were particularly vulnerable. Offensive, or defensive, construction work would become known and offer a tempting target for the Allied bombers; factories were likely to be attacked from time to time; movements within the communications network would similarly attract interest; but none of these factors exercised any influence on Le Portel. That most recent bombing over the weekend was presumably meant for vessels and installations in the port area in greater Boulogne. However, so far as the Portelois were aware, there was no actual or likely build-up of shipping, freight or military personnel in their neighbourhood which might encourage fresh raids.

The situation was akin to that in the fishing ports of Devon and Cornwall where many families of Portelois were well settled and into their fourth year as evacuees. An occasional incursion by one or more enemy aircraft which bombed or machine-gunned at random was enough to make everyone think that more of the same was to come. Sometimes it did, but more often it did not; and there was no point in fearing the worst. Live for today; let tomorrow take care of itself.

Civil defence organizations on both sides of the Channel recognized the need to be prepared for any eventuality. In Le Portel the fire service had devoted much of the previous couple of years investing in new equipment, improved techniques and better training[1] – in a word, modernizing, for anything that might happen as the war ground on. Mostly these were young men, aged 20 to 35, physically in good shape, sporty and energetic, mounting a round-the-clock watch with the vigour, attentiveness and humour typical of professionals in uniform doing a job that someone had to do, war or no war.

All of the emergency services in and around Le Portel were on standby that Wednesday – it was their routine after all – and everyone had made sure that their equipment was in order and their supplies were ready to meet any call. The firefighters were not alone; this was just as much the norm for the rescue crews and the ambulance and medical teams. Besides the professionals there were the volunteers in each of these areas, the difference being that they were part-timers and by implication less highly trained though equally dedicated. Full-timers and part-timers were united in their desire to maintain a constant state of preparedness in the knowledge that to waver could place property at risk and perhaps even cost lives – the lives of other Portelois.

That Wednesday was an unusually lovely late-summer's day, warm with the skies blue and cloudless, so different from the outlook presented by the weather forecasters across the Channel, whose judgement had prompted the decision to delay the Culminating Phase of *Operation Starkey* by 24 hours. The afternoon seemed to be ending as it had begun, all the signs being that there was a clear, bright evening ahead. It was the kind of day that thrust the war far out of mind – until the siren at the town hall in rue Carnot began accenting its mournful, wailing notes, to take up the familiar warning from other similar equipment on high points throughout the Boulogne coastal region. That particular alert came and went without causing much concern;[2] it was the next one that turned out to be 'the real thing' – a sampler, though this was not realized, for a night of destruction far beyond belief. It was to be a night to enrage, a night to expunge; a night without equal, a night without end.

From the outset the impression was that Le Portel itself was the target. Successive waves of aircraft swept over the town and, it seemed, unleashed their bombs on whatever was beneath them. The question that came to more and more lips that night was the question that was to remain unanswered for so long; the heavier the bombing, the more frequently it was asked; and the greater the destruction, the more pertinent it became: why Le Portel?

During that day, *Starkey* operations ranged right across the Pas de Calais, with airfields prominent within the key objectives coming under aerial attack. Around Boulogne, as evening approached, Cap d'Alprech and Fort de Couppes were among six groups of gun position targets chosen for the medium bombers and fighter-bombers of the US Air Support Command and RAF Fighter Command; the others were Pointe aux Oies, La Trésorerie and Fort de la Crèche, all to the north of Boulogne, and Hardelot, southwards along the coast and midway to Le Touquet. With the gun emplacements of Cap d'Alprech and Fort de Couppes targeted for the first time, attracting a carpet of high explosives with Le Portel caught in the middle, it is understandable that people in the town now considered that all of the planes had them in their bomb sights – them alone. It was an academic point that 45 minutes separated the starting points for two distinct air-raids. Time had little meaning, the two locations were each 'on the doorstep' and no one cared whether the bombs falling on Le Portel were meant for one gun position or the other. It was their town that was suffering, but why?

It was still daylight, the curfew yet to come, so there were people in the streets when the first planes appeared: American twin-engined Marauder medium bombers. Some, seeing the missiles falling from their bomb-bays, dived for cover as the first explosions tore homes apart in rue Jeanne d'Arc, rue Maréchal Foch, rue Bertrand, rue Jean Bart, rue Victor Hugo, where houses were set ablaze, and in other parts of the town.[3] Then the extent of the damage began to unfold: four rescuers using a shutter-blind as a makeshift stretcher to hurry an injured man to a nearby doctor's surgery already full to overflowing; dark clouds of masonry dust and grime starting to form above shattered houses; from cellar to cellar the hunt going on for those trapped alive.

Survivors who came through unscathed in this 'safe' town decided that enough was enough. In small groups, fearing worse to come, they edged their way through rubble-strewn streets, commencing the sad trek to they knew not where, troubled by their thoughts, burdened by the few essentials on their backs. If you knew that your immediate family was safe and with you, all very well; but what was to be done when a father, a brother, a mother, a sister had yet to come home from work? The family unit is important, particularly among the Portelois – so they tried to stay together. In life, in death, there is a compulsion to unite.

Picture it: a woman who gave birth prematurely lay dead in the cellar of her home, with her the baby and others in the family who had gone to her aid; a grandmother cried over the body of a child whose parents had just been killed; a woman who appeared unharmed was unable to make the smallest movement – understandably so, for she had come through when thirteen others had died around her, among them her husband and their three daughters.[4]

Faster than expected, night began to fall, the warm and cloud-free evening hastened by the sombre shroud hanging over this once trim town. Soon it would be transformed in its entirety, this town of brightly painted houses and narrow streets leading to the beach; its multistorey hotels which prior to the war welcomed visitors from near and far to enjoy the bathing facilities that made Le Portel such a popular spot each summer. Just minutes into the evening's raid, some of its buildings lay wrecked, collapsed into uneven heaps of wooden boards and crumpled brickwork that were formerly floors and ceilings, walls and fascias. Heavy and decorative cupboards and tables; beds, settees and chairs; linen and clothing; children's toys and treasured personal possessions – they were strewn everywhere. The pattern of familiar streets in this compact town would soon submerge into the rubble as houses toppled uncertainly, crashing down into roadways. The hours passed, quickly for the many who had so much to do; slowly, oh so slowly, for those who had to wait to see what would happen next. Soon they were able to guess for there was a fresh alert signalling the dread of further bombers probably on their way.

As the Pathfinders' TIs turned night into day, appearing as if giant fiery torches descending by parachute, more bombs crashed down on the wounded town. Red Cross teams continued a shuttle service, the ambulances taking more and more of the injured from Le Portel to the Saint-Louis de Boulogne hospital. It meant negotiating their way time and time again along badly holed, partially blocked streets. Clearly insufficient, despite the valiant efforts of crews and vehicles to speed the transportation process, the ambulances had to be reinforced by requisitioned motor cars. It was an uphill struggle, growing worse as the first phase of the raid ended and the second began – the planes' target having switched now from Fort de

Couppes to Cap d'Alprech, though the subtlety of this change in direction would have been missed by those on the ground. For them, the bombing just went on and on and on. All sense of time was lost; those working kept on working; those sheltering stayed where they were – waiting and praying, silently to themselves or taking up the familiar phrases of supplication from one mouth to the next.

Parish priest since 1936, l'Abbé Boidin was alerted by the sound of the aircraft carrying out the first attack of the evening and in minutes he was among his flock. Moving from house to house, cellar to cellar, he was there to give the kind of help – words of comfort, prayers of hope – that he knew was expected of him. On that single night he saw more sadness – and, yes, more courage – than ever before. Repeatedly he would be talking to people in one house only to pass by later to find that it had collapsed on them. Even more tragic was where homes which had been damaged earlier in the night, perhaps with dead and injured remaining, suffered a second time.

Throughout all of this would come the piercing shriek of high-explosive bombs dropping, the ground trembling as they went off, bringing down property and burying the occupants, whose own screams or moans added to the fearful cacophony. He must have known their feelings: that with so many bombs hurtling to earth, one must surely find them; and when it did, would they die then or later?; and what would it be like, all this physical pain, and maybe knowing nothing of the fate of their loved ones?

When the last bombs of the night had fallen, realizing that there was more that he could achieve elsewhere, l'Abbé set out on foot to Boulogne – there was no other means of transport available – to see what help was forthcoming from higher authorities.[5] There he met the *sous-préfet*, Monsieur de Villeneuve, and asked for his immediate help and support. The up-to-the-minute picture from the clergyman was confirmation of what the civic leaders in Boulogne had seen from their own vantage points and learned from other sources. Now well aware of the scale of destruction in Le Portel, the *sous-préfet* needed no further prompting before arranging for the local authorities throughout the Pas de Calais to assist the stricken town.

Boulogne's firefighters had already turned out, and, during the night, rescue organizations came from Calais and even from as far away as Béthune. Describing this as an 'all hands to the pump' situation would have been a ridiculous understatement, and the extent of the support given by so many organizations was nothing short of incredible. Local authorities superior to those in Boulogne made sure that Le Portel's fate was rapidly brought to the attention of government representatives in Paris and via them to the government in Vichy.

Marshal Pétain, as leader of the nation in the Vichy regime, received personal reports which triggered his individual role in the coming days. Meanwhile, with a massive effort marshalled first within Le Portel, then in Boulogne and quickly spreading further afield, active help came from the civil defence organization, the Red Cross, the fire services, hospital staff and community doctors. In the background, desperately trying to overcome the problems caused by smashed telephone links and other lost communications, administrators had duties of their own to pursue, ensuring that the earlier momentum was maintained and that everything ran as smoothly as possible.

Another clergyman, l'Abbé Bailleux, his cassock in shreds, moved quietly through the desolation to wherever he was needed. Trapped in a cellar or brought out and laid as gently and as carefully as possible on the roadway, the victims appreciated the spiritual comfort he was able to offer them. There were times, though, when a victim could neither hear nor understand; at a time like that the appreciation was that of a relative or friend, thankful that l'Abbé Bailleux was there, at the end of a life, to give the last rites.

That night the cellars must have saved many a life. Beneath or within a house, the cellar was the family's storage area, cool in the summer and ideal for food and wine. Sizes varied according to the type of property, the degree of comparative luxury depending on inclination and income. Air-raid precautions proposed cellars as a shelter from the bombs, either leaving them as they were or strengthening them where practical. To make them as acceptable as possible, families installed benches or easy chairs and ensured that there was ready access to provisions in case the air-raid alert was a long one. Some cellars would have been safer than others, but there was no point in making judgements of this sort. If you had one, you used it; if you were without one, you found shelter elsewhere.

That night, 8/9 September, Le Portel's cellars were given their toughest test and countless people of all ages must have owed their lives to them. As temporary shelters they performed as best they could and generally nothing else existed that appeared to offer greater protection. None would be much use in a direct hit even by one of the smallest high-explosive bombs in use on this occasion.

As bomb after bomb rained down, the people of Le Portel, sheltering in those cellars, would have been quick to accept that it only required one bomb to land on or close to them and there was probably little chance of survival. However, as people in many other places had already experienced, exploding bombs can cause the strangest effects, maiming some victims while leaving others without even a scratch.

Rescue workers could not shelter; they kept at it, ignoring the threat of bombs that could go off anywhere, on impact or later.* The best they could do was to throw themselves to the ground, which shook incessantly, benefiting from whatever instant cover was offered, and get their heads down. Bomb splinters merged with shrapnel from the gunfire to form a deadly hail of piercing steel. With each fresh incident, someone had to check for survivors, see if medical help was required and find out if anyone alive needed extricating from a prospective tomb – the dead had to wait.

For one man, a proverb had come to mind, the meaning of which he had found difficult to determine in the past. It was a simple phrase: 'Go where you wish, die where you must.' As he looked around, taking in the sheer horror of that night, he reckoned that he had no further need to question the truth of those few words.[6] Death had forced itself on so many in those few hours in Le Portel.

The task of locating and bringing out people buried in tons of rubble was a race against time, often using a human chain to shift rubble cleared by hand in the absence of proper tools. A persistent moaning or a sudden cry often gave the first clue, and then it was necessary to start digging, ensuring that neither the rescuers nor those trapped were allowed to be placed at risk. A sudden fall of a girder, a piece

---

* None of the bombs dropped in Phase I or Phase II was intended to explode by delayed action; any unexploded bombs found then or later were 'duds'.

of timber or masonry dislodged could kill, and already there was enough potential death and destruction when the bombers were overhead, their shapes caught by searchlight, their shadows cast by the moonlight.

No incendiary bombs were dropped, unless the bombers' illuminating marker devices are so categorized, but inevitably there were fires burning in the town. These had to be checked as a most pressing requirement because any blaze held back rescuers and the attendant medical teams, and also it was liable to act as a beacon to attract a fresh attack. If bomb-aimers saw a real conflagration developing it might just seem too important to miss. Water shortage hampered the firefighters that night; an ambulance ablaze set back the efforts of the medical teams; and fires in the target area that did burn out of control were visible even as far away as the Thames Estuary by planes returning home.

What was it like among the rescue teams, pursuing their task with renewed vigour as daylight broke over this shattered seaside resort? They could see with their own eyes what conditions were like in their immediate area; and they could hear with their own ears what it was like elsewhere when others who had been doing the same job in another part of the town were drafted in to help, because here it was felt the requirement was more pressing.

They learned of a doctor having to cut through a corpse to free a woman trapped at his side; three officers and three men from Boulogne fire brigade with two firemen from Le Portel, working for twelve hours to extricate injured and dead, killed when a further bomb fell in roughly the same place; rescue workers, having brought out as many as twenty-seven dead from one building, finding another later: a woman still sitting in a chair, dead, with the baby she was feeding alive in her arms;[7] the town hall untouched, the church damaged but not too badly, both turned into mortuaries; the incessant queries as to the whereabouts of relatives, punctuated, infrequently it has to be said, by a tearful reunion; life would never be the same again in Le Portel.

While the bombs fell, there was the knowledge that the next could be yours. At best the blast might hurl you to the ground unconscious or, worse, searing metal fragments might rip you to pieces. Short of either one or the other happening, you didn't dare stop because there was always someone else needing your help – a man trapped in a cellar; he has to be brought out, choking with masonry dust, shocked and bleeding, gasping for breath as he pleads for news of his wife and their children. At a time like this you remember that your family is somewhere else and you yearn for news of them – the wife, the children, whom you fear you may never see again.

The initial helplessness in the aftermath of the night's attacks could be seen in pleas to a clergyman and an administrator respectively;[8] 'My son, aged three, died last night. I'm off – and I'm leaving him with you.' . . . 'What must I do with my father, who has been killed? I don't want to stay here a minute longer.' The 'walking wounded', those unharmed but dazed, the frightened, the traumatized, all were there that night in Le Portel.

What were the thoughts of the Portelois in their cellars that night? Typically, perhaps, came this response:[9] 'We're waiting to die because this is inevitable. Homes are collapsing one after the other; the ground is shaking; and there's this dust that sticks in your nose, mouth, ears and eyes; your tongue is coated, your throat inflamed; and you dream of a little fresh air, but that's not to be.' When the whistle of falling bombs stopped, they ventured out of their shelters, only to be met with an uncanny silence. They often called the names of their loved ones, but without a response.

For those separated from their loved ones, making their way to the hospital in Boulogne was an alternative open to them in anticipation that they may have survived and, if injured, been taken there for treatment. This hospital, together with an emergency medical centre set up in Le Portel, coped with casualty rates far in excess of expectations. That so many pulled through is a testimony to the competence and care of doctors, nurses and ancillary staff at all levels, backed by able volunteers.

With more air attacks on the next day, greater credence was given to the thought that perhaps this was the prelude to an Allied invasion. There had been talk of this, certainly, with broadcasts from England that the day was soon to come, but there were no visible signs, nor was there confirmation through sources in the Resistance. Daylight revealed to the Portelois the horrific physical state of their beloved town; while a pilgrimage to the town hall provided an early indication of the frightful toll in human terms. Surely this was the end of this terrible ordeal at the hands of the people they knew as their friends?

In fact there was still more to come: more destruction, more deaths, more injuries, more pain. *Operation Starkey* called for the attacks on the gun emplacements north and south of Le Portel to be resumed in daylight on that, the final day, and already medium bombers on US Air Force bases in southern England were being prepared to home in on both targets. Routinely, these planes were to be under fighter escort, which was poised to take on the German air force and fulfil a principal objective of this complex deception plan.

A distant purr of aero-engines was the first indication; then the almost comforting sound of the AA defences springing into action at Mont Soleil and more distantly. Some eighteen Marauders were in the first wave, approaching from Boulogne and making a half-turn to sweep down rue Monseigneur-Bourgain to attack one set of guns. Seventeen of their colleagues, their flight paths coordinated, headed for the other gun position, with just 2 minutes separating these opening raids. Then the familiar 'cr-rump' of high explosives, the ground shuddering as if penetrated by a giant drill and the rising plume of dust as another building crashed down. Then there was no more to be seen, and the lure of the nearest shelter became irresistible.

The makeshift mortuaries opened their doors to further victims and in the town hall alone the number soon reached seventy-five – Portelois of all ages whose possessions had to be searched with infinite care as a first step towards identification. Initially there were no shrouds, little disinfectant and a shortage of coffins.[10] The team faced with this gruesome task were helped practically and spiritually by l'Abbé Boidin, 'a devoted and courageous man', so that in time it proved possible to put a name to most of those victims. The fact that many died in just their nightclothes did not help the identification process; but the fact that l'Abbé knew so many of his parishioners did help considerably.

Later the memorial columns in the press would unfold much personal tragedy to a wider audience: the repetition of family names such as Bourgain, Duhamel,

Germe, Gournay, Ledez and Libert, including babies less than a year old, and adults in their seventies and eighties; the spread of the churches and hospital chapels in which the religious services would take place – Arras, Boulogne, Desvres, Longueville, Outreau and Wimille among them; and the fact that their timing would be spread over as much as three months, marking the fact that some put up a brave struggle in hospital for survival and allowing for injured relatives to recover sufficiently to attend.[11]

Faced with the devastation, the total or almost total destruction of the vast majority of residential property and the loss of electricity, gas and water, Le Portel was ordered to be evacuated. Ahead of this action, Portelois who found themselves homeless were already in the process of leaving – 600 were accommodated in the Dezouteux school at Bréquerecque – and the act of abandoning bomb-battered shops and homes led to inevitable looting. This was curbed as effectively as possible by the population themselves and by the authorities, but with the town soon to be cleared of all of its inhabitants, and entry forbidden without the strictest control, a decision was taken to bring in an entire batallion of *gendarmes mobiles* to mount a lasting surveillance operation.[12]

It would be a considerable time before the Portelois could return to their shattered town – 93 per cent of which was destroyed, according to official figures[13] – and start to pick up once again the threads of normal life.

Chapter Eleven

Evacuation is Ordered

Out of the cellars, stunned by the frightful destruction all around them, the Portelois who had survived that night of terror emerged into the approaching dawn light unaware that already there were moves afoot for the total evacuation of their town. It was something that had never occurred before in France – an entire community as large as this one ordered to leave their homes,[1] or whatever shambles still existed that might be called a home.

As recognition of the plight of the Portelois spread as far as Paris and to the seat of government in Vichy, the authorities worked quickly together to arrange support in many ways. First came answers to the immediate needs with teams from distant towns rushing fire crews and rescue teams, many miners among them, to assist those in the immediate area. This relief was vital for those who were swamped by the sheer volume of the task that confronted them – dazed and about to drop with exhaustion following many hours of grappling with the debris and experiencing the personal tragedies that lay within it. There were medium-term needs to be met too: food and clothing to be organized; water supplies to be made available in key centres; shops and homes, open to all, to be protected from those posing as salvage groups who were carting away whatever provisions caught their eye[2] – even slicing fingers from the dead to plunder the rings they were wearing when the bombs crashed down.[3] There was also the longer-term requirement: where to house this number of people, how to move them and how to make sure that a welcome would be waiting for the distressed families.

From Paris, just as fresh air attacks began against targets in the Le Portel area, a special train commenced a journey of mercy to the disaster area to meet some of the most pressing demands. A government initiative, it came to be known as 'the miracle train',[4] its ten carriages including a travelling hospital with its own operating theatre, first-aid facilities, beds for 30 patients, an area for expectant and new mothers, a mobile kitchen with 2,400 litres of water and eight ovens, and clothing supplies sufficient for 2,000 people. Routed straight through to Boulogne, which was the closest station to Le Portel, it was eventually ordered on to Desvres because the coast was thought too vulnerable.

In Desvres by now, some hundreds of evacuees were assembled, the vanguard to reach this first staging post on the way to their new homes. Within 48 hours, thirty major operations were performed inside the train and two babies were born; in the region of 5,000 meals were prepared and distributed; and the clothing store was cleaned out, right down to the last pair of socks.

Three main localities were prepared to offer immediate accommodation to the Portelois in their time of need: the Marne region, a *département* to the east beyond Paris, which gave homes to the majority, plus Fresnicourt-le-Dolmen and Arras, both considerably nearer and within the *département* of the Pas de Calais.[5] These were the 'official' reception centres, though some families made their own arrangements and began a new life in other parts of the country, some nearer still and others much more distant, where the links with their former community were lost perhaps for all time.*

The people of the Pas de Calais had taken to the open road on a previous occasion in this war, of course, when the German armoured columns began their relentless thrust towards the coast in May 1940. In fact there was little similarity because then it was a matter of individual choice in a time of understandable panic. Now there was no alternative save for organized evacuation: if you could move, you moved; otherwise you were in the doctors' hands or helping to bring civil defence work in the town to an end.

It had been a traumatic experience. Encouragement to move away was hardly necessary, given the incentive brought on by fear – fear that the bombers would be returning and survival was questionable. Whether this was a prelude to an Allied landing in the Pas de Calais was pure speculation, although it was said to be for this reason that casualties being treated below ground in hospital in Boulogne were moved out of the area.[6] Could they be giving up their beds for potential victims from both sides, if the Allies were in fact about to make a bid against this most fiercely defended coastline in the whole of Europe?**

Other than the uniformed personnel charged with safeguarding property, the Germans alone would be staying put in Le Portel. In their much more protective surroundings, whether or not hits were scored upon them, German military casualties there appear to have been out of all proportion to those among the French

---

* A post-war report on the effectiveness of the evacuation of people from the Pas de Calais to the Marne between September 1943 and May 1946[7] noted that Le Portel was the first evacuation of a coastal town and recalled their flight in words that now seem effusive: the people of the town were having to make their way through a hail of bombs that defied description, on foot and carrying belongings gathered together in haste, the old and the infirm being hustled along among them. The refugees appeared to take the view that evacuation was a fate the next worst only to death; having now turned their backs on so much death, there were other uncertainties looming to burden hearts and minds. (*'Les réfugiés commençaient à connaitre qu'apres la mort, il n'y a rien de pire que l'évacuation'* – a phrase open to the widest interpretation!)

** Gen. Morgan, architect of *Operation Overlord* as well as *Operation Starkey*, presented Britain's Chiefs of Staff with a digest of his plan to secure a lodgement on the Continent from which further offensive operations could be developed – target date 1 May 1944. This showed that he examined and then ruled out the Pas de Calais as the assault beaches for *Overlord* (the D-Day landings in Normandy on 6 June 1944). In spite of the proximity to Britain, 'it is clear that it is an unsuitable area in which to attempt our initial lodgement'.[8]

civilians: reportedly two dead and five hurt out of an estimated 150/200 based at Fort de Couppes at that time.[9] Against the mounting number of non-combatant victims, this was miniscule, yet when the rescue operations were at their height in Le Portel, the site commandant even wanted to bring in townspeople to help to repair the damage to his precious fortress. He was overruled and also reprimanded, l'Abbé Boidin having brought his behaviour to the attention of higher authorities in the garrison at Boulogne.[10] There, the Germans had already 'done the decent thing' and, in response to an appeal from l'Abbé, put their soldiers at the disposal of the French for rescue and salvage duties in the town.

Evacuation orders were still being considered when from a cellar in rue Gournay-Hédouin came eight adults and a young child that night of 8 September, their home having been struck and collapsed around them, just their shelter intact.[11] There was no alternative but to claw their way through the rubble, saved by a miracle, in their opinion, and to go as a group to somewhere that was perhaps more secure. They decided on Equihen, to the south and even further from Boulogne, which had long been an Allied target. Time after time it was necessary to hurl themselves flat on the ground under the threat of fresh bombing. In rue du Beurre-Fondu there was a welcome offer of accommodation for the rest of the night, albeit on chairs. On the next day the evacuation instructions reached them, the movement of families towards the assembly points that morning being punctuated by renewed bombing as the US Air Force carried on where the RAF had left off in its onslaught aimed at the gun batteries of Cap d'Alprech and Fort de Couppes.

The sound of aerial warfare persisted with planes pulsating overhead, AA fire pounding them from the extra-noisy batteries of Mont Soleil and the screech, then the explosion, when the bombs were released. Inevitably there was anger all around – anger that surfaced as the French people saw more of their possessions going up in smoke; and anger among the Germans too, visibly so, when their gunners were seen to be directing their fire against a crew coming down by parachute after their plane was hit.[12]

The 'calm after the storm' was still some time away. One family had just arrived by lorry in the Place d'Eglise when a group of planes screamed overhead. They raced inside the church for cover, a bomb exploded with a mighty roar and the door blew apart; outside, the lorry was nowhere to be seen, gone without trace, presumably smashed to pieces by that bomb. Their transport gone, the family made its way to Hesdin-l'Abbé where a dance hall was put at the disposal of the refugees – no beds, but in situations like that the bare floor seemed as comfortable as a warm, soft bed.

This group was taken to Béthune by coach, on to Hébergés, where a ladies' college put them up for a week, and eventually to the village of Avize, in champagne country, where the more active among them helped to harvest the grapes. Later, when the influx dispersed at the end of the season, room was found for them in a house shared between two families. This group saw out the occupation without setting eyes on a single German soldier until it was their turn to flee ahead of the fast-moving Americans who liberated the area on 28 August 1944, and still kept going.[13]

Some of the evacuees were able, quickly and formally, to remember relatives and friends who died in the bombardment. Groups which found themselves in Arras within a day or two of the evacuation were able to join in a service in their memory in the cathedral of Saint-Vaast, conducted by the Bishop of Arras, Mgr Dutoit, whose generosity to the Portelois included a donation of 50 francs to each of them. It appeared that Pope Pie XII set aside a sum specifically for the refugees of Le Portel, and the *monseigneur*, who was his intermediary, added to this an amount on his own authority. Thus there were various donations of money from different sources, together with other forms of financial support in the months ahead. One of the least expected, though nonetheless most welcome, was the decision to release Le Portel owners and occupants from the obligation that year to pay their household taxes.[14]

From Arras and Béthune, special trains carried the refugees in their hundreds to Rheims and Epernay, the next staging posts and the points where families were further dispersed. Arriving in their new localities, some refugees found that accommodation in other people's homes was ready for them, while others temporarily had to sleep anywhere where there was floor space, perhaps on a bed of straw in a hall, until empty property could be requisitioned. As the evacuees carried only their barest personal belongings, essentials like plates, cutlery and bed linen had to be obtained at their ultimate destination. Many towns and villages in the reception areas gave willingly to collections organized for this purpose. In isolated cases the welcome was less friendly and it turned out that no accommodation was forthcoming for the Portelois[15] – no room at the inn, no room anywhere for these shocked and harassed victims of a bombardment that gave the impression of being utterly pointless.

Civic leaders in Boulogne joined such notables from Le Portel as the Abbés Ledoux and Boidin and town councillor Mlle Marie-Joséphine Bourgain in keeping attention focused on the plight of the people of Le Portel. In that first autumn and winter, members of this group travelled as far and as frequently as was possible in their determination to seek recognition and help for this now dispersed population.[16]

It was the rule rather than the exception in the evacuation that the local mayor and his colleagues, the clergy and the hosts themselves would be there to greet the refugees as they came in by rail or road. Some were received 'like royalty'. For instance, in Rilly-la-Montagne a champagne reception was organized by industrialists from the district – the management of a biscuit factory whose products carried a reproduction of the cathedral of Rheims, the principal city in the Marne.[17]

One family from rue des Hayettes, where not a house remained, settled in the village of Thil, about 8 miles from Rheims and in the part of France which received the greatest number of Portelois. Despite there being only 140 inhabitants, Thil set aside for this group splendid accommodation in a house with three rooms and a big kitchen totally furnished for them by the villagers. Another village in this same area, Loivre, took in five families which, in time, increased with the arrival of two members who had been seriously injured in rue Jean-Bart.

The quality of accommodation varied: some refugees were installed in veritable 'palaces', others where there was no electricity and panes of glass were cracked or missing from the windows. Irrespective of the facilities provided, the calm of the countryside brought new sights and sounds to the eyes and ears of the Portelois. It was good to get away.

It did seem that in the main the refugees were received with both kindness and generosity, as illustrated in one instance where, having just arrived in Tramery, a family was sitting by an open window when a man carrying a sack suddenly put a newly snared rabbit on the table in front of them without saying a word. In a flash he was gone, disappearing as quickly as he had arrived. It was, so the astonished family learned later, a poacher offering hospitality to the new arrivals in the way he knew best![18]

The younger refugees were able to resume school, but for the adults, finding work was a problem which appeared to be accented in some areas more than in others. Those just out of school that summer might have anticipated an apprenticeship leading to a career: no longer was that realistic. The choice of jobs was another limiting factor, not just on account of the war but because of this uprooting. Within the Marne it was noted that generally there was some work to be found for the menfolk, but there was scarcely any for the women. Agriculture proved to offer an opening for some, the railway for others; it was a matter of taking what was available in a district where already there were not enough opportunities to go round.

The change of setting was particularly noticeable. Le Portel was a close-knit community, yet it was comparatively large; circles of friendship were extensive and there was a sharp contrast for many who found themselves in small villages a fraction of the size and tiny in terms of population. There could be a sense of isolation if a family was billeted in a particular spot on its own, whereas morale would be much improved when a number of families were fortunate enough to be grouped close together.

Feeling remote could be a problem despite the friendliness of the environment. Vauciennes, in the Marne, boasted fewer than 100 inhabitants before welcoming the Portelois. Here, collecting the food due under the rationing system meant walking more than a mile into Damery or taking the train to Epernay and having to stay there all day because of the infrequency of the rail service. Being a refugee could have its benefits, though. For example, the privilege of receiving a double allocation of sugar was one way to sweeten the rigours of their new life!

Rheims provided work for some of the Portelois. For instance a young shorthand typist was taken on by one of the government departments to do a job which kept her in touch with others in the district. The chain of acquaintances that was forged in this manner seemed to grow longer and longer, and resuming contact with fellow Portelois must have been one of the happier aspects of this employment opportunity. The 'down side' was that being in a city of that size, with its rail network attractive for the Allies' bombers, the memories of the Le Portel attacks were still all too vivid.

Some found themselves in danger areas more remote from cities and towns like Rheims and Epernay. The champagne-producing area was a favourite with the Germans for establishing bases to build, supply and launch first their flying bombs and then their supersonic rockets. In time the local population learned of the whereabouts of these strange new weapons, as did the Allies eventually. It had been reassuring initially to get away from the coast with its obvious targets, but now that feeling of security was dwindling fast in the discovery that there were such tempting new ones in the neighbourhood.[19]

Vigorous effort went into keeping together the Portelois and maintaining their morale. It was easier in the Marne, and this was beneficial for those who chose to join the 'mass' exodus – *La grande dispersion* – rather than scatter as individual families, even if their destination was with others in the family or close friends. As well as the authorities, which built up a directory of Portelois giving both their original and their current addresses, the clergy were among the prime movers in ensuring that links were not broken and that contact remained for all who wished to stay in touch with the life of pre-bombardment times.

L'Abbé Boidin, his work finished in Le Portel now that the identification of the victims was as complete as probably it would ever be and now that he was satisfied that all was being done that could be done for the survivors, moved into the Marne himself in January 1944. He established an office in Rheims and, after a tour of the district to see who was where, he set two objectives: to arrange gatherings of Portelois in the various towns and villages and to make house visits. For everyone who was close enough, Rheims was the principal venue each Thursday, starting with a service at 11.00 a.m. followed by a meal of soup, meat and vegetables and the opportunity to talk and talk and talk. Numbers varied between 30 and 50 usually, but the record stood at 300 on 23 March 1944, with a photograph taken to make sure that the event would not be forgotten.[20]

On a motorcycle, l'Abbé Boidin made the rounds of his new parishioners in an example of dedication that also would not be allowed to dim in the memory of the Portelois. He brought groups together; he organized supplies of books to be sent to the refugees; he was always there to advise, to raise morale, to console and to stress that better times were ahead – it was just a matter of waiting.

Early 1944 saw the first departures from the Marne when the fishing community in Boulogne was able to operate out of Dunkirk, Gravelines and Calais, with an organization set up in Dunkirk to welcome crews. In fact some of the fishermen from Le Portel had already established a 'sea town' at Fresnicourt-le-Dolmen, a housing development near Barlin in the Pas de Calais which attracted families evacuated initially to the Marne. The term 'sea town' came not from its location, which was far from a sight of the sea, but from the intentions of its new arrivals to keep alive the spirit of Le Portel as a sort of 'new Portel'. The site had been intended as a youth camp, but circumstances dictated otherwise and its first occupants were the Portelois.[21] There were about fifty wooden huts there, on the edge of a wood.

Finding work was a particular problem, although the local mayor and others were keen to support efforts to secure employment. There were trees to be cut down, a factory between Verdrel and Barlin, and mining; and there was also the prospect of working on the railway, though the problem for some was that it meant having the Germans as employers. A number opted for Dunkirk and the chance to resume the livelihood that had been their family's for generations, the *Edith Cécile* being one of the fishing boats that provided the opportunity not only to return to sea but to do so in one's former vessel.[22]

In the 'new Portel' there was even their own chapel in which to hold services, although the church in Fresnicourt had to be used for baptisms and funerals because theirs had neither font nor catafalque. However, it was the venue for a number of weddings (in at least one instance, elsewhere, a Porteloise married not a Portelois but a young man from the next village to the one to which she had been evacuated). The chapel recruited its own choir and obtained a harmonium. On 30 January 1944 came the grand opening, and on 12 March its dedication service was conducted by Mgr Dutoit.

As a community it grew substantially, with a preschool for the youngsters to learn 'the three 'r's', and even to the extent that it attracted its own butcher's shop (a Portelois to be sure!). Naturally the practice continued where everyone helped each other with babysitting, dressmaking, knitting, looking for wood in the nearby forest for heating and generally lending a hand without waiting to be asked.

While some evacuees did not set eyes on a German before the liberation, others had them under their very noses. One young refugee from the ruins of rue Victor Hugo, having reached Cormontreuil, in the Marne and close to Rheims, found himself living in a building in which there were soon to be about thirty soldiers of the Reich, mostly lorry drivers who were conscripts to the field-grey uniform.[23] The welcome from the people of Cormontreuil was warm, right from the start, with the Portelois accepted individually and as a group. For the youngsters there was always something to occupy them and their school was enjoyable. Unlike some areas it was generally possible to get hold of chickens, eggs, rabbits, fruit and vegetables, this being a district with plenty of farms. For this particular evacuee, Cormontreuil became a second home; and for all evacuees (those 'courageous Portelois' was a term that many used), this second home would never be far from their thoughts in the succeeding years.*

In Le Portel, meanwhile, miners from across the Pas de Calais had been brought into the area to put their skills to urgent work in making wrecked buildings safe, helping the process of finding and recovering further bodies, and clearing debris where its presence was a hazard or an inconvenience. In Notre Dame cathedral in Boulogne, a week after the evacuation, Mgr Dutoit led a service to remember the dead – a service in which he was quoted as having denounced those responsible for the 'murderous bombing' and the 'slaughter' that it caused.**

Such a sentiment was expressed elsewhere and later, one instance being noted by a Portelois refugee anxious to return briefly to recover furniture from bomb-damaged property belonging to his family in rues du Bocage and Charlemagne-Pierrin. While in Le Portel he saw firemen still working amid the wreckage of the *Hôtel de l'Aéroport* where some fifteen people had lost their lives. One of the firemen, overcome by what he knew and what he was seeing, remarked to his colleagues as a plane passed high overhead: 'Here they come again, the murderers.'[24]

As the days and weeks passed, news came of more human tragedies, among them

* In Cormontreuil, Armistice Day 1993 saw an exhibition of photographs and documents recalling the bombing of Le Portel and the subsequent evacuation of some 300 Portelois to the district. To mark the fiftieth anniversary, Cormontreuil's mayor bestowed the *médaille de la commune* on his opposite number in Le Portel.[25]

** Mgr Dutoit reportedly used the word '*massacre*', which can be translated into its direct equivalent or as 'slaughter'.[26] It will be seen later that the post-war government in France referred to the martyrdom of Le Portel,[27] so perhaps 'massacre' is the more appropriate translation.

the report of a man rescued alive after four days, his wife and their four children, alas, all dead. As for a baby found alive in her dead mother's arms (also after four days), it seemed that rescue workers wished to adopt her; unfortunately the gesture would have been to no avail because she died, in the Boulogne hospital to which she had been taken with such care, on 1 November.[28]

By early November a total of 367 dead had been identified but there were still people who were missing and human remains so far unnamed.* To cope with fatalities on this scale, Arras had to send coffins to supplement Le Portel's fast-diminishing supplies. They came in 'knock-down' kits, carpenters among the Portelois having to assemble them. Of the estimated 1,200 injured between 4 and 9 September, some 400 were badly hurt and located in hospitals as far away as Paris.[29]

Meanwhile, what of the Allied landing that some Portelois believed must by then have been in progress? If anyone had the time, the opportunity and the inclination, there were vantage points offering sight of a curious smokescreen put down by planes and ships far out to sea on that morning of 9 September, south of Le Portel, while the town was commencing the mass evacuation. The 'invasion fleet' was there right enough, just as Gen. Morgan and *Operation Starkey* had intended, threatened as ever by those two big-gun emplacements.

---

* After more bombs fell on the now empty town, some nine months later, a further forty-three bodies were found. The torment of uncertainty did not end there: in one case, gruesome to contemplate and particularly distressing to the family, one male victim was not recovered until reconstruction work on the town was in progress. Part of the body was found in 1948, the remainder the next year.[30] The *Registres de l'Etat Civil* in Le Portel show 376 named dead (168 males aged between 12 days and 94 years; and 208 females aged between 2 months and 89 years), which includes some of the 38 deceased persons registered at 31 December 1943 as *inconnu* (unknown, by which was meant someone who was not, at that time, able to be formally identified). However, to the 376 identified dead must be added the names of those who succumbed to their injuries in hospitals as far afield as Paris (whose death would be registered somewhere other than in Le Portel), others beyond identification – multiple deaths among them – and those whose remains were never found. It is not unreasonable to perpetuate the term 'some 500 dead' - and to remember each one of them as do the Portelois – *Mort pour La France*.

Chapter Twelve

Invasion Fleet Sets Sail

Daybreak on 9 September 1943 saw the English Channel busier than at any time since the withdrawal of the British Army from beneath the noses of the encircling enemy forces at Dunkirk three summers earlier. Just as the 'little ships' had been shuttling backwards and forwards to pick up and bring back their human cargoes in full view of the Germans, the convoys assembling off the Kent coast this time were also clearly visible to the enemy across the water.

There was no attempt to hide the presence of these ships, which were gathering in the Culminating Phase of *Operation Starkey*, the climax of a complex plan to make the enemy believe that an Allied landing was imminent and to coax the German air force into one or more major air battles where the Allies could expect to have the upper hand. In fact, rather than try to keep the ships from being seen, considerable effort had gone into attempts to achieve the opposite result and to publicize their whereabouts.

Troop movements on a massive scale, involving thousands of soldiers, Canadians as well as British, deliberately created the impression that ports large and small on the south and south-east coasts were to be the starting points for the invasion forces. Distinctive flat-bottomed, utilitarian landing craft had been moved into position, the real ones supplemented by models so cleverly constructed that they would certainly pass all but the closest scrutiny. The troops learned the use of the various landing craft, going from the marshalling camps to the 'hards', and embarking and disembarking; while tanks, lorries, guns and stores were all carefully packed and unpacked in the darkness.

Gliders, hauled out of hangars on airfields in the Midlands and beyond, were meant to give further credence as if ready to receive more troops to drop silently out of the skies, an advance guard to do battle in the Pas de Calais. Radio traffic had increased commensurate with the amount and the kind to be expected when planning an amphibious operation on this scale. So far as the air element was concerned, squadrons of fighters, fighter-bombers, medium bombers and heavy bombers had already been making their existence known by sorties whenever the weather allowed the planned attacks. Airfields, marshalling yards and industrial targets had come under attack – though not military camps, as originally intended, which were left alone because of difficulties experienced in deciding whether the occupants were civilians.[1] The build-up was almost over. The crews were briefed, or were soon to be briefed, to carry out the final air operations.

The enemy were now to be thrown the last bone – the sight of fat and juicy convoys in a confined stretch of sea so invitingly close to their airfields in France, Belgium, Holland and Germany. They could have sailed under cover of darkness, which would have been a natural safeguard in ordinary circumstances, but the deception plan required the ships to be as obvious as possible. In daylight, surely, there was no chance that the Germans would miss them! There was a dual role: in themselves the ships were a target which should tempt German planes; and equally there was the assumption that they were an invasion force heading for the Pas de Calais, the bulk of the troops and their supplies on board. The precise spot that the Allies had chosen to disembark did not matter unduly, although the fact that the heavy guns in the Boulogne area had come under fierce attack was certainly one clue. Another would emerge by watching where the ships were heading. It was all too easy. The enemy were not meant to know, of course, that this huge landing force would not have gone to sea – and that all of the ships, mainly empty or virtually so anyway, would merely be doing a planned U-turn.

Airfields in and beyond the Pas de Calais were again key objectives for British and American planes in daylight, both on 8 September, the scheduled 'D-Day' for *Starkey*, and on 9 September, the actual D-Day. The 24 hour postponement had been introduced in anticipation of optimum weather conditions to suit both the naval and the air forces. As well as the enemy's air bases, however, in these final two days, selected gun batteries on and close to the coast became targets for the Anglo-American bombers – targets for the very first time in *Starkey*'s twenty-five day lifespan. This followed the original plan to the letter, although the scale of the attack had decreased in line with successive reductions to the allotted resources and on account of the weather. Gun batteries were, and remained, key targets for two reasons: the most powerful among them posed a threat to the convoys, the others a potential threat to ground forces in the event of a real landing. Thus the enemy would expect their gun batteries to become targets in the present situation. They would not be surprised if they were, but they would be if they weren't. For the Allies, however, the problem was that, with less weight to throw behind the punch, fewer positions could be attacked. The choice was critical, not only to reduce the effectiveness of those batteries which were selected but to enhance the deception.

In successive appraisals, *Starkey*'s coastal concentration was narrowed from Calais–Le Touquet to more or less Boulogne–Le Touquet, which removed all but one of the long-range gun emplacements described as being invulnerable to attack from the air. Nonetheless, the smaller frontage chosen for the pseudo-invasion remained fiercely aggressive, the entire coastline between Calais and Le Touquet being heavily fortified – the Pas de Calais was, after all, the most likely area for the Allies when seeking a foothold on the Continent – this year, next year, sometime, never . . .

The six groups of actually and potentially destructive firepower chosen to be on the receiving end of joint attacks by planes of the two air forces were all in a coastal strip no more than 10 miles from one end to the other, the north–south limits being just to the north of Wimereux and just to the south of Hardelot, Le Portel being roughly central. Moving southwards the objectives were codenamed *Millstone* (four 8 inch guns and three railway guns), *Pomeranian* (three 15 inch guns at La Trésorerie) and *Pumicestone* (four 10 inch guns at Fort de la Crèche), all north of Boulogne; *Religion* (three 8 inch guns at Fort de Couppes) and *Andante* (four 6 inch guns at Cap d'Alprech), respectively north and south of Le Portel; and *Menagerie* (a mixture of heavy AA guns and beach defence strong points at Hardelot), the most southerly of the series of broad, tempting beaches below Le Portel, which it would be assumed were the Allies' choice to disembark the troops from their landing craft.[2]

All gun positions between Calais and Wimereux had been discounted from this Culminating Phase of *Starkey* because the sea and air resources now available left the planners no alternative. It now meant making the best use of weakened punch-power to achieve the most of the original objectives. Le Touquet was the southern boundary in the initial concept, but Air Ministry decreed this 'off limits', so Hardelot, half-way to Boulogne and bristling with short-range armament, was substituted as the southern extremity.[3] The gun positions between Wimereux and Hardelot were thus the focus in this climax to *Starkey*, the targets for the fighter-bombers and the medium and heavy bombers of the RAF and the US Air Force, whose bombs would be aimed with the apparent and actual intention of reducing the efficiency of this lethal enemy firepower. There was no longer any intention to combine aerial bombardment with gunfire from British battleships homing in on the long-range artillery; no longer any intention to attack long-range artillery and/or beach defences at Equihen, Ecault, Mont Duchemin, Camiers, Ste-Cécile, Etaples or in the vicinity of Le Touquet.

Although each of the planes marshalled for this onslaught could have flown from one end of this 10 mile coastal strip to the other, dropping a part-load on successive objectives in no more than 2 to 3 minutes before disappearing from view, the bombing operations were coordinated in line with planned effectiveness of the overall concept. The programme recognized target priority, and the impact to be gained by the weight and frequency of attack. The governing factors were the number and type of aircraft released for *Starkey* and the effect on them caused by variations in weather conditions. Also to be taken into account was the compulsion to stay within War Cabinet limitations on targets where there was a risk of civilian casualties. This meant abiding by the agreement or the restriction which Air Ministry, as the government agency in such matters, passed down to the commanders in respect of each and every target in the lists submitted for formal clearance.

The eighty-six potential targets nominated on lists 8 and 9 for possible attack were part-and-parcel of the *Starkey* deception plan, their sanction or otherwise being integral to measures proposed to minimize harm to civilian life and property. When sent through to Air Ministry, those lists comprised forty-six potential targets among the beach defences from Calais to Le Touquet and, in the same area, forty potential targets among the coastal batteries and railway artillery, all viable possibilities in the Culminating Phase – the last 48 hours of *Starkey*.[4] Although all of the beach defence targets were cleared (except for six not approved for attacks by night), and the same was the case for the longer-range batteries (four not by night), both lists were subsequently pruned drastically, three in four ignored by the planning teams as being superfluous to the eventual requirements. The forty-six beach defence targets came down to nine, the forty big-gun targets to twelve, so that the punch could be delivered where it would be the most potent. Three in four of the potential gun-position targets were now saved from the threat of Allied bombs to enable all of the effort to be concentrated against the one-in-four absolutely critical objectives in this climax to *Starkey*.

So, targets within *Religion* and *Andante* would be attacked first by day on 8 September, then by night on 8 September and finally by day on 9 September. As these included the big guns considered to be the most threatening to the ships approaching the coast of France, these two objectives on either side of Le Portel would get priority treatment. The difference was this: when compared with the other groups of targets – *Millstone, Pomeranian, Pumicestone* and *Menagerie* – *Religion* and *Andante* would be subjected to a lethal sandwich comprising day-night-day attacks. *Millstone, Pomeranian, Pumicestone* and *Menagerie* would be targets by day alone, on successive days; *Religion* and *Andante* would be hit first by day, then by night – by more planes than at any other time – and then again by day.

So far as the population of Le Portel was concerned, the first deaths, injuries and wrecked homes attributable to *Starkey* came on 4 September when German E-boats and port installations in Boulogne Harbour were the intended victims of the Bostons, Mitchells and Venturas of RAF Fighter Command carrying out these attacks with fighter escort, a combined force of 238 planes being involved.[5] Port installations were hit, but not the E-boats; civilian property too, but not those E-boats.

There had been plenty of action inland, since the Preliminary Phase of the deception plan began on 16 August, but there was nothing much to be seen in this part of northern France, except perhaps the condensation trails of high-flying aircraft, the sound of distant gunfire and the sight of an occasional plane. There were no airfields, no marshalling yards or canal centres, no industrial targets, no ammunition dumps, no fuel oil stores, no military headquarters and no military camps or barracks deemed worthy of the attention of the planning teams. The coastal targets that did exist between Wimereux and Hardelot were being saved for the Culminating Phase – the last 48 hours of *Starkey*. This would be 'crunch time', when the convoys were preparing to sail – the last chance, perhaps the best chance, to entice the enemy's planes into the air and their ground forces towards the expected landing places. The war in the Mediterranean was 'hotting up', so if the Germans in the Pas de Calais could be persuaded to rush off in that direction, so much the better; and if the Russians saw that their British and American allies were taking some action in the West that might prevent German reserves from being despatched to the Eastern Front, all the better still.

Both the global picture and the pace of *Starkey* changed substantially on the evening of 8 September – the evening, concidentally, that saw the Italian government surrendering its forces unconditionally and a military armistice granted, its terms approved by the UK, US and USSR governments.

In the morning, offensive activity by the Anglo-American air forces had continued when the airfields at Lille/Nord, Lille/Vendeville and Vitry-en-Artois were targets for an assembled total of 144 Marauders and 18 Mitchells, supported by 38 squadrons of Spitfires and two groups of Thunderbolts. Nine enemy aircraft were destroyed, one probably destroyed and five damaged for the loss of four Spitfires and their pilots. This operation was followed by an attack on Mardyck airfield by Typhoon bombers and on Abbeville marshalling yards by twelve Venturas, with the support of twenty Spitfire squadrons.[6]

It was not until evening, though, that the intensity of *Starkey* began to be experienced by people in that 10 mile stretch of coast between Wimereux and Hardelot, via Boulogne and Le Portel. The ferocity of what the Allies had in mind with their ploy became evident when 12 Mitchell medium bombers of 98 Squadron and 6 of 180 Squadron, flying together from Dungeness to a point 2 miles south of Hardelot, parted company 6 miles east of Boulogne to attack their respective targets concurrently at 1745 hours. The two box formations of 6 released 45 × 1,000 lb bombs on *Pumicestone* (Fort de la Crèche) – three hung up because of an electrical failure and were jettisoned before returning home – while the single box of six attacked *Millstone* (Pointe aux Oies) with 24 × 1,000 lb bombs, a combined 30 tons. Then came 32 Marauder medium bombers of the US Air Force's 322nd and 386th Groups, making separate attacks on *Pomeranian* (La Trésorerie) between 1800 and 1815 hours, dropping more than 40 tons of bombs. This time the bombs were smaller, 500 lb, but there were more than twice the number released on the other two targets. In the half-hour either side of 1800 hours, it was the turn of the beach defences at Hardelot, codenamed *Menagerie,* to come under attack from twin-engined, high-tailed Whirlwinds of RAF Fighter Command with two 250 lb bombs apiece and the bomb-carrying version of the single-engined Typhoon fighter (nicknamed 'Bomphoon'), each with two 500 lb bombs. The aggregate was 5 tons of bombs on Menagerie, and it brought the total on these four locations to some 77 tons.[7]

The Mitchells were flying from RAF Station Dunsfold, where 98 and 180 Squadrons had been joined by a detachment from a Dutch squadron, No. 320, based at Lasham, which brought 14 aircraft with full crews, plus 14 reserve crews, to reinforce the effort being put into this Culminating Phase of *Starkey.*

The Whirlwinds belonged to 263 Squadron at Warmwell, Dorset, its pilots having been recalled from leave on 5 September to operate temporarily in No. 11 Group from RAF Station Manston. Of the 16 serviceable Whirlwinds, 12 were mustered for the evening attack but only 7 completed the operation, the other 5 returning early, all with mechanical trouble of one sort or another. The Bomphoons, 7 in number from 181 Squadron operating out of No. 124 Airfield, New Romney, Kent, closed this part of the proceedings. They took off at about the time the 'Whirlibirds' were approaching Hardelot – getting ready to dive from nearly 3 miles high and release their bombs at an altitude of between 4,000 and 5,000 feet.

In the Le Portel area, the first bombers had come and gone by now, *Religion* (Fort de Couppes) being the opening target for US Air Force Marauders, 18 of them from 323 Group dropping more than a hundred 500 lb bombs (23.88 tons in total) at 1715 hours – a half-hour before RAF planes began their raids on *Pumicestone* and *Millstone,* the gun positions north of Boulogne. *Andante* (Cap d'Alprech) was attacked 45 minutes after *Religion,* 18 Marauders from 387 Group dropping one bomb more than their compatriots had aimed at the other Le Portel target, bringing to 215 the total of 500 lb bombs released against the two targets north and south of the town.[8]

Attacking in formations of 6 aircraft flying at 500 foot steps between 11,000 feet and 12,000 feet, 16 of the American planes suffered damage from AA gunfire, seemingly faring rather better than those bombing *Pomeranian* where 21 planes were battle-scarred and one entered into a skirmish with one of the several enemy aircraft seen in the area.[9]

The 50 tons of high explosives dropped on the Le Portel guns (actually 47.99 tons) compares with the 75-plus tons (actually 77.23 tons) dropped that evening against the other four groups of gun positions. However, both tonnages pale against the 678.10 tons (250 lb bombs up to 4,000 lb 'blockbusters') that would be released that night, 8/9 September, in the Bomber Command attack on *Religion* and *Andante*.

It could have been still worse – or could it? – but for the onset of unfavourable weather conditions that grounded aircraft and also forced the 24 hour postponement of 'D-Day', the day the ships were to sail. The original intention, which was presented to the Chiefs of Staff Committee as late as 26 August, saw *Starkey* expecting RAF Bomber Command to carry out night attacks on two successive nights on enemy coastal gun positions; on the penultimate night, as many OTUs and Wellington squadrons as 'Bomber' Harris could spare and on the ultimate night not less than 200 sorties by OTUs, plus Wellington and Stirling squadrons. It also allowed for the possibility of a repeat effort if 'D-Day' had to be postponed after the first of these two bombardments had been launched.[10]

No one need speculate as to whether or not *Religion*, *Andante* and therefore the town and townspeople of Le Portel too were thus spared from penultimate-night bombing and the potential horrors of a consequential 'double whammy'. HQ Bomber Command had issued definitive orders for *Starkey* operations on the night of 6/7 September. These comprised a PFF-led raid by an all-Wellington force comprising 16 aircraft from No. 1 Group and 10 from No. 6 Group with 16, 23 and 21 aircraft respectively from Nos 91, 92 and 93 OTU groups – 100 aircraft, exactly, when including the Mosquitoes, Halifaxes and, on this occasion, Lancasters (3 from 7 Squadron), detailed to do the target-marking. The Le Portel coastal batteries were not, that night, the 'target for tonight'; instead, the dubious distinction of introducing this final segment of the *Starkey* scenario was bestowed on other cleared objectives a comforting few miles away – the big guns of La Trésorerie.[11]

With D-Day happening on 9 September without more delay (and the planned night bombing on 6/7 and 7/8 ruled out by the weather), no further effort needed to be sought from 'Bomber' Harris. So far as he was concerned, what he had dismissed as being 'a piece of harmless play-acting' – this 'comparatively futile operation', this 'academical study' – was over. *Starkey* was behind him, Bomber Command's job done with Pathfinder-led raids on the nights of 30 and 31 August and 2, 3 and 8 September totalling 387 effective sorties for the loss of a single OTU Wellington. Free from distraction, he could proceed with the overriding task of demolishing, once and for all, Germany's means to continue the war.

The original plan proposed as many attacks by heavy bombers by day as by night, the Americans to contribute 3,000 sorties by day, the British 3,000 sorties by night. Besides the verbal lashing from Air Chief Marshal Sir Arthur Harris, with the consequent scaling-down, Gen. Ira Eaker, Commanding General of the US 8th Air Force, raised his own objections for much the same reason. Eaker protested that he had been given a clear directive to destroy German industry, and any diversion which would prejudice this task would be unacceptable.[12]

In the event, British-based American 'heavies' were employed on a number of occasions additional to that historic time when five US Air Force Fortresses joined the RAF for a first taste of bombing in darkness. In one, on 31 August, 315 Fortresses were despatched to attack targets in France and the Low Countries, but found them obscured by clouds with the exception of Amiens/Glissy airfield. The temptation was strong, as many as 105 aircraft going into the attack on this single airfield, releasing 315 tons of high explosives with what were described as 'good' results. Results overall were less satisfactory. Four Fortresses were lost – three, tragically, due to a collision on the way out – and a fifth was reported missing, presumed lost to enemy action. In this respect the score was possibly even: five enemy aircraft claimed as destroyed, one claimed as probably destroyed and one damaged.[13]

Huge groups of Fortresses, massing over southern and eastern England – a familiar sight those days to watchers on the ground – formed early on 9 September, D-Day. An even larger total could have been counted than on previous occasions, and this time whatever cloud cover began appearing over the Continent was not enough to hide the intended targets. Timed to meet the requirements of the *Starkey* planners, while RAF Fighter Command was carrying out its first attacks of the day and the convoys were assembling in the Channel, eight forces of four-engined bombers were taking off from the USAAF bases. The 1st Division had 140 aircraft with three targets, the 2nd Division 63 aircraft with two targets and the 3rd Division 128 aircraft with three targets. These 331 'heavies' were provided with 224 fighters to give them cover against German defenders in critical stages of their flights, as far as Paris and in broad daylight from start to finish.[14] It was the biggest air operation of its kind in any of the three stages of *Starkey* with 555 planes – the fastest and furthest-ranging single-engined aircraft available for escort duties and the highest-flying, largest and heaviest bombers in the European theatre of operations.

Beauvais-Tille airfield was the first to come under attack, fifty-nine Fortresses of 3rd Division leaving the English coast behind them at 0725 hours at Shoreham. Routes and timings for the other targets were carefully coordinated with a half-hour spread between the first and last of these wings of Fortresses and Liberators crossing the coast between 0750 (Selsey) and 0818 hours (South Foreland). The destinations were Paris (20 aircraft mustered and secondary targets selected – factories producing ball-bearings and aero-engines) and Beaumont-sur-Oise (49) – completing the contribution by 3rd Division's Fortresses; Lille/Nord (37), Lille/Vendeville (52) and Vitry-en-Artois (51) – 1st Division's Fortresses; and St Omer/Longuenesse (28) and Abbeville/Drucat (35) – 2nd Division's Liberators.

The fact that the four-engined bombers were flying towards enemy territory from three directions appeared to confuse the ground controllers.[15] The fighters they were meant to be guiding were unable to make contact with either the 1st or 2nd Divisions and the minimal combat that did take place was confined to a quarter of an hour. It was long enough and effective enough, however, from the *Luftwaffe*'s point of view, to ensure that two of the bombers failed to return home. Indeed, these raids on key airfields attracted the bulk of the enemy's reaction on this day, with *Luftwaffe* wings from Cambrai and Beauvais and its squadrons from Evreux airborne in some strength. Some 100 to 120 fighters were sent up to engage the

Fortresses on the way into and out of their Beauvais and Paris target areas. Apart from Paris, all of these raids were on airfields, the results ranging from 'poor' to 'fair' to 'good', according to reports given at subsequent crew debriefing sessions when the Americans returned to their bases.

On that D-Day morning these 331 US bombers released a total of 611.30 tons of high explosives.[16] It can be noted that as many as eight airfields and factories, stretched inland as deep as Paris, took a pounding less than that inflicted against the *Religion* and *Andante* gun positions at Le Portel in the night just gone. A force of night bombers less than three-quarters its size dropped a greater tonnage – heavier by 11 per cent – than its 'day shift' colleagues. There were good reasons for the individual loads being reduced. Needing less fuel because the distances were shorter, the 234 bombers leaving their airfields by night to home in on Le Portel could take on board a greater weight of high explosives (678.10 tons) than those that had to penetrate far further into France.

The two air forces combined their medium-bomber capabilities closer to home with a series of early morning raids on the six groups of gun emplacements between Wimereux and Hardelot – raids which produced further heartache for the Portelois in the period between dawn and the mass evacuation. The USAAF alone turned its attention to *Religion* and *Andante*; the RAF alone to *Pumicestone* and *Menagerie*; and there were combined attacks on *Pomeranian* and *Millstone*.[17] All six groups of guns had already figured in attacks the previous evening.

At half-hourly intervals, *Religion* (Fort de Couppes) was the objective for four waves of American Marauders with a mixture of 500 lb and 600 lb bombs – 18 coming in at 0745 hours and dropping a 108 × 500 lb bombs; 16 dropping 88 × 600 lb and 6 × 500 lb; then 18 dropping 90 × 500 lb and 12 × 600 lb; and finally 13 dropping 72 × 600 lb and 6 × 500 lb. At the same time, other Marauders belonging to the same four 54-strong bomber groups in US Air Support Command attacked *Andante* (Cap d'Alprech) with the same combination of high explosives – 17 dropping 96 × 500 lb and 6 × 600 lb; 18 dropping 108 × 600 lb; then 17 dropping 87 × 500 lb and 18 × 600 lb; and finally 17 dropping 96 × 600 lb and 6 × 500 lb, all attacks pressed home in the face of intense AA gunfire.

The USAAF had casualties as well as setbacks. Five of the six members of a crew in No. 387 Group were killed at Chipping Ongar, Essex, in a crash on take-off due to poor visibility, and another crew fell victim to AA fire after leaving the target; No. 386 Group lost a plane shot down over the target before releasing its bombs, apparently the result of a direct hit by flak in the bomb bay; and one of No. 322 Group's planes, taking a direct hit on the port engine, spun into the water 3 miles off the coast. Some sixty-four of the 202 Marauders attacking that morning were hit by AA fire – one in three – and in one instance the damage forced an emergency belly landing on return to base. Each of the four groups despatched a maximum effort fifty-four aircraft, with No. 387 Group trawling up a further two as spares. In the event, besides the one lost on take-off, nine were ineffective because bomb-release equipment failed, and four returned early – three with engine trouble and one through becoming lost from its formation while flying in cloud before leaving the English coast.[18]

In the immediate and wider area of *Religion* and *Andante*, 134 of these twin-engined American planes dropped 399 × 500 lb and 400 × 600 lb bombs, a total of 196.20 tons. It brought to close on 1,000 tons (actually 922.29 tons), the amount of high explosives intended for them in the attacks of 8 and 9 September, day and night combined, by RAF Bomber Command and the USAAF. The number of bombs, excluding the TI incendiaries dropped by Pathfinder Force, amounted by now to 1,014 in the daylight hours and 2,243 at night, a total of 3,257 bombs ranging from 250 lb to 4,000 lb.* It will never be known precisely how many fell where intended, although a study of investigations carried out in the aftermath of the bombardment would be able to produce some telling comments on the degree of accuracy achieved by the bomb-aimers. It would even be possible to compare the effectiveness of American results, in raids carried out in daytime using visual identification and visual bombing of their targets, with those of the RAF by night.[19] RAF crews on the 'night shift' were relying on primary marking with sophisticated radio-positioning and aural-signalling equipment followed by visual backing-up and then bombing visually on the markers.

While the weight of the *Starkey* bombing offensive on D-Day was directed against *Religion* and *Andante*, with their big guns judged capable of firing 20 miles and 14 miles respectively, the other targets north beyond Boulogne and south towards Le Touquet were coming under attack too. A quarter of an hour earlier, at 0730 hours, RAF Fighter Command made simultaneous raids on *Pomeranian*, *Pumicestone* and *Millstone*, with *Menagerie* its target just an hour later. It was the opening of a series of bomb attacks that final morning to harass the defences while the ships made their way as if to deposit the troops and their supplies on the broad, sandy beaches. Exactly where would still have been unclear because directions could be changed to confuse the opposition. With Hardelot the particular focus for raids against beach defences along this stretch of coast, apart from those which were adjacent and subsidiary to the sites of long-range guns, the Boulogne/Hardelot/Le Touquet area must have appeared the favourite to Germans trying to analyse the situation.

Pomeranian (La Trésorerie), which took the brunt of the bombing the previous evening – the USAAF alone, with 187 × 500 lb in two separate attacks within a quarter of an hour – now became the target for an increasing number of aircraft in successive waves. First came two boxes of 6 Mitchells from RAF Fighter Command carrying a mix of 1,000 lb and 500 lb bombs, then two further waves of Marauders belonging to the US Air Force. The first 15 planes dropping 90 × 600 lb bombs, the next 18 dropping 96 × 500 lb and 12 × 600 lb, to produce an aggregate 69.51 tons.

Pumicestone (Fort de la Crèche) received a return visit from the RAF, whose Mitchells were joined by the Venturas of No. 21 Squadron at RAF Station Hartford

---

* In correspondence with the author, Boulogne journalist Guy Bataille refers to contemporary police documents reporting shells fired from ships adding to the damage caused by bombs, even as far away as Ambleteuse. *Starkey* documentation, however, shows that attacks against the coastal artillery were left entirely to the RAF and USAAF once the plan to use battleships was abandoned. It has to be assumed, therefore, that any shells fired from ships in fact came from German anti-aircraft guns carried on board vessels in port or off the coast, which were known to have supplemented the fixed defences during the night of 8/9 September.

Bridge, and this time a new component was introduced – delayed action bombs. Besides 1,000 lb bombs conventionally set to explode on impact, one in two 500 lb and 250 lb bombs carried by both types of aircraft had 30-minute fuses to increase the confusion among the gun crews,[20] the combined loads dropped by the 24 aircraft totalling 31.70 tons. At *Millstone* (Pointe aux Oies), the first raids by 11 RAF Mitchells (the 12th lost formation in cloud over the South Coast and returned to base) saw 23 x 1,000 lb and 40 x 500 lb bombs being dropped, one 1,000-pounder having hung up. Again, one-in-two of the smaller bombs were fused to go off with a half-hour delay. Subsequent attacks by 17 and 18 USAAF Marauders delivered a further 30 x 500 lb and 180 x 600 lb bombs, an aggregate 74.11 tons in 75 minutes.

Against *Pomeranian* and *Millstone*, the Americans flew in formations of up to eighteen, ostensibly 'bombing on the leader', many of them sustaining damage from AA gunfire, which was experienced in appreciable amounts, especially at *Pomeranian*. Against both *Pomeranian* and *Millstone*, also against *Pumicestone*, the Venturas and Mitchells despatched by the RAF flew in formations of six, again following the aim of the leader – the Mitchells all coming from a single airfield, RAF Station Dunsfold, and provided in equal numbers by 98, 180 and 320 Squadrons. AA fire was described as only moderate except at *Pumicestone*, where it was heavy and accurate.[21]

Thus these three long-range gun positions were attacked by a combined Anglo-American force of 115 aircraft within the space of 80 minutes. They dropped 175.31 tons of high explosives in 682 bombs of between 250 lb and 1,000 lb. The motive was clear: *Millstone* comprised fixed guns and railway artillery inland from Wimereux; *Pomeranian* was the site of three 15 inch guns at La Trésorerie – 'invulnerable to air attack', like three other sites nearer to Calais, according to Bomber Command experts; while *Pumicestone* was the Allies' name for Fort de la Crèche, a clifftop battery between Wimereux and Boulogne with four 10 inch guns.

Further down the coast, Hardelot (*Menagerie*) received a return visit from Fighter Command's Whirlibombers of 263 Squadron and 30 minutes later from other Bomphoons, this time provided by 3 Squadron at Manston. Suitably escorted, their 'calling card' was more pronounced than that of the previous evening but the technique was similar: dive bombing from 14,000 feet on this dispersed target (actually seven separate targets, including two adjacent six-gun batteries, all within an area stretching ¾ mile along the coast and a mile or so inland).[22] In two waves, a half-hour interval between them, the twenty-three fighter-bombers carrying out this attack (compared with fourteen) dropped 7.37 tons of high explosives to bring the bomb tonnage to 12.05 tons. This was small by comparison with the bomb loads inflicted on the coastal guns, but in the Allies' eyes these were no more than beach defence positions – the armament and the gunners protected more by bricks and sandbags than concrete bunkers that were partly subterranean. Nevertheless, *Menagerie* was important within the framework of *Starkey*.

Incidentally, to the consternation of those on the ground on the home side of the Channel, one of the Bomphoons (which each carried a 500 lb bomb beneath each wing) committed the sin of scoring an 'own goal' in this operation. The ORB at their home base, Manston, noted that the attack on the Hardelot guns was performed quite successfully and without incident, 'apart from the jettisoning of one bomb which hung up, in the middle of our runway – fortunately at "safe"'.

The Mitchells from Dunsfold had to find alternative landing grounds because of changeable weather conditions, which prevented Manston's dive bombers from operational flying again later in the day. While 3 Squadron took off but was recalled immediately, 263 Squadron, similarly briefed to attack an enemy airfield, received its instructions to abort while taxiing out to the runway.

Even so, Fighter Command alone carried out more than 2,000 sorties during that day, encompassing tiny UK-produced Spitfires that were dedicated to far-ranging escort duties to the American-built twin-engined bombers, whose job was to blast those six groups of targets down from Wimereux and the further-afield aerodromes. In a number of airfield attacks, during an operation that demonstrated the versatility of a particular aircraft built in British factories, Typhoon fighters escorted Typhoon bombers. As well as providing protection for the bombers, escort planes that day were busy putting up an aerial umbrella, over-flying the seaborne forces from 0545 to 1700 hours and patrolling the beaches from 0700 to 1100 hours. More than one in three of them were Spitfires – 786 sorties out of the 2,006 flown on D-Day were by Spitfires,[23] their pilots continuously scanning the coastal skies in search of enemy planes, which were nowhere to be seen in that part of France.

These operations were not without loss. Two Fortresses, three Marauders, one Typhoon and two Spitfires failed to return to their bases, although the Typhoon's pilot was known to be safe.[24] A fourth Marauder was lost even before these attacks began – it crashed on take-off, suffering the casualties already described.[25] As occurred the previous day, German AA guns were spirited in their efforts to prevent the bombers from reaching their targets; and to deter those which did so by making sure the curtain of fire was sufficient to influence the determination to take proper aim. All three Marauders lost in action were shot down by the AA guns ringing *Religion* and *Andante*.

Air cover for the mini-armada of 355 ships began at first light for vessels forming into the assault convoy to head for France, and for the merchant ships whose course would keep them nearer home. At various times during the night the assault convoy craft had sailed from Richborough, Dover, Rye, Newhaven, Shoreham, Portsmouth and Southampton to be off Dungeness by 0700 hours. Pilots and crews in the bombers heading for France and the fighter pilots who were to provide protection must have wondered about the presence of so many vessels whose course certainly appeared to be towards 'the other side' – another 'Dieppe', perhaps, or the 'real thing', because there were half as many ships again as carried the Canadians to Dieppe.* There must be something special going on because all the planes were decked out in new markings – black-and-white stripes – to make them stand out to those on the ships, in the air and (maybe!) to the soldiers surely soon landing in France.

Correspondents were gathered by now to provide reports for the media, some positioning themselves on the cliffs between Dover and Folkestone, others ready to go 'into the thick of it' aboard ship. In graphic reports, British newspapers would

* Then, a 6,100-strong force (more than four-fifths Canadians) sailed cramped aboard 237 ships[26] to mount this costly operation. The Canadians alone suffered 3,369 casualties, over 900 of them fatal.[27]

the following day cover the troop concentrations, the aerial bombardment and the disposition of the armada.

If anyone had any preconceived ideas about the composition of an Allied invasion force, they could not possibly have matched this strange sight. There were vessels large and small, from self-propelled Thames barges to 10,000 ton merchant ships; river boats to cross-Channel pleasure steamers; nippy destroyers to lumbering landing craft built to carry tanks as well as troops; a river gunboat, motor gunboats and even motor launches.[28] All were formed into pre-assigned groups, shepherded skilfully to pass through mine-free waters – a mile-wide assault force that was really no more than a lot of 'sitting ducks'. Those on board were about to stare down the mouths of German long-range guns capable of blasting them right out of the water – guns that by now, mercifully, the RAF and the Americans would have silenced if all was keeping to plan.

There were twenty-one groups of surface vessels in all, widely separated and varying in number, size and composition, assembled from Dungeness north-eastwards to Richborough (Pegwell Bay) and westwards to the Solent. While these vessels were proceeding in the direction of the mine-swept passage off Dungeness, the twenty merchant ships would be 10 to 12 miles south of Shoreham and steaming eastwards, parallel to the coast. It was their job to appear to be a heavy military force following up the assault troops.

It was a 2 hour voyage to nowhere. Come 0900 hours, HMS *Albrighton*, a Hunt Class destroyer serving as the HQ ship, heading the lead group would transmit the code word Backchat, the signal for the senior officers of the various groups to order their vessels to turn 180 degrees. The French coast would be ahead one minute, between Boulogne and Le Touquet, an uninviting and hostile environment; the next, the English coast would beckon, the disembarkation venues of Stokes Bay, Southampton, Hythe, Deal and Newhaven ready to provide a warm welcome later in the day.

There was a minimum number of men on these vessels, the big merchant ships and the escorting destroyers manned as usual but the landing craft empty. Generally the single concession to the danger of aerial attack was the presence of fast-firing guns, their crews on the alert and ready for any call to action stations, intent on inflicting maximum damage to any enemy aircraft attacking the expedition. The fighter squadrons providing the air umbrella for the most critical period were a comforting sight; still, on-board defences put the power to fight back in the crews' hands. Overall, the loads embarked on the landing craft constituted a mixed bag: trucks with Vickers twin machine-guns, tractors to add bulk, Bofors guns and other weaponry. The several thousand soldiers that one would have expected to find in them were now about to resume battle-training across the length and breadth of Britain. Their task, the exercise known as *Harlequin*, ended when everyone had transferred from their permanent bases to temporary accommodation across southern England – an operation to test the effectiveness of the Army's plans to move large numbers of troops into reception areas in a pre-invasion situation.

The twenty merchantmen, each of them around 10,000 tonners, were there to give substance to the 'invasion force' as a direct result of Churchill's involvement in *Starkey*. These vessels had sailed from the Solent so as to be 10 miles off Beachy

Head by the time the assault force was due to about-turn. Having made their presence felt, orders would be given to withdraw from whence they came, minimizing the risk of attack by the enemy by air, sea or coastal guns. A well-aimed bomb or a well-placed shell could sink one of these ships, costing seamen's lives and prejudicing the chain of vital supplies destined for the British ports.

Cover of up to seventy-two aircraft was provided for the convoys by RAF Fighter Command from 0700 hours to 1000 hours, and then very considerably reduced as the enemy 'appeared to show no interest whatever in the convoys'.[29] Hostile reconnaissance was limited to an area south of the Isle of Wight/Dungeness in the west and off Dunkirk in the east at the outset of the operation, including a look-see probe by two enemy aircraft in the Selsey Bill area, one of them, an Me 109, being shot down.

Some 165 landing craft were among the 355 vessels in this naval assault force, including 24 which were equipped to 'make smoke', a prime requirement of this component of *Starkey*. A smokescreen was needed to mask the ships' movement when it was time to carry out the 180-degree change of direction. It would hide the real intentions from German eyes on shore and it would help to protect the ships from attack. The 64 tank landing craft added credibility to the mini-armada; the 11 destroyers supplied the firepower to beat off attacks from both air and sea, as well as the speed to dash hither and thither in response to varying conditions. No one knew what might happen. The remaining 91 vessels were there as if about to perform a mixture of tasks, either transporting men and equipment to France or loaded with supplies to be used when the first of the troops stormed ashore. There were 5 cross-Channel steamers, which in happier days had taken Londoners to France on a day's outing, and in the darker days of war brought soldiers back from the beaches of Dunkirk; there was a river gunboat, HMS *Locust*; and there were barges which used to ply their trade up and down London's river, between the great docks and the sea.

It would be hard to imagine a more motley collection of seagoing vessels than these. It was, however, all that could be spared. The intention was to assemble the biggest and most impressive fleet seen in the Channel in years – a force with sufficient conviction to deceive the enemy. The problem was that shipping was at a premium and landing craft production was yet to match demand. There had to be landing craft in the assault force for realism – while dummies were acceptable ashore for deception purposes, it would take real ones to go halfway to France and back again.

RAF Fighter Command's Bostons, already committed for bombing airfields and gun emplacements, now had another purpose to fulfil. While some of the shipping could help to create the smokescreen to cover the withdrawal 10 miles from the French coast, plus that supplied by the two dozen landing boats fitted for laying smoke, ten Bostons were brought in to extend the smoke cover for a 20 minute period ahead of the turnaround signal. There were more of these smoke-producing planes on standby, but the weather – unpredictable as ever – took another turn for the worse, clamping down and preventing take-off.[30] The crews were not alone in being briefed for a role in the climax to *Starkey*, then having to sit tight because increasing mist closed the airfield or some other meteorological condition caused a cancellation. Just when the situation seemed stable, a change in the weather would upset the operation. It had been like this from the start; and it would end the same way. Capriciously, the weather conditions had turned out better the previous day – the day originally intended for 'D-Day' until the forecasters were given their say.

The RAF's activities extended beyond laying smoke and protecting shipping, further even than attacks on the coastal batteries. With the convoys fast approaching their home ports, Tactical Air Force planes were busy. Some 23 Bostons with Spitfire escorts were despatched to begin an afternoon's offensive operations by bombing Monchy/Breton airfield. Further impetus came with 12 Mitchells attacking Bryas Sud airfield, 8 Venturas attacking Merville airfield and 12 Bomphoons attacking Coxyde airfield, each time with fighter cover. Some 50 tons of bombs were dropped in these four raids, the bomber crews describing their results as ranging from fair-to-good to excellent. The fighter pilots reported mixed results: a lame FW 190 shot down and two Me 109s probably destroyed for the loss of two of their own – one, ironically perhaps, apparently hit by AA fire rather than going down in combat with opposing fighters. The plane was seen to go into the sea off Dunkirk.[31]

Activities began to tail off as the afternoon progressed, the weather again turning against the aircrews. Further attacks on six airfields were called off, as were fighter sweeps intended for Biggin Hill, Hornchurch and North Weald wings, whose planes were detailed for the Lille, Courtrai and Flushing areas to round off *Starkey*.[32]

Reporting on what the Admiralty, War Office and Air Ministry described in a joint announcement on 10 September as 'a full-scale amphibious exercise', British newspaper correspondents referred to the medium and light bombers flying out 'to smash the airfields and coastal defences' in northern France – 'the explosion of their bombs like thunder . . . the vibration felt on the English coast'.[33] It seemed totally one-sided. On the 'invasion' craft, no one saw an enemy aircraft, submarine or E-boat, and not a single enemy weapon was turned against them. The announcement reported record numbers of sorties in a day by RAF Fighter Command and by bombers and fighters of the USAAF. This 'most successful' exercise saw 'valuable lessons learned'.

Being much less dramatic, no doubt, there was no mention of the contribution by the 'spy planes' on the final day of the 'exercise'. While deteriorating weather conditions hampered offensive operations by aircraft of the Anglo-American air forces, reconnaissance and photographic sorties by the RAF's single-seater Mustangs and Spitfires were nonetheless maintained throughout the day, from soon after 0630 to almost 1900 hours.[34] It was their role to provide camera evidence enabling intelligence specialists to get some idea of the effectiveness of the *Starkey* operations overall – troop and transport movements as well as the results of bombing.

Based at RAF Station Benson, Berkshire, 541 Squadron set the highest standards in this kind of work, which provided the fastest means of determining the impact of bombing on key targets whether deep into Germany – a familiar pre-*Starkey* routine – or along the French coast, often taking their pictures from 3 or 4 miles high.

British and Dominion pilots from this squadron carried out a series of such flights each day between 3 and 9 September, with the Boulogne area providing 'targets' for its airborne cameras on all seven days.[35] They had no idea what to expect in their lone sorties. One of them, posted to flying duties with 541 only on 2 September, flew operationally for the first time the following day and, while photographing Cherbourg, received a baptism of fire from the port's AA guns. A Canadian colleague, trying to photograph Boulogne on the same day, found opposition of a different sort, the weather turning against him. Calais and shipping in the Channel were successfully captured on film, but due to cloud conditions he could manage only distant oblique shots of Boulogne on that occasion.

It was one of these missions, Sortie E174 – flown by an Australian pilot between 1000 and 1140 hours on 9 September and producing prints 'of excellent quality' – that revealed damage to military objectives to the north and south of Le Portel, including the first indication that 'chiefly residential' property in a built-up area had suffered 'very severely' as a result of the attacks on *Religion* and *Andante*, an assessment made on those photographs by the specialists of the Central Interpretation Unit (CIU) based at RAF Station Medmenham.[36] Part of frame 4037, on which their report was based, is reproduced in the plate section. Timed at 1045 hours, the full frame shows an area covering just over one and a half square miles – roughly 2,350 yards by 2,000 yards, scaled 1:10,200 on the original print before magnification.

Pilots in 541 Squadron were familiar with the photo-interpretation duties being performed at Medmenham – five of them had made a visit there as recently as 10 August when bad weather put a block on photo-reconnaissance sorties. They appreciated the need for clear, sharp images on the prints they brought back, recognizing that doing their best required steady flight, straight and level, when over the target area – maximum concentration each and every time, irrespective of enemy opposition.

The primarily *Starkey* sorties over the Channel ports were generally completed within 2 hours, but one of their number had been as far as the Baltic (6 hours 40 minutes) on 21 April and to Berlin (5 hours 10 minutes) on 19 February, the latter 'probably the finest sortie ever carried out by a photo-reconnaissance pilot'. For him, Boulogne/Dieppe/Le Havre on 4 September (1 hour 40 minutes) must have seemed relatively tame.*

By the time the last photo-reconnaissance aircraft touched down, 325 such sorties had been flown by the nine Mustang squadrons of Nos 35 and 39 Wings in the eleven days of active reconnaissance, all without fighter escort and for the loss of only three planes.[37] Of these, 249 were described by the Air Force Commander as 'successful'. Flying Spitfires, 140 and 541 Squadrons contributed 11 and 10 sorties respectively.

The aerial photographs obtained by these lone fliers would be revealing – these and others taken by bomber crews, plus the words of fact and interpretation accompanying them, which would soon put *Starkey* into stark perspective.

---

* The 541 Squadron ORB noted that this pilot, Fl./Lt J.R. Brew, spent 45 minutes over Berlin and obtained an 'almost complete mosaic', having photographed 'almost the whole city'. He was awarded the DFC on 9 July 1943, just four days after a narrow escape over Paris when, having obtained photos of the target, his engine cut due to an empty wing tank. The engine did not restart until the glide had taken him down to 12,000 feet. He climbed 'flat out' to regain operational height and returned with 'no more unpleasant incidents'.

Chapter Thirteen

Rebuilding Homes . . .
Rebuilding Lives

With Marshal Pétain showing an immediate and personal interest, the plight of the bombed-out Portelois could not have been brought to the notice of anyone in higher authority among their countrymen in wartime occupied France. He had been made aware of the impact of the bombardment on the town and the subsequent dispersal of the civilian population. He was familiar with the extent of the evacuation programme and the steps taken to care for the injured survivors, some of whom had been taken as far as Paris in the 'miracle train'. He knew all about it having seen this lavishly equipped mobile medical and reception centre for himself during a visit with M. Pierre Laval, his head of government in the Vichy regime under the German occupation.[1]

In l'Hôtel du Parc in Vichy on 9 October, a month after the bombardment, Marshal Pétain received a delegation representing the Portelois.[2] In it were clergymen – l'Abbés Ledoux and Boidin – and councillors – Le Portel's deputy mayor, Mlle Marie-Joséphine Bourgain (it was said that in her family alone as many as thirty-five were dead),[3] with the Mayor of Boulogne, M. Brevers. During this visit the Marshal received first-hand reports of the bombing and the rescue operations, and he heard the delegation's acknowledgement of the assistance given so far by the government. The main reason for being there was to seek continuing support. So the group stressed that much more help was necessary and focused individually on some of the main needs still to be fulfilled – clothing for those who had left the area and the means to succour the estimated 200 people clinging on to what life remained amid the ruins of their shattered homes.[4]

Having set aside the sum of 100,000 francs for such help to be made available right away, the Marshal invited the delegation to stand alongside him the next morning for a moving ceremony rather like a mini-Changing of the Guard in peacetime London. The high spot came when a huge banner comprising the French national colours of red, white and blue was raised at the main entrance to the l'Hôtel du Parc while a military band played the French national anthem, the *Marseillaise*. It must have been an extremely emotionally charged occasion with the humble Portelois seen by curious onlookers to be occupying a place of honour in the presence of their head of state. The message that he gave the delegation before he left them that morning was surely intended as a morale booster to be transmitted to all Portelois wherever they might now find themselves: 'Stick together and don't lose your spirit.' For the Portelois, who always stuck together anyway, it would have been a superfluous enjoinder; their spirits may have been down at the time, but they were not about to disappear.

The following month in the heart of Paris the plight of the Portelois received further and even wider recognition when, on 27 November, in the world-renowned Cathedral of Notre Dame no less, the community was represented at a memorial service to the estimated 500 men, women and children who lost their lives. The service was held in response to a suggestion by a Paris-based committee that had been set up to help the victims of the bombardment. Agreeing to it, the Archbishop of Paris, Cardinal Suhard, proposed that the scope should be extended to include all other citizens of France who had been killed in air-raids on their country.[5]

Particular care was taken with the interior decorations to ensure that this occasion became as fitting a memorial as possible, even to the presence of the French tricolour draped on high above the massed pews of worshippers. The national flag was unfurled outside too, above the huge front doors, where it made history by being displayed openly in Paris for the first time since the German occupation.

A 100-strong detachment of the Garde de Paris formed a guard of honour for the arriving dignitaries, at their head the representative of Marshal Pétain, Col. Bonhomme, and among them the representatives of M. Laval and his heads of departments, together with the Princess of Broglie and a delegation comprising members of various medical teams. Germany itself and units of its occupation forces were represented too, alongside the international Red Cross and the civil defence organizations in France.

At the side of the Archbishop of Paris, who was conducting the remembrance service, stood l'Abbé Ledoux, one of the few inside Notre Dame that morning with personal experience of the suffering in his now-empty parish. Of course, he was not alone with harrowing memories of aerial bombardment; greater Paris itself had suffered, as had other cities, and in the congregation were those who knew this well – the mayors of districts within the industrial suburbs.

At that moment Paris was quiet, the silence no more pronounced anywhere than within this great cathedral where the bomb victims of Le Portel and France at large were being remembered. Elsewhere in France, elsewhere in Europe too, the bombers would be back and, inevitably, there would be more deaths, more injuries, more destruction.

So far as the newspapers were concerned, for reasons of control and timing, what had happened in Le Portel failed to make any impact until several days after the last bombs had fallen and the last stragglers in the mass evacuation had left. News of the bombardment in one of the Pas de Calais papers, the *Télégramme*, appeared under a heading announcing that Anglo-American aircraft had 'sown the seeds of death yet again', with more than 400 bodies recovered from the rubble of Le Portel, the seaside resort close to Boulogne, and that rescue teams had gone to its help from across the region. Close scrutiny of its columns would have revealed an earlier clue as to the fate of this resort.[6] The wider readership would probably have been curious about the purpose of a brief reference to the inhabitants of Le Portel being able to leave the restricted zone without having to show their passes, an identity card being sufficient to satisfy the authorities in the event of their being stopped.

On the radio, on the same day as the newspaper report identifying Le Portel as having been a target of Allied bombers, came a report of 460 deaths, many of them in Le Portel.[7] Just as the death toll increased in subsequent publications, so did the scope of information made known to the public about events in the aftermath of the bombardment: a Le Portel factory asking for the new addresses of its employees so as to be able to forward their wages; sixteen people accused of looting a bakery in Le Portel; access to Le Portel being banned because of the risk from collapsed buildings and hazards to health; the whereabouts of personal property recovered from addresses in Le Portel; an open letter of thanks from the evacuees of Le Portel to their hosts in Béthune. Piece by piece the facts were becoming known to the outside world, the world outside the abandoned town of Le Portel – in places far away from Le Portel, 'The Town That Had To Die'.

In fact Le Portel was to suffer from further bombing, the incident that was the most devastating to the hearts and minds of the scattered evacuees being substantial damage to their church. Remarkably, in the September 1943 bombardment the building had escaped the worst of the devastation (as had two prominent statues in other parts of the town, the *Calvaire des Marins* and that of the *Vierge de la Falaise*)[8] – protected by the hand of God, it was tempting to say. Within 24 hours of the Allies landing in Normandy, at about 10.00 a.m. on 5 June 1944, the church was largely destroyed by a combination of high explosives and the consequential fire. The news of this loss was given by Boulogne's mayor in a letter to the parish priest, l'Abbé Ledoux, who had long since moved to Fresnicourt-le-Dolmen.

Administratively, Boulogne had taken over responsibility for Le Portel since the evacuation. It must have been a distressing task for his worship to have to be the bearer of such news; he could be excused, therefore, for asking the clergyman to relay it to the Portelois. A priest, he wrote, would be better able to find the right words to calm the absent parishioners whose latest blow was shared by everyone in Boulogne. He reminded the reverend gentleman of the 'watchwords' of Boulogne – courage, faith and hope – adding that, soon, Le Portel would live again.[9]

Liberation came to Boulogne before Le Portel. In September 1944, in their advance down the coast, Canadian soldiers hounded the enemy forces into and through 'Fortress Boulogne'. They were not easily dislodged – Hitler had demanded that this stronghold would survive[10] – and the commandant, Lt-Gen. Ferdinand Heim, stayed put to the bitter end. In fact, with poetic justice some will say, Le Portel was where eventually he was forced into surrender by the constant pounding of his Cap d'Alprech bunkers.

With an estimated 7,000 defenders, Fortress Boulogne stretched along the coast and deep inland, from Wimereux in the north to Equihen in the south, by way of Boulogne and Le Portel. Flowers gave their names to many of these encampments – *Pantoffelblume* for Cap d'Alprech and *Seerose* for Fort de Couppes, for example. Among those 'flowers' the scent of defeat was less pleasant by 4.32 p.m. on 22 September when white flags appeared,[11] finger-pressure eased on the waiting flamethrowers and at last the guns fell silent.

For the liberating troops, Le Portel would have appeared in grim contrast against the reception in other towns in the Pas de Calais. The destruction was staggering, the desolation beyond belief; the landscape stark, the silence eerie. There were no people thronging the streets, no laughing faces; there were no flags unfurled from the upper windows, nothing stirred but what few curtains still remained with their signs of age and the dust that permeated everything in the bombardment a year earlier. The Portelois were many miles away, some already free of the Nazi oppression while others were yet to enjoy this experience. Not for the Portelois the satisfaction of watching the rounding up and imprisonment of the occupying troops, unarmed and cowed – the soldiers in the field-grey uniforms whose presence in the surrounding gun positions had triggered the demolition of their beloved town.

Afterwards, though a long while afterwards, one of the first notabilities to visit Le Portel was Gen. Charles de Gaulle, leader-in-exile of the French people. The war in Europe was over and the familiar figure, so tall, so imposing, made his way through what was left of the streets. Town councillors 'bent his ear' to be sure that before he left he would be in no doubt that Le Portel needed help to help itself. There is a story about this visit that may be apocryphal but nevertheless is worthy of a further airing. It seems that two old men approached him, both Portelois, apologizing that there was no one to welcome him – '*mon Général*' – because Le Portel was now 'no more than a resting place for its own dead'.[12] An exaggeration, perhaps, but nonetheless a telling phrase to enhance the history of this proud town.

In reality, some of the townspeople were there several months earlier, during the first winter of liberation, as a visiting journalist discovered while roaming the district in the first days of January 1945.[13] In the shadow of the cliffs, waiting for low tide, a number of fishermen were about to collect mussels from around Fort de l'Heurt, that distinctive landmark in the bay where Napoleon's soldiers – and just recently Hitler's – manned their guns against the threat of seaborne attack from the British. One of the group had lost an arm in the bombing – as well as a son and a daughter – and he was clearly trying to make a bit of a life for himself in the only way that he understood. Strictly speaking he had no right to be there – none in that handful of fishermen on the beach should have been in these parts. As the journalist went on to point out to his readers, the authorities had good reason to continue stressing that no one should consider returning to Le Portel until conditions could be improved sufficiently to suggest a safe and healthy existence.

The civic authorities in Le Portel had already turned to Canada for whatever help might be forthcoming from that country, especially from the French Canadians, by writing to Gen. Vannier, Canadian Ambassador, in Paris. It was pointed out that it was Canadian soldiers who captured 'Fortress Boulogne'; that only 74 homes out of the 1,800 in Le Portel prior to the war were capable of repair; that more than 500 of its former 8,500 inhabitants had been killed; and that after the evacuation, under the eyes of French policemen who could do nothing about it, the Germans had stolen possessions that the townspeople had been forced to leave behind – even floorboards, doors and windowframes. The ambassador went to see for himself, to establish what assistance was needed, and in a subsequent letter of thanks wrote that both he and his wife had been most moved by the warmth of their welcome.[14]

Meanwhile, life continued more normally elsewhere. In front of a crowd of 10,000, Valenciennes beat Lille 3–2 at football, there were the regional boxing championships continuing apace, and news came that, in Berlin, Hitler had broken a five-month silence to give a New Year message on the radio to the German people.[15]

By agreement between the maritime authorities of Britain and France, Boulogne had been opened as a fishing port from Boxing Day 1944 – subject to strict control on the movement of boats and crews.[16] In the opening weeks of the New Year of 1945, an initial group of twenty children returned to their homes in Boulogne, Wimereux and Outreau after evacuation to the Vosges region of France. It was party time too, with groups celebrating the return of former prisoners of war. Others banded together with amusements and gifts to try to make life a touch easier to bear for children who had been orphaned in the tragedy of war.

There were continuing signs that life was beginning to return to normality, albeit slowly. One such indication was when it became known that port workers in Boulogne had discharged their first commercial cargo since the occupation – 1,200 tonnes of jute destined for the textile factories of northern France.[17] There was some semblance of normality being resumed, although living conditions were pitiful.

In readiness for the return of the Portelois, a fresh round of financial assistance was promised, with 150 francs for each household plus 50 francs per person; those who were on their own were to receive 100 francs.[18] By Easter of that year – it was early, with Good Friday falling on 30 March – an estimated 300 people were back home,[19] if 'home' was the correct term for families gathering up the threads of life.

By a strange twist of fate it was the abandoned gun batteries – the very ones whose presence on their doorstep had triggered the town's destruction – that helped to provide the desperately needed accommodation.[20] There was little else left to provide any cover, any privacy, any hope.

Ignored was the unwelcome, unsatisfactory and unhygienic nature of these massive and forbidding concrete bunkers that the Germans had set up as part of the Atlantic Wall defences on the clifftops and other vantage points around Le Portel. They became a shelter for the night as the Portelois with nowhere else to stay were able to meet family members and friends with whom contact had been lost for so long. They were a base, too, while seeing what needed to be done to repair wrecked homes and rebuild shattered lives.

As a 'welcome home' for the first to arrive, Easter Monday was chosen for an indoor basketball event organized by one of the sports clubs, *l'Etoile Sportive Saint-Michel*.[21] Those 'returnees' had spent the past eighteen months or so in other parts of France. Within a fortnight, however, the first of the families from the greater Boulogne area who made the journey by fishing boat to Britain were back home too. The problem was that the Portelois among them had no homes to go to. As a consequence, Desvres became a staging post along the rough road to rehabilitation, just as it had for so many of their townsfolk in the aftermath of the bombardment – a horror that these particular Portelois had escaped by having settled in Britain when it occurred.

By now the war in Europe was coming to a close, with the Allies racing for Berlin. Tuesday 8 May 1945 saw the end of hostilities, an event marked in Boulogne by a ceremony in the open air beneath an azure sky, the sun blazing down, while everyone stood in respectful silence for a minute of solemnity and private thoughts. Military, naval and civilian organizations were represented at this ceremony – the British Army among them – where Boulogne's mayor, M. Eugène Canu, expressed the feelings of those present in an address, remembering all who had died to restore peace to France and the rest of Europe. Over the loudspeakers too came the voice of Gen. de Gaulle in a national message of hope – words meant to console, sustain and unite.[22]

In fact – and all the more tragically because it happened in Le Portel – within 48 hours Boulogne would be mourning one more of its citizens, a boy aged 15, whose death came as a direct legacy of the war just ended. He was among a group of children looking for souvenirs when some grenades exploded, fatally injuring him and seriously injuring four others.[23] Although probably unrelated to the bombardment, Le Portel had suffered yet another wartime tragedy involving explosives – though this time it appears more likely that they were of German origin.*

The burden of overseeing the task of making Le Portel live again now fell largely on someone who had done so much for the town prior to the war and so much for its evacuees after the bombardment – Mlle Marie-Joséphine Bourgain. Coming from a family of wholesale fish merchants, with a background in community service, Mlle Bourgain, who was only just into her 40s, on 26 May 1945 became the first post-war mayor to be elected by the town council.

The initial steps had already been taken to establish what was necessary to create new homes and roads, and new educational and recreational facilities. There was an early surprise when the civic authorities realized that in terms of available land, thanks largely to incursions due to national and local government requirements, Le Portel had actually shrunk to two-thirds of its size a century ago while its population had quadrupled![24]

Glancing at the map shows Le Portel to be a narrow coastal strip a little over 3 miles in length and less than half a mile deep at its widest point; it is hemmed in by the sea on one side with Boulogne at its northern end, and with Outreau as its southern end and inland neighbour. Expansion out of the question, this town-in-waiting would have to make best possible use of the limited land at its disposal.

The civic leaders put their case vigorously yet succinctly to the government-appointed architectural planners based hundreds of miles away in Clermont-Ferrand. They argued that while before the war the built-up area comprised some 60 hectares (150 acres) – out of about 250 hectares (625 acres) available – the initial plan appeared to utilize only about 100 hectares (250 acres).

Furthermore, 'though you are not from our region', the planners should recognize that no longer could one contemplate cramming people into alleyways without breathing space or room to move; the war had left Le Portel with not a single dwelling capable of providing accommodation without substantial repair; there was only one school apiece for infants, boys and girls, whereas before the war two were needed; there was nowhere for indoor or outdoor sports; there were no public gardens and there was a need for at least two; there was no market-place or covered market; there was no public baths, no medical centre and no information centre, let alone the various other facilities essential for community life.[25]

---

* Before that first peacetime summer was over, Le Portel would be numbed by yet another tragic accident when three more children, aged 5, 7, and 8, were killed when a shell that one of them had found in the grass beside a derelict German tank exploded.[26] The relics of war were all around – to the extent even that the homes of those youngsters were abandoned blockhouses.

Prefabricated barracks from Hesdin, originally housing German military personnel, were sought for transfer to Le Portel, the larger one to house those brought in to help in the reconstruction of the town, the smaller one to be used as a cinema – the only form of communal recreation then available.

Ingenuity proved to be the salvation for many a returning family. They carted away what materials could be found amid the devastation of Le Portel to put a roof over their heads. The term for these makeshift homes was '*demie-lune*'; the term for the occupants which reflected their task was 'beavers' – among them, it transpired, was a future mayor of the town.

Elsewhere, for example in the Moulin Bleu district towards Boulogne, which was yet to be built on, prefabricated buildings were erected. Plans were laid for Le Portel's first HBMs – *Habitations à Bon Marché* – low-cost homes to ease the burden for low-income families.

For many years Le Portel would be adopting rigorously a policy that other authorities dared not introduce: rigidly sticking to providing accommodation in Le Portel solely for the Portelois and effectively barring potential newcomers.

In the town itself, as 1947 gave way to 1948, there were still well over a hundred homes in more than thirty streets – nineteen in one street alone, Rue Carnot, one of Le Portel's principal thoroughfares – awaiting what were described as 'urgent repairs'.[27] Normality was a long, long time ahead.

While repairs to individual properties continued, plans for the reconstruction of the town were proposed, discussed, revised and accepted, the Portelois themselves pressing at all stages for what they believed to be best. In the course of time, interest inevitably focused on the former Boulogne-Alprech airport, but nothing came of it. The devastation caused by the fifty or so bomb craters was not the real problem: these could be filled in and the whole area levelled to make way for new facilities. The difficulty was a matter of space. Looking ahead, as was sensible, any prospect of making Cap d'Alprech the site of a regional airport seemed doomed to nosedive – there wasn't sufficient room for the length of runway that the post-war planes were going to need for take-off and landing.[28] It was the end of an era. Boulogne's airport, opened just weeks before war came, gave way to agriculture – to the chugging of farm tractors instead of the whine of jet engines.

By the summer of 1945, upwards of 300 Portelois were back and the number of returning evacuees began rising, slowly at first and then more sharply. Days and dates held scant significance, save for those of 4, 8 and 9 September 1943, which were remembered two years on by poignant ceremonies; in the town hall, where Doctor Léon Godart, a future mayor of Le Portel, so carefully read out the seemingly endless list of bombardment victims – M. Libert-Rentier enunciating *Mort pour la France* after each one . . . in the ruins of the church, where Mgr Lepretre, an archbishop whose own family came from Le Portel, conducted a service . . . at the war memorial close by, where the unknown dead (identified only as 'No. 252') was laid finally to rest . . . and at the communal grave in the town cemetery where children each placed a floral tribute at the foot of each simple wooden cross.

That day, former prisoners of war had carried the coffin of the unknown victim from the town hall to the war memorial for interment, the cortège proceeding through shattered streets, the houses that lined them still incapable of sustaining family life in this immediate post-war period. The selection of the coffin containing the remains of the unknown victim had been entirely random, chosen in fact by a Portelois who had lost his sight in the bombardment[29]; whether a close relative or a friend, this was nonetheless someone special, a 'someone' who had been lost without hope of ever being found. To quote the words of Mayor Jean Coppin as he faced the catafalque on which rested the coffin of that unidentifiable loved one, he or she would henceforth be known as '*Le Parent Portelois de septembre 1943*'.

In that second anniversary of the bombing, any other demonstration of public feeling connected with the war would have been entirely superfluous. And so it was, but not for this reason, that a fortnight later the first anniversary of Le Portel's liberation slipped by without recognition, which is precisely the way that this date has been allowed to go unnoticed in successive years. Why celebrate, when the Allies had merely passed through their town without actually liberating its people? How could this be a 'liberation' with the town empty, the Portelois gone, that September day in 1944? A year on and there was too much on the minds of the Portelois then present to think about the Liberation; and there was so much to be done to restore their homes.

A year later and the population had grown tenfold with upwards of 3,000 Portelois now back. Many children were among them, so emphasis was placed on reopening the classrooms as quickly as possible. Easter 1946 saw a resumption of these facilities.[30]

By now, volunteers had begun sifting through the rubble of the church, pulling out and gently renovating items of religious significance that could be used when services resumed, first when the present building was made safe for this purpose and then in the replacement church. Until demolition in 1952, what little survived of the original church provided spiritual comfort for a reduced congregation while plans were laid and money sought for the post-war Church of St Peter and St Paul on its former site in the town centre.[31] The foundation stone was laid on 19 October 1952 and inauguration took place on 13 March 1955 by the Bishop of Arras, Mgr Perrin.

Meanwhile, Le Portel had been honoured with the Croix de Guerre and Silver Star from the French Government, the authority signed in Paris on 11 November 1948 by Max Lejeune, Minister for the Armed Forces. The citation did not mince words. It recalled the martyrdom of the town. It used the phrase 'crushed by the devastating bombing of 4, 8 and 9 September 1943 that decimated its population', and it described Le Portel's suffering as a sacrifice in the service of the country.[32]

Circumstances at the time compelled the vast majority of the victims to be buried in a communal grave. Subsequently, a distinctive memorial was built at the end of the central pathway through the town cemetery. On an apocalytic theme, the commemorative design is the work of a former prisoner of war, an artist who chose to live and work in Le Portel rather than return to his native land, Germany.[33] There are no words – anyone going there who does not know its meaning goes away unknowing. It is possible to interpret the purpose as the town wishing to mourn alone. Townspeople know why the memorial exists; it is as if the grief that it represents should be theirs and theirs alone.

Photograph taken during an attack on the harbour area at Boulogne by RAF Mitchells on 6 September 1943. Thirty aircraft dropped 46 tons of bombs. Bombs are bursting on 'E' and 'R' boat pens and quays at the Bassin Loubet and there are hits on the Artillery Arsenal too. In a two-phase attack on Boulogne harbour two days earlier, when the RAF dropped 100 tons of bombs, some fell in Le Portel killing seven people.

Photo: Imperial War Museum (C. 5797)

La tragédie du Portel

4, 8, 9 SEPTEMBRE 1943

RÉCIT DE GUY BATAILLE

Forty years on, Le Portel's mayor arranged for an illustrated brochure to be produced to commemorate the bombardment; Guy Bataille's account contributed further important facts but only now has the full story come to light.

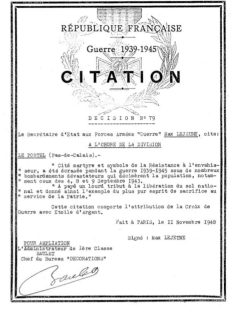

RÉPUBLIQUE FRANÇAISE

Guerre 1939-1945

CITATION

DECISION N° 79

Le Secrétaire d'Etat aux Forces Armées "Guerre" Max LEJEUNE, cite:

A L'ORDRE DE LA DIVISION

LE PORTEL (Pas-de-Calais).–

" Cité martyre et symbole de la Résistance à l'envahis-
" seur, a été écrasée pendant la guerre 1939-1945 sous de nombreux
" bombardements dévastateurs qui décimèrent la population, notam-
" ment ceux des 4, 8 et 9 Septembre 1943.
" A payé un lourd tribut à la libération du sol natio-
" nal et donné ainsi l'exemple du plus pur esprit de sacrifice au
" service de la Patrie."

Cette citation comporte l'attribution de la Croix de
Guerre avec Etoile d'Argent.

Fait à PARIS, le II Novembre 1948

Signé : Max LEJEUNE

POUR AMPLIATION
L'Administrateur de Ière Classe
BAULET
Chef du Bureau "DECORATIONS"

Le Portel was honoured with the Croix de Guerre with Silver Star on Armistice Day 1948; the citation, reproduced here from the original held at the Town Hall, acknowledges the martyrdom of the resort. Citation, brochure and other material from the town archives kindly made available following author's approach to Mayor Paul Barbarin, 24 June 1994.

General de Gaulle visited Le Portel on 12 August 1945 and saw for himself the destruction suffered during the bombardment – and listened intently to the statistics prepared for him and the call for his help.

Photo: *La Voix du Nord*

An area of Le Portel close to the present town market-place.

Another area of Le Portel, closer to the seafront. Both these photographs are from the same private collection. The post-bombing state of one of the main hotels can be seen in the foreground on the right.

Photos: Duval family archives

élégué aux Sapeurs-Pompiers : Messieurs les Membres de la Délégation Spéciale ; le Capitaine BOUHEZ, Commandant le Corps des Sapeurs-Pompiers, Chef du Centre de Boulogne-sur-Mer ; Messieurs les Officiers, Sous-Officiers, Caporaux et Sapeurs du Corps des Sapeurs-Pompiers ; Messieurs les Officiers, Sous-Officiers, Caporaux et Sapeurs Honoraires ont la douleur de vous faire art du décès de

LIEUTENANT
BONVOISIN Pierre
SOUS-LIEUTENANT
BOURGOIS Georges
ADJUDANT
GOURNAY Joseph
ADJUDANT
JONQUET Albert
SAPEURS
CREUSE René
CALOIN Jean
et MARIE Henri

Monsieur Jean-Baptiste PONT ; Madame DUHAMEL-PONT ; Madame Marguerite COPPIN-DUHAMEL et ses enfants ; Monsieur et Madame LERETRE-PONT et leur fils ; Monsieur et Madame PONT-LIBERT et leurs enfants ; Monsieur et Madame PONT-COPPIN ; les familles PONT, DUHAMEL, MELIN, DESCAMPS, BERLIN et PAUCHET ont la douleur de vous faire part de la perte quelle qu'ils viennent d'éprouver en 3 personnes de

Madame PONT-PONT
Agée de 64 ans
M. Adrien DUHAMEL
47 ans
Mme DUHAMEL-PONT
42 ans
M. Adrien DUHAMEL
21 ans
Mme Thérèse DUHAMEL

Madame Veuve MAGNIER-LIBERT; Monsieur et Madame LIBERT-DE-RYCKE et leurs enfants ; Madame Veuve MAGNIER-MACQUINGHEN ; Mademoiselle Marcelle GOURNAY, en religion Sœur Cécile de Saint-Jean ; Madame Veuve MAGNIER-DION et sa fille ; Madame Veuve MAGNIER-GOBERT et sa fille ; les familles LIBERT, MAGNIER, GOURNAY, CUVELIER ont la douleur de vous faire part de la perte cruelle qu'ils viennent d'éprouver en la personne de

Monsieur Jacques LIBERT
Agé de 72 ans
Madame Jacques LIBERT
née Marie GOURNAY
Agée de 69 ans
Monsieur Jules
MAGNIER - LIBERT
Agé de 50 ans
Marie-Angèle MAGNIER
Agée de 21 ans
Juliette MAGNIER
Agée de 17 ans
Louise MAGNIER
Agée de 15 ans
Monsieur
Jean-Baptiste GOURNAY
Agé de 59 ans
Madame
Jean-Baptiste GOURNAY
née Cécile CUVELIER
Agée de 63 ans
Yvonne GOURNAY
Agée de 22 ans

décédés accidentellement à Le Portel, le 8 septembre 1943.
Et vous prient d'assister au Service funèbre qui sera célébré le Jeudi 23 septembre, à 9 h. 30, en l'église Sainte-Thérèse de l'Ave-Maria, où l'on se réunira.

Vous êtes prié d'assister au service qui sera célébré le Mercredi 10 novembre, à 9 heures, en l'Eglise d'Outreau pour le repos de l'âme de

M. Fernand DUFRENNE
Employé de chemin de fer, 49 ans
Madame DUFRENNE
Née Céleste DUFOSSE, 46 ans
M. Eugène DUFRENNE
21 ans
Mlle Fernande DUFRENNE
16 ans
Mlle Jeannine SORRET
16 ans
M. Edouard DUFOSSE
Retraité du chemin de fer, 59 ans
M. Robert DUFOSSE
17 ans

décédés dans la nuit du 8 au 9 septembre au Portel.
De la part de
Madame Veuve SORRET et ses en-

Vous êtes prié d'assister au Service funèbre qui sera célébré le Mercredi 3 novembre 1943, à 10 h. 30, en la Basilique Notre-Dame de Boulogne, pour le repos de l'âme de

M. Jean-Baptiste GERME
Patron de Pêche du chalutier B. 1432
Monsieur Pierre DARRE
Marin à bord du chalutier B. 1496
Monsieur
Louis-Joseph BOULARD
Marin à bord du chalutier B. 2000
M. Jean-Baptiste LIBERT
Novice à bord du chalutier B. 1857

décédés accidentellement à Le Portel, le 9 septembre 1943.
De la part des familles GERME, DARRE, BOULARD et LIBERT ; de Messieurs DELPIERRE, Armateurs à Boulogne-sur-Mer; des équipages des

---

Monsieur Pierre LEDEZ, fils (Le Haillau, Gironde) ; Gabriel LEDEZ (Le Haillau, Gironde) ; Madame Veuve LEDEZ-BOURGAIN et ses enfants (Le Haillau) ; Madame M. Isabelle BOURGAIN, en religion Sœur Isabelle de l'Eucharistie, Petite Sœur des Pauvres ; Monsieur et Madame PAINSET-LIBERT et leurs enfants ; Monsieur Gabriel BOURGAIN (en captivité) ; Monsieur Louis-Marie COPPIN et ses enfants ; les enfants des feus BOURGAIN, LIBERT, LEDEZ, COPPIN, PAINSET, SAUVAGE.
Ont la douleur de vous faire part de la perte cruelle qu'ils viennent d'éprouver dans les personnes de

Madame Veuve
BOURGAIN-SAUVAGE
81 ans
Madame Veuve
LIBERT-BOURGAIN
54 ans
M. Jean-Baptiste LIBERT
18 ans
Monsieur Gabriel
LEDEZ-BOURGAIN
50 ans
Madame Louise
LEDEZ-BOURGAIN
49 ans
Mlle Marie-Gabrielle
LEDEZ-BOURGAIN
23 ans
Monsieur Louis-Marie
LEDEZ-BOURGAIN
18 ans
Madame Marguerite
COPPIN-LIBERT
29 ans
Marguerite COPPIN
3 ans

An extract from a larger display of funeral notices from newspaper columns in the aftermath of *Starkey*, reproduced in one of a series of publications, *Nos villes dans la tourmente*, produced during the war.

Le huit-neuf septembre mil neuf cent quarante trois,
à _____ heure _____ est décédé à
a été trouvé le corps d'un homme paraissant âgé de 16 à 18 ans, assez grand, cheveux blonds vêtu d'un veston en toile bleue de travail, d'un pantalon de même tissu avec une pièce à hauteur de la braguette, d'un pull avec kaki, caleçon à grands carreaux, gilet de corps en coton grenat, chemise flanelle de coton à lignes bleu, chaussettes de laine bleue avec jarretières de caoutchouc provenant d'un pneu d'auto. Dressé le dix septembre mil neuf cent quarante trois à quatorze heures sur la déclaration de Emile Delhaux, chef .... de Division à la Mairie de Boulogne-sur-Mer, qui lecture faite à signer avec nous, Charles Brévès, Maire de Boulogne-sur-Mer.

The Registres de l'Etat Civil in Le Portel show 376 named dead, including 38 registered at 31 December 1943 as '*Inconnu*' (i.e. not yet formally identified). One such was this fair-haired boy perhaps 16 to 18 years old.

LA DESTRUCTION DU PORTEL

(8-9 SEPTEMBRE 1943)

Un aspect de la commune après le bombardement

Dans les premiers jours de septembre 1943, la région boulonnaise avait été particulièrement survolée par l'aviation anglo-saxonne sans que la population habituée depuis trois années à des passages aériens fut particulièrement alarmée.

Mais le samedi 4 septembre, fâcheux symptôme, le Portel était bombardé à deux reprises. Il y avait des dégâts dans plusieurs rues et l'on avait ramassé sept tués et six blessés.

Les trois jours qui suivirent furent relativement calmes. Le 8 septembre au matin la population assista avec émotion aux funérailles de plusieurs victimes de ce bombardement parmi lesquelles il y avait deux enfants, âgés de dix et onze ans. Le temps était doux, c'était une belle et calme journée d'arrière-saison.

Brusquement, le soir, un peu avant huit heures, de grosses formations de bombardiers anglo-américains apparurent au-dessus de Boulogne. Comme d'habitude les habitants croyaient que ce n'était pas « pour eux », se bornèrent à admirer la formation des escadrilles qui passaient à haute altitude.

Dix minutes plus tard, les avions, au nombre d'une cen-

taine, étaient déjà de retour et leurs premières bombes tombaient aussitôt sur Boulogne même, puis aux environs de la Grande Armée.

Du haut du beffroi, le sous-préfet et le maire de Boulogne assistèrent au bombardement de la banlieue boulonnaise et de ses agglomérations.

Puis le Portel fut pris comme cible... La destruction méthodique du Portel était commencée.

Le nombre des appareils et les attaques répétées tous les quarts d'heure pendant plus de deux heures provoquèrent dans le centre de la commune des démolitions extrêmement importantes, entraînant la mort d'un grand nombre d'habitants, ensevelissant ceux que la rapidité de l'attaque avait empêché de rejoindre les abris.

— « La puissante déflagration des explosifs projeta à une très grande hauteur de véritables nuages d'une fine poussière faite de plâtras et de terre pulvérisés que le vent poussa vers Boulogne où elles retombèrent lentement comme les cendres du Vésuve s'en vont au loin dans la campagne napolitaine. »

Le bombardement n'est pas terminé que déjà des équipes de sauvetage comprenant une centaine d'hommes dont un certain nombre de prisonniers libérés arrivent au Portel. Avec les magnifiques

> ## Le Portel violemment bombardé par l'aviation anglo-américaine
> ### On compte déjà 400 victimes
> Des familles entières gisent sous les décombres
> Plusieurs centaines de réfugiés — la station balnéaire ayant été évacuée — n'ont rien pu emporter, pas même leur argent
>
> Boulogne-sur-Mer. — La station balnéaire du Portel a été violemment bombardée dans la journée de vendredi, par l'aviation anglo-améri... compte déjà 400 vi... été entièrement... scène...

This extract from the post-bombardment series *Nos villes dans la tourmente* recalls that the *sous-préfet* and the mayor of Boulogne watched the night bombing from *le beffroi* – 'The methodical destruction of Le Portel had begun . . .'

As Force Commander for *Operation Starkey*, Air Marshal Sir Trafford Leigh-Mallory acknowledged that this operation did not achieve its object of compelling the enemy to engage in air battles of attrition 'under conditions advantageous to us'.

Photo: Imperial War Museum (CH. 11943)

The Air Force Commander, Air Vice Marshal H.W.L. Saunders, reported post-*Starkey* that bad weather 'seriously restricted' air operations and the effort achieved was 'considerably below' that which was originally planned. Even so, some 25,227 RAF and USAAF sorties were flown.

Photo Imperial War Museum (CH. 7956)

Air Chief Marshal Sir Arthur T. Harris, Air Officer Commanding-in-Chief, RAF Bomber Command (left), talking to Lieutenant General Ira C. Eaker, Commanding General, US 8th Air Force; both were 'very disturbed' that *Starkey* would cause a 'fearful diversion' from their joint offensive at 'possibly the most vital stage of the bomber war'.

Photo: Imperial War Museum (CH. 11543)

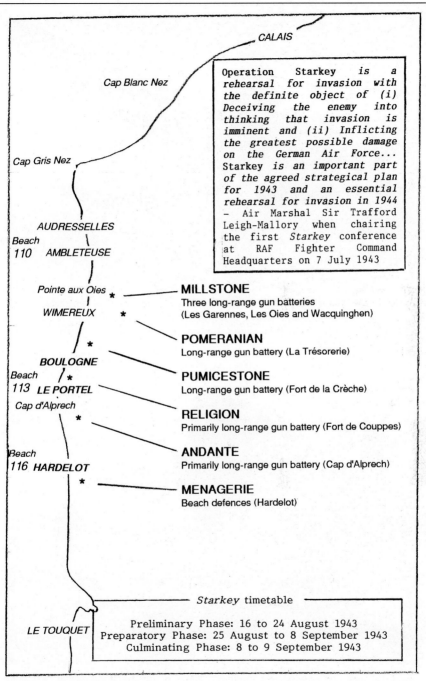

CALAIS

Cap Blanc Nez

Cap Gris Nez

AUDRESSELLES

Beach
110 AMBLETEUSE

Pointe aux Oies *

WIMEREUX *

*

BOULOGNE

Beach / *
113 LE PORTEL

Cap d'Alprech

*

Beach
116 HARDELOT

*

LE TOUQUET

Operation Starkey *is a rehearsal for invasion with the definite object of (i) Deceiving the enemy into thinking that invasion is imminent and (ii) Inflicting the greatest possible damage on the German Air Force...* Starkey *is an important part of the agreed strategical plan for 1943 and an essential rehearsal for invasion in 1944* – Air Marshal Sir Trafford Leigh-Mallory when chairing the first *Starkey* conference at RAF Fighter Command Headquarters on 7 July 1943

MILLSTONE
Three long-range gun batteries
(Les Garennes, Les Oies and Wacquinghen)

POMERANIAN
Long-range gun battery (La Trésorerie)

PUMICESTONE
Long-range gun battery (Fort de la Crèche)

RELIGION
Primarily long-range gun battery (Fort de Couppes)

ANDANTE
Primarily long-range gun battery (Cap d'Alprech)

MENAGERIE
Beach defences (Hardelot)

Starkey timetable

Preliminary Phase: 16 to 24 August 1943
Preparatory Phase: 25 August to 8 September 1943
Culminating Phase: 8 to 9 September 1943

The 'invasion rehearsal' coastline and the seven long-range gun batteries considered most likely to threaten the ships heading towards Boulogne–Le Touquet shortly after dawn on 9 September 1943 in the climax to *Starkey*. Anglo–US bombers attacked all of them, plus the beach defences at Hardelot, on 8 and 9 September.

A Mosquito Mk IV of 105 Squadron – the first squadron to receive these remarkably versatile aircraft which they used to carry out the RAF's first successful daylight attack on Berlin. The squadron moved into Pathfinder Force in time to join 109 Squadron for *Starkey* marking/bombing operations.

Photo: Imperial War Museum (CH. 7781)

Getting the bombs into position for loading a Halifax of 405 Squadron, whose operational debut with these aircraft was in the Thousand Bomber raid against Cologne on 30/31 May 1942. By the time of *Starkey*, when 405 and 35 Squadrons were the back-up markers, with all the crews flying Halifaxes, 405 Squadron was already re-equipping with Lancasters.

Photo: Imperial War Museum (CH. 6609)

Wellington Mk Ic belonging to 214 Squadron before re-equipping with the four-engined Stirling bombers used during *Starkey*. In the night attacks of 8 September 1943, Wellingtons were flown by pupil crews in the OTUs as well as by crews from front-line squadrons, and that night the Wellington contributed the greatest number of effective sorties – 111 out of a total 249.

Photo: Imperial War Museum (CH. 1756)

A Stirling Mk I of 218 Squadron which took part in both phases of the night bombing against the two coastal gun sites considered 'the most dangerous' to the assault convoys due to sail to within 10 miles of the French coast the following morning. Stirlings carried two-thirds of the high explosive tonnage dropped in those raids.

Photo: Imperial War Museum (CH. 16996)

One of 180 Squadron's Mitchell II bombers arriving back at RAF Station Dunsfold on 9 September 1943; Mitchells and other aircraft carried out a daylight bombing 'shuttle service' across the Channel that day – the climax to *Operation Starkey*. Three squadrons of Mitchells from Dunsfold attacked the coastal guns at Fort de la Crèche, La Trésorerie and Pointe aux Oies.

Photo: Imperial War Museum (CH. 11037)

Marauders of the 386th Bombardment Group, based at Boxted, Essex, lined up ready for take off; this was one of four USAAF groups engaged in the daylight bombing of *Religion* and *Andante* alone and, with the RAF, *Pomeranian* and *Millstone*. The 270 Marauder sorties dropped a total of 390 tons of bombs on these four coastal-gun sites.

Photo: Imperial War Museum (KY. 11894)

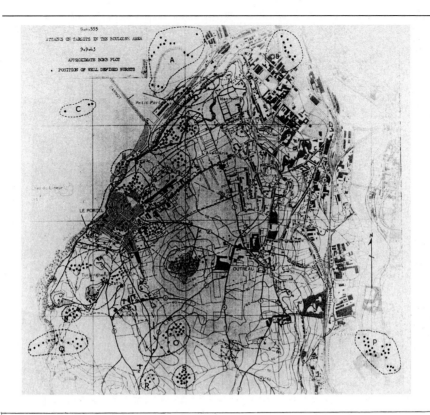

SECRET
(AMERICAN CONFIDENTIAL)
13.9.43

INTERPRETATION REPORT SA. 555

ATTACK ON TARGETS IN THE BOULOGNE AREA ON 9.9.43

(i) INFORMATION RECEIVED ON THE ATTACK

(a) This report is based on photographs taken during a daylight attack on Coastal Defence targets in the Boulogne Area by 202, possibly more, aircraft of U:S. VIII Air Support Command on 9.9.43 at 0745 to 0945 hours.

(ii) BOMB BURSTS OBSERVED ON AND NEAR THE TARGET

The heaviest concentration of bursts is noted in and near the town of Le Portel. There are concentrations in the Port of Boulogne, on the Railway, the jetties and the wet dock. Several probable hits or near misses on gun positions are noted

USAAF records show 134 out of 202 Marauders attacked the two targets nearest Le Portel on 9 September. The Central Interpretation Unit report (Crown copyright and reproduced by permission of the Controller of Her Majesty's Stationery Office) and the original of the related bomb-plot illustration (shown at top) are held in the PRO (AIR 40/905).

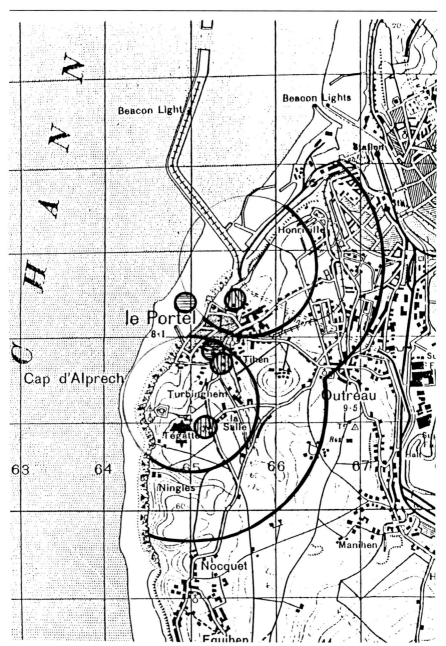

Two Target Indicators (TIs) attracted 60 per cent of the bombing in Phase I, while a single TI (which split into three parts, straddling a mile and shown with vertical shading) attracted 75 per cent of the bombing in Phase II; their misplacement shifted both 'targets' from the gun sites to the town itself. The circle circumferences shown represent distances of half a mile and one mile from the respective aiming points, the northerly one being *Religion*, the Phase I target, the other being *Andante*, the Phase II target.

Author's annotations on War Office map GSGS 4040, which is reproduced with the permission of the Director of Military Survey.

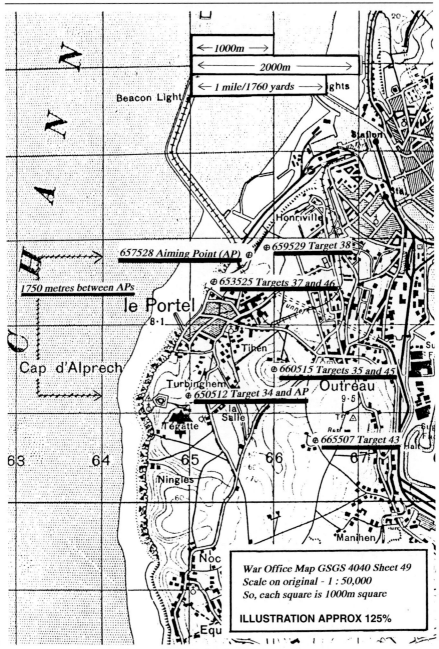

A section of War Office map GSGS 4040 Sheet 49, each square being 1,000 × 1,000 metres, superimposed (by the author) with the two Aiming Points for *Religion* and *Andante* and the grid references for the seven targets at five locations within these two sites.

Map reproduced with the permission of the Director of Military Survey.

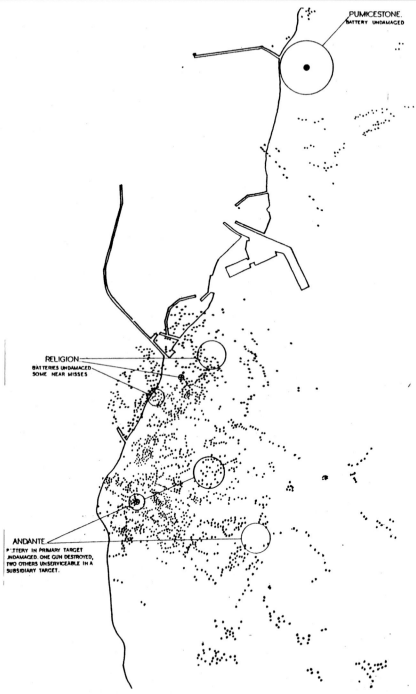

The following labels appear within the image:

PUMICESTONE.
BATTERY UNDAMAGED

RELIGION:
BATTERIES UNDAMAGED.
SOME NEAR MISSES

ANDANTE.
BATTERY IN PRIMARY TARGET
UNDAMAGED. ONE GUN DESTROYED,
TWO OTHERS UNSERVICEABLE IN A
SUBSIDIARY TARGET.

Bomb-crater plot including the area of the five pinpoints that comprised *Religion* and *Andante*, prepared by the Central Interpretation Unit at RAF Station Medmenham from photographs taken during Sortie E174 (one is published on facing page). All five locations are ringed; the small circles with a cross are the respective aiming points for the night bombing. The original of this illustration is held in the PRO (AIR 14/2692 – A.W.A.S. No. 650 of 24 March 1944).

Aerial pictures taken on the morning of 9 September 1943 – shortly after the last of the bombing raids on the coastal gun batteries in the Boulogne area – produced target-damage prints that CIU described as 'excellent quality'; this print, 4037 from Sortie E174, showed that 'chiefly residential' property in Le Portel suffered too – 'very severely'. The original of this photograph is held in the PRO (WO 205/449).

More than fifty years on, Fort de Couppes still shows signs of wartime fortifications; in the distance is Cap d'Alprech, similarly retaining visible evidence. On the lower ground between them nestles the town of Le Portel.

Photo: Richard Cumming

This name-plate in Le Portel is a unique commemoration of the bombardment by Allied bombers in 1943; there is a plaque in honour of 'An Unknown Victim' (right) at the base of the town's war memorial. The night of 8 September saw the heaviest bombing, the highest casualties and the most damage in the 16-hour time-span of this bombardment.

In the town cemetery stands this memorial to all the victims of the bombardment; the commemorative design was the work of a former prisoner of war, an artist who chose to live and work in Le Portel rather than return home to Germany.

Photo: Richard Cumming

Though the presence of the enemy attracted the bombardment, it was the British, numerically the largest force among the participants, who carried it out, making them unwelcome in certain quarters for some years.[34] The lack of understanding locally for the tragedy of Le Portel, the absence of apparent reason and the inability to comprehend served only to sustain the feeling that the town's suffering was in vain and for an unidentifiable cause. If there was bitterness towards Britons it was not difficult to appreciate if less easy to condone.

Forty years after the bombardment, Mayor Paul Barbarin echoed the words of many Portelois throughout the intervening period by asking, in the preface to a commemorative booklet entitled *The Tragedy of Le Portel, 4, 8 and 9 September 1943*, why the Allies demolished it. He recalled that successive waves of bombers, coming from England, 'wiped out' Le Portel; as near as made no odds, the bombardment 'razed it to the ground'. No one looking for the reason had been able to discover the truth. He had heard it said that the only explanation sometimes advanced was that the bombardment was a diversionary move linked to the Allies landing in southern Italy.*

Since those days, M. Barbarin wrote, no confirmation had come to justify the bombings, although a number of historians had turned their attention to the subject, notable among them being M. Guy Bataille, then editor-in-chief of the newspaper *La Voix du Nord* in Boulogne. The mayor had invited Bataille to compose the text for that commemoration booklet, in which was reproduced – both as a photograph and translated into French – a letter replying to one he had sent in 1980 to Prof. R.V. Jones, one of Churchill's foremost scientific advisers.[35]

This appears to have been the closest that anyone anywhere had come to getting an 'official' answer to that long-standing question. In the letter, Jones opened by stating that he was not involved in the Le Portel bombardment – 'because this was carried out primarily to destroy coastal batteries' – but he had pursued Bataille's inquiry with some of his former colleagues.

Some of the target-marking at night was inaccurate, the letter stated, and many bombs fell on the town instead of on the planned aiming points. Le Portel 'was certainly not bombed deliberately, but it had the misfortune to lie in the centre of an area that the Germans had heavily fortified'.

In that commemorative booklet, Barbarin put the deaths of the Portelois in the bombardment in the same category as those who fell while in the armed forces or in the resistance organizations, and those who were deported and never seen again. With the combatants who lost their lives, the civilians who were killed by the bombs were, he said, equally victims who gave their lives in the struggle for peace, the liberty of France and the final victory.

Ten years later, Barbarin inaugurated a further programme of events to keep fresh in the hearts and minds of the Portelois the memories of the bombings. Every family had been hit in one way or another: one or more of their number being among the 500 dead, one or more among the 250 severely injured. These fiftieth anniversary

* The timing supports that hypothesis – that night of 8/9 September 1943 saw British and American troops preparing to go ashore near Salerno in a 0330 landing codenamed *Avalanche*.

activities included an exhibition opened by former mayor Marie-Joséphine Bourgain, who was there at the time; a journalist addressed a public meeting, recalling what had happened during the bombardment; a special service was held in the Church of St Peter and St Paul; and sprays of flowers were laid at the memorial to the civilian dead of Le Portel.

In the columns of *La Voix du Nord* the tragedy of the bombardment of Le Portel was unfolded once more. The town was 'struck off the map', in the journalist's words on that occasion. Was it an error, or tactics, on the part of the Allies? There was a theory that this was the prelude to a landing but, the article declared, for most people in Le Portel the reason for the bombardment was still a mystery fifty years on.[36]

Members of the town's historical society (*CHP*) have kept the subject alive in successive issues of its annual publication, the informative and much-respected *Le Portel – Notes et Documents*. For example, in 1983 there was the suggestion that the British wanted to test the defences of Le Portel ahead of another Dieppe-type landing; alternatively that there was a direct relationship between the destruction of the town and the need to divert the attention of Axis troops from an intended landing in Italy. In 1993 the point was made that still there had been no real answer to the question as to why this 'massacre' took place. Wrong information? Mis-aiming? Preparing for a simulated landing? This latter possibility was considered perhaps the most likely because of people having reported the movement of Allied shipping, minesweeping and an increase in radio contact.

The questions may linger, but life in this coastal resort has been shown to move on with increasing pace. The 'prefabs' are gone now, the last pulled down in 1990, though some of the bunkers have survived them – outliving their presence but not their usefulness. Life has come back to Le Portel, with its neat homes, supermarkets and family-run 'corner shops', its welcoming hotels and restaurants where succulent fish dishes and inviting pastries are specialities. To a stranger it will seem as if the Second World War had passed by Le Portel; the crumbling concrete and the myriad memories of *Religion* and *Andante* are not evident and need seeking out.

The population is approaching 11,000; there are some 4,450 houses and 2,900 flats; and boundary revisions have swelled the size to 385 hectares (950 acres). Amenities sought in the aftermath of the bombing have come to Le Portel: the 20 hectare (50 acre) Parc de la Falaise, with hides from which to study migrating birds, three-star camping facilities overlooking the sea, indoor swimming pool and sports grounds among them.

In their book, *The North of France*, Michael Barker and Paul Atterbury advocate a short excursion to Le Portel: 'This new town has a definite feeling of civic pride, being very spruce and well-kept, without the usual dead hand of so much post-war urban planning – probably because the architects maintained the old street pattern.'

M. Laurent Feutry, elected Mayor of Le Portel in 1995, a person too young to have experienced the destruction of his native town, holds the view that while the people of Le Portel must never forget the wartime tragedy, peace and the passing years create a different complexion. Memories are for those who were involved; the town does not go out of its way to recall that particular black September – even the monument inaugurated on 8 September 1963 to the bombardment victims carries no inscription, the names of the known dead and descriptions of the unidentified dead being secreted carefully within it.

A souvenir booklet produced by the tourism office traces a pictorial history of the town through postcards: its fort built at the command of Napoleon Bonaparte, its growth as a seaside resort, its importance as a fishing port, and, less overtly, its martyrdom in the Second World War.

Mayor Feutry says of the achievement of post-war reconstruction:[37]

Visitors will see little of the Le Portel of the 1930s and 1940s, for ours is a town reborn. Physically, it was destroyed; spiritually, such a fate was something our citizens just could not accept.

Few communities will have had to face such a challenge, I am sure, but we are confident that we have risen to it. People coming here will see that construction work is still continuing, however, because to the Portelois, satisfaction is an ideal well worth the wait.

Chapter Fourteen

The Inquest Opens

In the aftermath of the bombardment that 'struck off the map' the seaside resort of Le Portel in the first week of the fifth year of the Second World War, aerial photographs were the only means the Allies had to achieve an immediate assessment of the effectiveness of the target-marking and the bombing. However, it was not the impact on the town but the effect on the fortifications there and elsewhere that interested those whose eyes were 'glued' to the photographs. In time, the more detailed the study, the more comprehensive would be the overall 'picture' to determine the degree of success gained by the Anglo-American air forces in the climax to *Operation Starkey*.

Set against the entire air effort put into *Starkey*, which it will be remembered was severely curbed by unseasonal weather, the attacks directed towards the two groups of gun positions at Le Portel may seem almost paltry in cold statistical terms – between 1½ and 2 per cent of the 25,000-plus offensive, defensive and other sorties flown in the twenty-five days of this British-led deception ploy. Or, to put it another way, for every Bomber Command plane that was detailed to bomb *Religion* and *Andante* in the blistering two-phase night assault on the eve of the convoys sailing, 100 RAF and USAAF planes were involved in carrying out other aspects of the operation.

In addition to 20,461 offensive sorties throughout the Preliminary, Preparatory and Culminating Phases of *Starkey*, there were 537 reconnaissance sorties; 1,492 shipping-protection sorties; 1,531 other defensive patrols; 782 air/sea rescue and other patrols; and 424 sorties by Bomber Command, the last figure embracing those detailed against the two groups of guns at Le Portel on 8 September and against inland targets on a further four nights previously – a grand total of 25,227 sorties by the RAF and USAAF throughout Starkey[1] – all this despite the weather.

During *Starkey*, RAF losses were 84 aircraft while the USAAF lost 115, all but 8 of them being the huge four-engined Fortresses, which were generally flown with a nine-man crew. Compared with these admitted 199 Allied losses, the RAF claimed to have destroyed only 136 enemy aircraft, although another 18 were 'probably destroyed' and a further 71 damaged.[2] As Air Marshal Sir Trafford Leigh-Mallory would have to recognize, *Starkey* failed to do what it was meant to do where the German air force was concerned.[3]

Subsequent top-level reports produced a wealth of facts, analyses and comments on the deception operation and the air activities that formed a substantial part of it. Particularly revealing are those on the attacks against *Religion* and *Andante*, which were the most critical of all the big-gun positions in the eyes of the commanders who ordered the 'mini-armada' to sail on 9 September 1943. These attacks, on the one night alone, accounted for some 9 per cent of the total tonnage dropped throughout

Starkey. Those 678.1 tons of high explosives were more than half as much again as in the heaviest daylight operation. Add to this figure the 48 tons in the 'curtain raiser' that evening and the 196.20 ton *coup de grâce* next morning and the combined 922.30 tons delivered against *Religion* and *Andante* between 1715 hours and 0915 hours is greater even than the preceding total for any 24-hour period in *Starkey*'s overall 25 days (891 tons against airfields and other targets on 3 September).[4] For the record then, RAF and USAAF activities combined, for every 100 offensive sorties carried out during *Starkey*, as few as 2 were against the *Religion/Andante* guns; but for every 8 tons of bombs dropped throughout *Starkey*, 1 ton was directed towards those two 'most dangerous' batteries among the seven that were judged 'most likely' to threaten the make-believe invasion fleet sailing to and from the French coast.

Anglo-American bombing raids comprised 4,252 effective sorties: 3,040 by the USAAF – which included 1,451 by the four-engined Fortress and Liberator bombers – and 1,212 by the RAF – the Typhoons, Whirlwinds, Bostons, Venturas and Mitchells of Fighter Command, plus Bomber Command's contribution by means of night attacks on the gun batteries and the forest dumps. The 7,656 tons dropped were split 16 per cent against the coastal guns and beach defences, 32 per cent against transportation, industrial and other targets and 52 per cent against airfields – a prime purpose in *Starkey* being to destroy as many enemy planes as possible in the air and on the ground.

In respect of the bombing attacks which occurred closest to Le Portel, there were three aspects to be reviewed: the target-marking and bombing procedures; the results of those attacks; and their relevance to *Starkey*, which could now be considered in its entirety. In various documents, Bomber Command specialists and the Air Force Commander covered the first two aspects; while the overall commander and the three force commanders covered *Starkey* at length. Those formerly highly secret reports contained information and statistics which, once assembled into a cohesive format, take this present study significantly beyond the material published piecemeal since Prof. Jones' disclosure in his letter made public in France in 1983.[5]

In it he explained that, owing to technical faults, some of the target-marking in the night attack of 8 September was inaccurate, resulting in many of the bombs falling on Le Portel instead of on the planned APs. In the foregoing pages the actions of the Mosquitoes and Halifaxes of Pathfinder Force were reconstructed (see chapter eight), as were those of Main Force (see chapter nine). The focus can now turn to what happened as a result of those actions, as revealed by the findings of the various studies carried out at the time and no longer classified 'Top Secret' or 'Secret' material.

Post-*Starkey* documentation recalls the Plan of Attack.[6] With this as the starting point it is confirmed that the method of target-marking was identical for Phase I (against *Religion* – Fort de Couppes) and Phase II (against *Andante* – Cap d'Alprech). Pathfinder Force Mosquitoes 'will mark the exact A/P with TI red. Other Mosquitoes will also mark the A/P with TI green using a modified technique [Baillie beam instead of Oboe].' Pathfinder Force Halifaxes, the 'backers-up', were to maintain the marking, aiming their TI greens at the TI reds or the Mean Point of Impact (MPI) of the TI greens. Main Force aircraft – the Wellingtons and Stirlings from operational squadrons in Nos 1, 3 and 6 Groups and the Wellingtons from the operational training units in Nos 91, 92 and 93 Groups were to aim at TI reds or

MPI TI greens. There was a clear instruction to Main Force units: 'Bombs to be brought back if no TIs seen.'

The first report from Bomber Command's ORS which contains comments critical of the target-marking procedures employed that night, refers to 'a new technique' tried out by half of the Oboe aircraft 'with little success'. Accuracy as a whole 'was not good enough for such small targets'. Neither of the two main targets 'appeared to have been damaged', according to this report.[7]

What happened in the attack was described in detail in a subsequent report,[8] also from ORS, which was introduced with the explanation that the Phase I attack was 'against a special coastal target at Le Portel, near Boulogne'; that Phase II was a similar attack 45 minutes later 'against a second objective near Cap d'Alprech, about 1 mile further south'; that both attacks lasted about 15 minutes; and that they were carried out 'under excellent weather conditions'.

The reconstruction has already shown that the first Oboe Mosquito despatched to mark the Phase I AP did not do so and that the first TI greens to go down were dropped at 2202 hours by W-William, a Baillie beam Mosquito of 109 Squadron. The report shows that these fell in two sections, half going into the sea and therefore extinguished (TIs were intended to continue burning on the ground), the other half landing on the foreshore as much as 960 yards west-south-west of the AP. The TI greens dropped by K-King, a backer-up Halifax from 405 Squadron, fell still further from the AP – a distance of 1,200 yards away to the south-south-west. The report stated that the next two backers-up refrained from dropping their TIs as no TI reds were seen, and that there was a gap of 3 minutes before the TI reds dropped by H-Harry, an Oboe Mosquito of 109 Squadron, went down. Though these reds were right on schedule, by now the raid was half over. The result was that '60 per cent of the Main Force bombed on the first two greens, the main weight of the attack thus falling to the south-west of the AP'.

In fact the reds from H-Harry were closer to the AP than the greens, falling about 550 yards to the north. Within the next 3 minutes the reds were backed up with greens from three Halifaxes of 35 Squadron and two Halifaxes from 405 Squadron. These fell at distances varying between 150 and 2,300 yards south of the reds. Most Main Force aircraft bombed on the reds, the report stated, but the bombing was scattered and no marked concentration developed around the AP. The third and last Mosquito dropped its target-marker at 2213 hours – V-Vic of 109 Squadron, using the Baillie beam. This was the closest yet among the primary markers, the greens falling 360 yards south of the AP. By this time the Main Force attack was nearly over, so this had what the report described as 'little influence' on the course of the raid.

Phase I had opened 4 minutes late; Phase II, on the other hand, 45 minutes afterwards, opened on time, at 2243 hours. Salvos of reds from E-Edward of 109 Squadron, an Oboe Mosquito, and greens from S-Sugar, a Baillie beam Mosquito from the same squadron, dropped almost simultaneously. The greens fell 1 mile east of the AP and did not attract any bombing, the main attack centring on the reds, on which 75 per cent of the Main Force bombed. The report made an interesting observation on these reds, an observation with significant repercussions on target-marking in the future. The report found that this salvo of reds unfortunately fell in three parts, each separated from the next by 800 yards. The whole salvo was thus spread out over a distance of 1 mile, and the Main Force bombing tended to follow a similar pattern. All of the backers-up except one bombed on these reds [which stretched to the north-east from about 350 yards south-south-east of the AP], and an excellent concentration of green TIs was achieved within 500 yards of the AP.

Phase II was practically at its end, the third and last of the primary target-markers, R-Roger, a Baillie beam Mosquito from 109 Squadron, dropping TI greens at 2254 hours. They were photographed in the air, 600 yards west of the AP, and never seen again, presumably disappearing into the sea.

There should have been five Mosquitoes dropping primary target-markers in each phase. In the event, in each phase only one aircraft carrying reds and two with greens completed their missions. The report has shown that their markers ranged from 360 yards to 1 mile from the AP, while those of the backers-up Halifaxes, visually marking, landed between 150 yards and more than 1¼ miles from the TIs on which their own markers were aimed. In a section of this report, headed 'Appreciation and Comments', it was noted that 'on neither of these attacks did the accuracy of the primary marking reach the high standard required for attacks on this type of target'. The range errors were reasonably low, the line errors of the Baillie beam, on the other hand, were very large, the mean line error of all Baillie beam greens dropped being about 1,000 yards. Apart from 'the inaccuracies of the technique', another 'very serious source of error' was introduced owing to the fact that TIs released in salvo fell in the form of a stick. This phenomenon, 'which has been noticed on previous occasions', was very marked in the case of the reds dropped by the Oboe Mosquito in Phase II – E-Edward – which were spread over a distance of 1 mile. The report noted:

It seems unlikely that this is due entirely to errors of the barometric fuse of the TI bomb, causing the TIs to burst at different heights because, in order to account for a spread of 1,600 yards, a difference in bursting height of the order of 17,000 feet would be necessary. It seems, therefore, that the fault probably lies in the distributor mechanism rather than in the TI itself.

With regard to the bombing, which it will be understood was to be aimed on the Pathfinders' TIs, the Main Force bombing appears to have been more concentrated in Phase II (Cap d'Alprech) than in Phase I (Fort de Couppes), 'possibly owing to the fact that a large proportion of Phase I attackers were OTU crews'. (As many as one in two planes attacking the Phase I target were from the OTUs, compared with only one in five in Phase II.)*

---

* These are the figures: Phase I, 53 sorties by Stirlings of No. 3 Group, 19 by Wellingtons of No. 91 Group and 35 by Wellingtons of No. 93 Group; Phase II, 23 sorties by Wellingtons of No. 1 Group, 51 by Stirlings of No. 3 Group, 12 by Wellingtons of No. 6 Group and 22 by Wellingtons of No. 92 Group. Thus, 50 per cent of Main Force crews in Phase I came from the OTUs compared with 20 per cent in Phase II. Some 35 per cent of the effective sorties carried out overall in the two raids comprised OTU crews – 76 out of the 215 Main Force aircraft attacking (the 5 USAAF Fortresses having been excluded from these figures).

The 'Conclusions and Recommendations' noted that:

the line error of the Baillie beam is at present far larger than is permissible for attacks on very small targets, and unless this difficulty can be overcome it is doubtful if it will qualify to replace Oboe, even for attacks on short range targets.*

It was also noted that:

a very serious source of error in marking may be introduced owing to the fact that the TIs do not fall in salvo. This, whilst not of great importance in area bombing, becomes critical in the case of precision marking.

The report had no need to explain 'line error' (which averaged about 1,000 yards with the Baillie Mosquitoes' TIs). However, this term meant that those TIs had been plotted on the ground as much as 1,000 yards wide of a direct line between the ground station and the AP. If, 'as seems possible', there was a systematic error, it could be counteracted by offsetting the beam by the required amount in the opposite direction. The extent of error that came to light in this unique comparison with Oboe was clearly too great for confidence, especially when recognizing that with a problem of this sort, the error grew with target distance.

Bomber Command's ORS, which produced that report, did not let matters rest with those comments, despite the strength of this criticism. It stated that:

if further operations using the Baillie beam method of bombing are contemplated, tests are desirable to determine the causes of the errors occurring so that they can be eliminated . . . [that] careful checking of the bomb distribution gear is essential to ensure the TIs fall in salvo . . . [and that] where very accurate marking is required, the use of a marker bomb which bursts on the ground (such as the Ruby Spot Fire) would give better results.**

Had lessons been learned? It is assumed so, because a further report from ORS, issued six months after Bomber Command's night attacks on the two targets,

---

* That the Baillie beam gave, by comparison, a poor result, would have been 'no surprise to Oboe pilots', according to *Pathfinder Force*, by Gordon Musgrove.

** In use for only nine months by this time, TIs were naturally still being developed to achieve improved target-marking capabilities. For greater accuracy against small targets, non-cascading TIs would become operational later; and there would be alternative forms of illumination triggered by the TI when it began to burn on the ground – an intense crimson flame or white-burning magnesium.[9] Concurrent with these enhancements, Pathfinders first on the scene with H2S ground-imaging equipment (blind markers) dropped flares with their markers. Then other crews (visual markers) attempted to identify and mark the AP by the light of those flares, using a different-coloured marker which would take precedence over any other colour for the attention of all following aircraft. However, if the visual markers were unable to identify the AP and drop their markers, then the raid would proceed with the backers-up using yet another colour of TI, aiming for the centre of all the original markers. Main Force would then take the backers-up markers as their AP, that is to say, adopting normal 'Paramatta', to use a name that will be familiar to Bomber Command crews.[10]

recalled them in still more detail.[11] The lambasting continued with the target-marking being described as 'unsatisfactory' and the marking accuracy with the Baillie beam as 'poor'. Complete elimination of the marking error could not be expected, it conceded, 'but a great improvement would accrue from a reduction of it, and steps have already been taken in this direction'. With target-marking errors included, the overall average aiming error that night was 1,000 yards; the bombing error alone, it said, was of the order of 500 yards.

The report acknowledged that target-marking had been seen to be better since the attacks on *Religion* and *Andante*, which were situated in an area of 'very poor' Oboe coverage, only one channel being available. To supplement this, 'the experiment of using the Baillie beam for tracking and an Oboe ground station for releasing was tried'. That method 'proved rather inaccurate, and is unlikely to be used again'. The Oboe coverage had now been improved and 'much better marking is now usually obtained'.

With *Religion* and *Andante*, 'provision of adequate marking was rendered difficult by the fact that for two of the three Oboe channels the angle of cut was much too low and for the third it was just good enough'. Further, 'owing to technical failure, only 1 Oboe Mosquito and 2 Baillie beam Mosquitoes attacked in each case in spite of the fact that a reserve Oboe aircraft was flown as usual'. The marking accuracy by the Baillie beam technique was 'poor' and the Oboe salvo on *Andante* was spread along track over a distance of no less than a mile, 'in spite of its being released with tolerable accuracy'.

In the month after the attacks against *Religion* and *Andante*, Pathfinder Force noted (in an internal publication with the title 'Precision') that its Oboe squadrons 'were not exactly overworked'.[12] Apart from leading the last heavy bombing of the month with some 1,000 tons dropped on Bochum, 'they marked the APs in the attacks on ammunition dumps and coastal defences, and thus assisted in the invasion rehearsal at the beginning of the month'. The Mosquitoes of 105 Squadron flew 36 sorties in the month (16 successful, 17 Oboe failures and 3 early returns), while those of 109 Squadron flew 52 sorties (28 successful, 23 Oboe failures and 1 early return). The figures suggest that that period must have been a 'bad patch' for the Oboe precision-marking system with just one in two Oboe-equipped Mosquitoes completing their missions – 45 per cent of those 88 sorties in that month of September 1943 were formally catalogued as 'Oboe failures'.

A contemporary Bomber Command report for verbal-only communication to its aircrew members was optimistic in its tone.[13] APs for the 'two area attacks in the vicinity of Boulogne' were selected to cover predetermined areas in which enemy coastal defences were sited. Night plots revealed that 'a high degree of concentration was achieved', although from day photography it was 'difficult to give accurate assessments of the comprehensive results of these attacks'. These comments came in a summary of operations carried out by Bomber Command in the week ending 12 September 1943, which also recorded the fact that in the period 1 January to 31 August 1943, the tonnage of bombs dropped by Bomber Command (102,532 tons) exceeded by 12,203 tons the combined total for the years 1940, 1941 and 1942.

How successful was the bombing on the coastal defences in the vicinity of Boulogne? Photo-reconnaissance on and around 9 September enabled a 'performance table' to be produced within Bomber Command which covered the attacks on the Le Portel gun positions by day as well as those by night.[14] Direct separation of the results of day bombing and night bombing was not possible, one crater in a photograph looking much like another, but experienced photo-interpretation specialists were nonetheless in a position to reach conclusions as to the likely relative contributions of the Anglo-American bombing force. Against *Religion* (groups of guns at Fort de Couppes), Bomber Command achieved an estimated 20 hits against the long-range guns that were the prime target (USAAF Marauders by day, 32 hits) and 11 hits against the AA/CD dual-purpose guns at Moulin Bleu, the subsidiary target (USAAF Marauders by day, 25 hits). Against *Andante*, Bomber Command achieved an estimated 17 hits against the long-range guns (USAAF Marauders by day, 14 hits); 23 hits against the AA/CD dual-purpose guns at Mont Soleil (29 hits by day); and 8 hits (2 hits by day) against the six-gun battery furthest south and furthest inland of all five objectives in the *Religion/Andante* target groups. The prime targets – which took an estimated 83 hits between them – were respectively 350 and 400 yards square; the subsidiary targets (an estimated 98 hits) 200, 200 and 370 yards square.

In the daylight attacks on all five groups of coastal batteries (which brought in *Millstone* – Pointe aux Oies; *Pomeranian* – La Trésorerie; and *Pumicestone* – Fort de la Crèche), a formation of 18 Marauders achieved an average aiming error of 500 yards, less than 3 per cent of the bombs dropping in an area 200 yards square around the AP; with Mitchells and Venturas, 750 yards (less than 2 per cent); and other formations, this time flying into intense AA fire – it was 'moderate' AA fire in the other attack – 1,200 yards (less than 1 per cent). It will be recalled that Bomber Command, by night against *Religion* and *Andante*, achieved a bombing error of the order of 500 yards.[15]

So much for *Religion* and *Andante*, the night and day attacks on them and the disclosure that not only was the target-marking for the night attacks unsatisfactory, in neither of them did the accuracy of the primary marking reach the high standard required for attacks 'on that type of target' – in other words, attacks where the target was small and the marking needed to be precise.

On the subject of precision, just how accurately placed were those 4,000 lb, 1,000 lb, 500 lb and 250 lb high-explosive bombs that the multinational combined force of experienced and trainee crews released in the vicinity of the threatening big-gun emplacements to the north and south of Le Portel in the massive night raids of 8 September?

The odds were that, whatever the accuracy, there would be damage and casualties beyond the perimeter of any site that the planners nominated for attack within the welter of military targets open to them, both there and further afield in occupied Europe. It was too much to hope for a comfortably wide, civilian-free belt around airfields, ammunition and fuel dumps, gun emplacements and so on.

In the aftermath of bombing attacks, no matter which side was involved, it would be a consequence of war that there would be civilian victims. There would be dead and injured who had the misfortune to be in buildings shattered by bombs which missed their targets – some by many miles. It had happened before in France, certainly elsewhere already in the Pas de Calais region of northern France.

As the survivors in shattered homes in Le Portel were struggling out of the rubble, RAF photographic sections on the airfields which sent out the bombers to attack *Religion* and *Andante* were preparing to start a familiar routine once the planes were back at the dispersal points.

By 1942 most bombers operating at night carried cameras and photoflashes, their introduction having proved that most of the bombing left much to be desired regarding accuracy.[16] The bomb-aimer's thumb pressure on the release mechanism simultaneously allowed the bombs and the photoflash to fall and activated the camera. By analysing the results, using skills born of long experience, specialists could plot the position of a particular plane when its bombs hit the ground. Even with a single photograph per plane, in a major attack there would be several hundred prints to be examined.

Determining factors were known – for instance, the compass course that the plane was following, its speed and altitude, together with the time the camera functioned – so that careful plotting enabled conclusions to be drawn before daylight photography revealed where bombs had actually fallen. It was not infallible: apart from the camera or the 'flash' sometimes failing to operate, there were human failings to take into account. Trying for a photograph was no mere routine – the procedure was particularly demanding on everyone on board. The reason was that keeping the plane flying straight and level until the photoflash exploded was essential, even though the bomb bays should by then be empty.

Bombs are falling objects and take a predetermined time to reach the ground. Aerial photography must compensate for this, theoretically the 'flash' exploding and the camera shutter open at the moment the plane is above the bombs' impact point. So pilots would grit their teeth and crew members feel on edge, the plane and its occupants facing increasing risk from AA or fighter attack. Only after the required timespan could the plane break away, and a crew member check the flare 'chute to ensure that the photoflash was no longer there. (If it remained and ignited accidentally, the plane and all inside it could easily be consumed by flames.)

If all went well, the centre of the resulting photograph would show the precise point where the bombs fell – hopefully near the intended target. Direction from the AP was determined by the plotter referring to the compass bearing of the plane. In both phases of this attack there was sufficient photographic evidence for those experienced in this work to be able to form a significant impression of the bombing results. Fortunately all planes returned safely, most of them with photographs on which to judge their performance based on distance and direction from the AP.[17]

One of the pupil crews, No. 18 OTU's W-William, the first of all the aircraft to take off from the twenty-nine airfields involved in the twin raids, found themselves plotted within 1,200 yards of the AP in Phase I; while another from this unit was plotted almost twice as far off-target. It demanded the skill (or judgement plus good fortune) of No. 3 Group's Stirlings to manoeuvre themselves onto the right heading and sufficiently near to place their bombs 'as close as dammit is to swearing'.[18]

As for the biggest of all the bombs that night – the two 4,000 lb bombs dropped in Phase II by Polish crews in 300 Squadron – the signs were that the first slammed down some ¾ mile north-north-east of this AP, the other further away still – 1 mile north-north-west according to the initial photo-plot.[19] Both were thus well outside the assumed ½ mile average error of the RAF's bomber force at the time of Air Chief Marshal Sir Arthur Harris's protestations against the wisdom of *Starkey*.

One of Bomber Command's plots not only provided comparative results between the participating groups, but also included the American bombardment group, which was working with No. 3 Group and making its debut that very night in night operations. This plot indicated that only two of the five Fortresses came within 3 miles of the AP when concluding the Phase I bombing on what remained a cloudless night with bright moonlight, generally good visibility over the target areas, only moderate opposition from AA fire and few combats with enemy fighters.

Taking the same yardstick, their bombs dropping within 3 miles of the AP, a progressive improvement emerged among the OTUs – 41 per cent in No. 93 Group (with thirty-five Wellingtons attacking in Phase I), 50 per cent in No. 92 Group (22 attacking in Phase II) and an even more respectable 59 per cent in No. 91 Group (nineteen attacked in Phase I).

It was to be expected that the performance of the operational squadrons would better the best of the 'freshmen' crews. Compared with them, No. 3 Group, with a total of 104 Stirlings in the two attacks, achieved 89 per cent in the first attack and 80 per cent in the second; Nos 1 and 6 Groups, with the remaining 35 Wellingtons effective that night, both produced 83 per cent whose cameras put them within 3 miles of the AP.

Even more interesting would be some form of analysis to highlight what level of accuracy was achieved closer to the target – say within a 2 mile circle or nearer still. In fact, further data subsequently available did enable more detailed results to be determined. Bomber Command's ORS reported on photographs 'from 91 of the 132 aircraft which participated in Phase I and photographs from 94 of the 125 which were in Phase II'. This took a different approach: the Pathfinders (whose results would be counted on to be 'top of the class') were included in this examination and the emphasis was placed on the night's best performances. This ORS study came more than a fortnight after the attack, and it established that in both Phase I and Phase II, 74 of the bombers were plotted to within 1 mile of the respective APs.[20] In Phase I, 13 of the bombers were within ½ mile of the AP and 14 within ¼ mile; in Phase II, where the bombing was seen to be more concentrated, as many as 48 were within ½ mile and 18 within ¼ mile. As these were coastal targets, even some of the closest bombs fell harmlessly into the sea – as did many, mercifully, that night.

Overall, the indications were that in excess of 80 per cent of the bombing was within 1 mile of the AP (17 per cent within ¼ mile); looked at the other way, however, one bomb in five fell wide of the target by at least 1 mile. One of the more experienced crews managed to drop their bombs well over 3 miles away, perhaps with good reason. Others, whether practised or newcomers, were surely 'off the map' altogether, with or without some plausible explanation.*

Although none of the reports quoted so far dwell on it, the results in both phases

---

* Studying raids on Friedrichshafen (20/21 June 1943), Montbeliard (15/16 July 1943) and Le Creusot (19/20 June 1943), all 'precision raids carried out under good conditions of weather against light defences', Bomber Command ORS (in a report issued after *Starkey*) determined Main Force error of between 400 and 600 yards. If full advantage was to be taken of the current aiming capabilities of Main Force, 'more reliable marking is required when small targets are attacked'.[21]

were dissipated through absent target-markers. The primary markers' reds were all-important in each as the spot to back-up and to bomb; yet only one set of reds was dropped each time, instead of two. The greens that were intended for precision release were critical too; but each time one in three was missing. It was noted, however, that in Phase I (the first red being missing), 60 per cent of Main Force bombed on the first two greens; and that in Phase II, 75 per cent of Main Force bombed the one red to go down, though what was intended as a single beckoning flame-red pinpoint ended up as three separate ones straddling a distance of 1 mile, and the bombs of Main Force tended to follow a similar pattern.[22]

A careful examination of the mission records and subsequent reports labelled 'Most Secret' at the time has thus enabled the presentation of a clear picture of the night's events. The emerging facts have put the bombing into perspective both as a discrete episode and as a contributing factor in the overall operation. Publicly for the first time, this reconstruction has been able to explain why it was that these attacks turned out to be much less effectively, less positively, spearheaded than the instigators of *Starkey* had intended in the climax build-up.

What, then, did the bombing of those coastal gun batteries achieve in material results? Detailed study of aerial photographs revealed only one direct hit on a prime target – it was on one of the 15 inch guns at *Pomeranian* (La Trésorerie, a battery that was judged to be 'invulnerable to bombing attacks'), causing damage but not destruction. There were near misses on two other prime targets – at *Religion* (Fort de Couppes) and *Andante* (Cap d'Alprech). The other prime targets were undamaged – *Pumicestone* (Fort de la Crèche) and *Millstone* (the three batteries at Pointe aux Oies). In a subsidiary target at *Andante* (Mont Soleil), one 88 mm AA/CD gun was destroyed and two others made unserviceable. Overall, as many as eight guns in total were probably put out of action for not less than 6 hours.[23] The tally, then, among the thirty-nine guns comprising the five codenamed batteries that were singled out in *Starkey* as being the most menacing armament in the whole area came to scarcely more than this: one of the twenty-one most powerful guns damaged and one of the eighteen smaller ones destroyed.

So who did the most damage? That same report determined that daylight bombing (mainly Marauders) achieved not only the single direct hit but also most, if not all, of the near misses. Night bombing 'does not appear to have hit either of the two primary APs', although undoubtedly damaging subsidiary defences and communications.*

As for *Starkey*, Air Vice Marshal Hugh Saunders' comprehensive post-operation summary as Air Force Commander recalled that the air operations in the Culminating Phase were to concentrate on seven gun-battery positions considered by the Naval Force Commander to be those most likely to engage the assault convoy during its sea passage from Dungeness towards Le Touquet and withdrawal therefrom: *Millstone* (with three discrete positions), *Pomeranian*, *Pumicestone*,

---

* A brief entry in *The Bomber Command War Diaries*, by Martin Middlebrook and Chris Everitt, passes judgement on the 8 September 1943 night raid by concluding that it 'was not successful'. It noted that 'the marking and the bombing were not accurate' and 'the battery does not appear to have been damaged'.

Religion and *Andante*. *Religion* and *Andante*, being considered the most dangerous, Bomber Command was requested to put its 'entire allocated night effort to the area bombing of these targets'. The remaining five positions (as well as *Religion* and *Andante*) were to be bombed in daylight by medium bombers only.

He concluded that:

> the fact that the assault convoy was at no time fired upon by the coast defence guns on the morning of D-Day indicates that although the guns were unlikely to be knocked out completely, heavy and medium bombers can cause casualties to gun crews and disrupt communications and otherwise cause confusion, thus reducing the efficiency of these defences.[24]

Churchill, still in North America for the Quebec Conference, received a swift and succinct summary on *Starkey*. With the ships safely home from their 'voyage to nowhere', Britain's Chiefs of Staff had sent him a message, quoting the Force Commander,[25] to say that the operation had been completed; that the sailing of the convoys produced no enemy reaction from air or surface attack, or by fire from coastal artillery; and that the intensive programme of air operations was also virtually unopposed. The air operations included bombing enemy coastal artillery on the night preceding and the morning of the final day, and it appeared that definite damage and dislocation to some batteries resulted.

It went on to report that the preliminary minesweeping operations by day between 31 August and 3 September had caused the enemy to open fire with their coastal artillery and to resort to air minelaying at night. This and slight reconnaissance activities during the Preparatory Phase were positive indications of some enemy interest which might have produced reaction on the final day. In this, however, the Chiefs of Staff were disappointed:

> We have thus not obtained the air battles and additional attrition of the German Air Force we had hoped for. It is too early to assess negative results, such as the extent to which *Starkey* has assisted in pinning down the enemy land and air forces in the West. On our side, *Starkey* has proved most valuable training experience for the Navy and Army. The US Air Force cooperated wholeheartedly with the RAF in the air programme.

All three senior commanders produced separate post-operation reports on *Starkey* – Air Vice Marshal Saunders as Air Force Commander; Gen. Sir Bernard Paget, Military Force Commander; and Commodore John Hughes-Hallett, Naval Force Commander. Air Marshal Sir Trafford Leigh-Mallory drew on these when sending his own report to COSSAC – Gen. Morgan – as well as attaching them as appendices.

Saunders focused on some of the problems that had existed during the operation, for instance the impact that changing weather conditions had made on its effectiveness. He noted that bad weather 'seriously restricted the scale of air operations which had been planned' and that 'the total effort achieved during the operation was necessarily considerably below that which was originally planned'.

In the last ten days the Germans had concentrated the bulk of their long-range bombers on the Western Front in Belgium and Holland, and used them for defensive minelaying off Boulogne. There was therefore evidence that the enemy were taking precautionary measures to meet an operation, but none 'to suggest that they appreciated the real scope of the operation, or that it was likely to be a serious attempt at invasion'.[26]

As for the climax of the operation, the main problem in the planning of the Culminating Phase was that of dealing effectively with enemy long-range coastal batteries which threatened the passage of the naval assault forces 'in view of the limited amount of bomber effort available'.[27] It had been hoped, he recalled, to secure the assistance of heavy bombers of the US 8th Bomber Command in this connection, 'but it was decided that, for the purpose of this particular operation, they would be better employed in attacking enemy airfields on D-Day'. The Allied effort, therefore, had to be confined to attacks by medium bombers by day and 'area' attacks by bombers of RAF Bomber Command at night.[28]

Bomber Command undertook to supply some 250 sorties on the night before 'D-Day', and it was hoped to provide some 300 medium bomber sorties on 'D-Day', relying on Marauders, Mitchells and Venturas, the Bostons being required to lay smokescreens. It was appreciated that this effort would be insufficient to deal with all of the enemy long-range gun positions and it was decided, after consultation with the Navy and Army commanders, that the effort should be concentrated on the seven gun-battery positions which were considered by the Naval Force Commander to be those most likely to engage the assault convoy. The original plan also envisaged attacks on the known beach defences between Boulogne and Le Touquet. As it was now not possible to spare any medium bomber effort for this task, it was allocated to fighter-bombers, the group of defences called *Menagerie*, at Hardelot, being selected.

Referring to the two-wave night attack ahead of 'D-Day', Air Force Commander Saunders' report stated that 'the two objectives were accurately marked by the No. 8 (Pathfinder) Group force of Mosquitoes and Halifaxes' and that 'a high percentage of the bomber crews reported having accurately sighted on the "markers" and a good concentration resulted'.

In respect of lessons learned by the Army, Paget came up with two points: that it would have been 'impossible' in eleven weeks to have planned in full detail a combined operation, including the assault and subsequent operations on the other side; and that the importance of producing a complete security and deception plan before the start of executive planning was 'clearly demonstrated'.[29]

As for the Navy's views, Hughes-Hallett was of the opinion that the failure of the enemy to react 'can only be fully explained on the assumption that he did not believe that any serious attack was intended'. He pointed to two possible reasons: one, that repeated warnings to the French population may have compromised security; and, two, the fact that the operation 'only included a most trifling diversion of the night bomber effort may have convinced the enemy that but little importance was attached to it by the Allied Command'. From the naval point of view, this was an operation of 'considerable value' – 'viewed as an exercise'.[30]

As Force Commander, Leigh-Mallory acknowledged that *Starkey* did not achieve its primary objective of compelling the German air force to engage in 'air battles of attrition under conditions advantageous to us'.[31] Its fighters were generally unwilling to engage those of the RAF and USAAF, the general indication being that they were being held in reserve to oppose bomber attacks of deeper penetration. Such air fighting as did develop was in the Allies' favour. As for the coastal guns, Leigh-Mallory said that while it could not be claimed that their failure to open fire on the assault convoy was due to complete inability, it was reasonable to assume that their efficiency was seriously reduced.

He concluded by giving British newspaper editors a pat on the back for their subsequent help when formally urged to cooperate in 'damping down' 'Second Front' speculation aroused by the Quebec Conference, the institution of regulated areas and increased troop movements all occurring at about the same time that summer.*[32]

A US 8th Air Force digest for 1 to 15 September 1943 noted that attacks connected with *Starkey* 'dominated a large part of the period'; on the last day 'a record 1,217' of its planes were airborne on operational missions. The operation provided valuable experience but 'failed to provoke the hoped-for major air battle'.[33]

The Americans were clearly relieved that the heavy-bomber contribution of its 8th Air Force had been scaled down at the urgent request of the commanding generals from the initially proposed 3,000 sorties to the eventually accepted 300-minimum sorties. Since *Starkey* 'turned out to be a very disappointing operation, it is just as well that it cost the strategic bombing forces little in diverted effort. The Germans failed to react as briskly as expected. Clearly they had not been deceived, and clearly also they were determined not to risk their precious fighter defenses in an air battle in which they were outnumbered and which was not likely to be of decisive importance'.[34]

But why *did* the enemy fail to react in the manner that the mounting of *Starkey* was intended to achieve? Back to the Air Force Commander's report. Drawing conclusions from the experience gained throughout the operation, Air Vice Marshal Saunders began with a positive achievement: that in the narrow waters of the Straits of Dover it was possible to maintain, simultaneously for several hours, two adequate air 'umbrellas' giving air superiority over the Channel and assault beach areas, which enabled the assault forces and formations of unescorted medium bombers to proceed to their tasks and targets unmolested.[35]

On the enemy's 'complete failure' to react to the operations on 'D-Day', he suggested two main causes: that the enemy was at no time deceived into thinking that a serious landing was intended; and that under those circumstances he decided it was 'impolitic' to engage the Allied fighters over the Boulogne area or over the assault convoy. Why? He stood to gain nothing because of the Allies' fighter superiority, and he wished to conserve his fighter forces to meet the constant threat of attack by the Fortresses. He had already reinforced his fighters in the Beauvais and Lille areas by some sixty aircraft, and during the morning of 'D-Day' he had

---

* Confidential guidance issued by the Ministry of Information on 16 August 1943 stressed the importance 'that exaggerated public expectations of large scale continental operations should not be raised prematurely'.[36]

sent down additional aircraft from Holland to patrol Belgium. The enemy was not going to allow his fighters to be drawn away in any strength from their main defensive positions, thus exposing himself to the risk of unopposed air attack on Germany.

Addressing the hypothesis that the enemy had appeared to appreciate that a full-scale landing was not intended, Saunders suggested that this may have been due either to his having had information that the extent of the Army participation in the operation amounted to little more than an administrative exercise (*Harlequin*) or else to a firm conviction that there could be no serious invasion threat from Britain at that time. The enemy's almost complete lack of overland reconnaissance, both prior to and during the operation, lent colour to either hypothesis, the Air Force Commander concluded.[37]

Thus, on the facts as presented so far and subsequently analysed, *Operation Starkey* can hardly be counted as a resounding success – no air battles, no moves against the convoys, no reaction at all from the enemy. Nonetheless, one component within the master plan has been resounding ever since, and that is the impact that the savage bombing of the guns of *Religion* and *Andante* has had on the town and the people of Le Portel.

Chapter Fifteen

Murder – or Accidental Death?

Is it really surprising that generations of Portelois have questioned the reason for the destruction of their town? Surely not, when apparently some forty years were allowed to pass before anyone carrying the authority of the eminent scientific adviser Prof. R.V. Jones 'came off the fence' over the nagging possibility that the Le Portel bombardment was a deliberate act, by the Allies, against the French people in a French town. In those circumstances, bereft of answers for so long, the Portelois could be excused for suspecting that the motive for the bombardment remained secreted in locked cabinets behind closed doors in London, Washington or even in post-war Paris. Why us – why Le Portel?

Well, was this an act of murder or a case of accidental death? Bitterness was excusable while the sights and the suffering, the grief and the gravity of the situation remained so vivid. No doubt it was perfectly understandable that Mgr Dutoit, when conducting a memorial service in the cathedral in Boulogne so soon after the event, should speak of the 'murderous bombing';[1] and that a fireman later, working amid the ruins of a shattered hotel in Le Portel, should describe incoming aircraft as 'murderers'.[2] After all, a town had been flattened, the population decimated and the survivors dispersed. Yet the true targets were barely touched, and, ironically, the firepower of both those big-gun positions, at Fort de Couppes and Cap d'Alprech, was apparently overestimated when these actual targets of the Allied bombers were being chosen in Britain.*

In an emotive environment, the blunt and accusing word 'murder' comes quickly to the lips; later, dispassionate jurors will more likely incline towards an alternative verdict on the grounds that there was no intent to kill.

This was not a deliberate attack – we have this on the authority of Professor Jones, scientific adviser to the British prime minister of the day, after he raised the subject with some of his former colleagues in response to an approach from a Boulonnais with a mission to seek out the truth. Of course it was not deliberate – this is patently clear from the wealth of detail now on record in the foregoing pages. So, accepting that the town of Le Portel was not bombed deliberately, what new 'can of worms' has been opened, if any, with the introduction and publication of fresh evidence?

No query over basic fact existed at the time of the bombardment and none has surfaced in the fifty-plus years afterwards. The core fact is beyond all doubt: it is that the terrible toll that this Pas de Calais seaside resort suffered in September 1943

---

* Fortifications specialist Lucien Vasseur post-war put size and range of the major guns at both Fort de Couppes and Cap d'Alprech below those of the *Starkey* planners.[3]

was the result of bombing by Allied warplanes – planes of the British and American air forces. Those bombs caused that death and destruction; there is no question mark over that. It is undeniable that friendly forces carried out the bombing; it is indisputable that the bombing caused such devastation; it is necessary only to address the reason for the bombing and the reason for the death and destruction. Research into once-secret contemporary documents now provides unequivocal statements on both counts, so it remains only to seek a rationale, and to argue the justification – assuming that there was justification – both for the raids of 4, 8 and 9 September 1943 and for their tragic consequences. For the last time, then, why Le Portel?

The question was asked when the survivors came out of their cellars after those raids – the ones in daylight on 4, 8 and 9 September and those by night on the 8th. It was asked when the Portelois realized the extent of the intolerable toll on their town and its people that this series of attacks had inflicted: some 500 killed, around 1,200 injured and approximately 93 per cent of the buildings damaged. The question was still being asked as recently as the fiftieth anniversary, when *La Voix du Nord*, the daily newspaper circulating in Le Portel and throughout the Pas de Calais, carried a commemorative article in which it was noted that for most people in Le Portel the reason for the bombardment was still a mystery.[4] It should no longer be necessary to ask why Le Portel was made to suffer all those years ago. Since the facts are now crystal-clear, it should no longer be pertinent to suggest that doubts continue to exist, unless anyone asking the question is doing so in the sense of questioning why the life of a particular person has been saved while that of another has been taken away.

The Allied bombs that pulverized Le Portel were not meant to fall on the town but on coastal batteries outside it. They missed their mark – time and time again – and the causes have been determined by reference to contemporary documentation. On the occasion of the fortieth anniversary of the bombings, in 1983, Prof. Jones' letter to the historian Guy Bataille brought into the open the aspect of inaccuracy in the way that the APs were marked for the night bombers whose task was to destroy those gun-battery targets. As this appears to have been the first 'official' explanation for the deadly bombardment of Le Portel, it was clearly a highly significant milestone in efforts among the Portelois to seek as much information as possible on the subject – a subject that has shown no inclination to 'go away'. So, the professor's contribution can be regarded as an appropriate starting point for a definitive study, a dispassionate overview that here pulls all the strands together for the first time.

It is not sufficient to blame target-marking inaccuracy – anyway, day bombing missed too; it has to be determined, first, why those targets were selected. Remember, Le Portel had been relatively free of attack for over three years despite the presence and proximity of offensive and defensive guns – guns large and small. There had to be cause for this situation to change; without a target, or targets, there would be no need to bomb. And while there were no bombs there would be no damage and no one hurt. So why was it that Le Portel of all places had to fall the unwitting victim to such incredible havoc and misery? Why was it that Le Portel was nominated 'The Town That Had To Die' – if this was the case?

What happened to Le Portel can be correctly described as an accidental bombardment, since all of the bombs that fell in and around the town were intended for military targets, not for civilian residents. In this context the apologetic term 'consequence of war' springs to mind – although civilian deaths numbered in tens of thousands rather than in hundreds were equally a consequence of war. Hamburg, Dresden, London, Hiroshima – all will be remembered. Leaving aside the 'friendly fire' factor and acknowledging that Le Portel's fate was on a much reduced scale, it is nonetheless possible to draw comparisons which show that what this town suffered was in itself distressingly severe on two counts: casualty figures and bomb tonnage.

It is a fact that German bombs killed fewer people in that memorable night raid on Coventry on 14/15 November 1940 than the Allied bombs on Le Portel – Churchill wrote that, of all the raids Britain had sustained, this was the most devastating.[5] The death toll in Le Portel also surpassed that in the tragically historic bombing of the Billancourt Renault factory on 3/4 March 1942 when 235 bombers were despatched to form the largest number of aircraft directed against a single target at that stage of the war. Then, some 367 French people died – a death toll more than twice that inflicted so far in any RAF raid on a German city.[6] Boulogne, an obvious military objective and on Le Portel's doorstep, figured in 123 bombing raids during its 1,582 days of German occupation, the heaviest loss of life occurring on 13 May 1944, in the build-up to D-Day, when a total of 103 civilians died.[7]

Turning to bomb tonnage statistics (the weight of bombs dropped), the fact that the targets and town of Le Portel received 678.10 tons of high explosives in the massive night attack of 8/9 September alone is also significant; it was heavier than the weight of bombs unleashed on Berlin in a night raid carried out by the RAF six months earlier (1/2 March 1943: 664.9 tons by 297 aircraft).[8] It was greater even than the tonnage dropped in a night raid on Berlin, again by the RAF, just the week previous to the attacks on Le Portel (3/4 September 1943: 631 tons, killing 568 people according to contemporary German figures.)[9] All that high-explosive, all those bombs – and all for two groups of guns.*

Statistics apart, other reasons exist for what some may regard as a rather belated focus on a locality and an episode that belongs to the past, the war of 1939–45. The bombardment of Le Portel happened; and it won't go away, however unpleasant it may be to have to recall the tragedy and the reasons for it occurring, all those years ago.

There is no suggestion that the incident has been 'hushed up' and buried under a shroud of secrecy these past fifty years. That point having been registered, there will no doubt be a school of thought in Britain and America, if not in France, that it should have remained out of the public domain on the grounds that no one gains when the perpetrators are needlessly reminded of the disturbing results of their actions. Consciences may possibly be tweaked, but this was wartime, orders were orders and, anyway, no one said that the *town* of Le Portel was to be bombed.

The justification for this focus comes in the fact that the bombardment of

---

* A comparison that is perhaps easier to assimilate is this: that fewer high explosives were dropped and fewer people killed in the Thousand Bomber Raid on Cologne in May 1942.[10]

Le Portel stood – and remains to this day – unique in the circumstances that caused such death and destruction. It was unique, certainly, because this horrific bombing by Allied aircraft on a French town occurred not in a situation of reality but during an act of pretence.

It is an extraordinary episode. Le Portel did not suffer because the bombing was required as a prelude to the invasion of Europe; the town was destroyed and its people killed, maimed and evacuated as a direct consequence of a theatrical ploy. It lost its life, by accident, in a major operation planned and executed with the object of deceiving the enemy into supposing that a large-scale Allied landing was imminent. Perhaps Le Portel merits a place of honour in the annals of 'friendly fire', but, if it does, note well the distinction that while the town was hit by 'friendly' bombs that missed, the bombing itself was ordered under the guise of reality. It was a let's-pretend situation, 'play-acting' with no intention to commit *any* Allied troops to *any* assault . . . empty boats, empty threats. This is the essence of the matter. This is, after all, the *real* tragedy of Le Portel.

Now that there is a comprehensive and objective account that fully integrates *Operation Starkey* and the bombardment of Le Portel, it becomes possible to determine the rationale – and of course to debate the wisdom of decisions that were taken at the time. Doubtless the motives for the deception plan overall were admirable, and perhaps even unavoidable, at that stage of the war. But could the same be said for the decision to bomb the gun batteries codenamed *Religion* and *Andante* at all, let alone with such apparent frenzy, given bombing error rates of the time and the proximity of a built-up area? The guns of Le Portel were just one small part of the overall strategy, the significance of the town of Le Portel presumably lost in the midst of the detailed planning for what would be but a single step in *Starkey*. The importance of Le Portel surfaced only much later – it was, regrettably, 'The Town That Had To Die'. No one appears to have realized the potential risk – the danger to French lives and property – in time to do anything about it.

It is imperative that the bombardment is kept within its true context: the importance hinges not on the fact that this seaside resort was virtually wiped out in a series of bombing raids carried out by RAF and USAAF planes but that the bombardment occurred because *Starkey* demanded it.

Starkey had been introduced to the top echelon of the participants as being an important part of the agreed strategical plan for 1943: an 'essential rehearsal for invasion in 1944' with the definite objects of deceiving the enemy into thinking that invasion was imminent; and inflicting the greatest possible damage on the German Air Force (see p. 16).

Regard the attacks on targets in the vicinity of Le Portel as being fundamental to the success of *Starkey*, and all falls into place. The conclusion is inescapable: Le Portel was in the wrong place at the wrong time. Despite Boulogne being its neighbour, despite the defences circling the town, it largely escaped the worst of earlier air-raids in this part of the Pas de Calais. Unfortunately, when circumstances demanded otherwise and the focus across the Channel turned on it, Le Portel made the supreme sacrifice. No one intended it; no one foresaw it; but it happened all the same – another of those 'consequences of war', but this one – emphatically, tragically – way out in a class of its own.

While the war progressed, some of the facts about the British deception plan were released to the general public (though not its name or its aim), and some of the facts about the bombardment of Le Portel became known too. However, the extent of the knowledge made available through the media depended on which side of the Channel you lived. Both 'sides' made the most of the opportunity, although the military armistice in Italy, the Allied landings there and the Soviets' continuing offensive earned the headlines.

In Britain, after the 24-hour postponement for what was in fact an inaccurate weather forecast, the climax to *Starkey* on 9 September 1943 became a public relations exercise with war correspondents on board the ships for a slice of the action and assembled on the clifftops overlooking the Straits of Dover for a grandstand view. There was national and international representation in the press corps, the aim being to avoid any contention that this was an aborted landing, which it was reckoned would be the nub of the message that the Germans would try to spread. The newspapermen reported the bombardment of the coastal defences, even to the point of naming Hardelot as one area under attack, but there was no mention of Le Portel.[11]

In France, however, it was what happened to Le Portel that provided the 'meat' for the propaganda machine; though it must have been recognized that an Allied armada had sailed and about-turned, there was no reference to it. Via their own newspapers, produced under censorship restrictions as were those in Britain, the French learned that Le Portel had suffered dead and injured in their hundreds and that schools, churches and other public buildings there and elsewhere were victims of Anglo-American air attacks.[12] Marshal Pétain's personal interest and the memorial service in Notre Dame in Paris, the best-known cathedral in the whole of France, heightened public attention on the plight of Le Portel and the Portelois, all now gone from the town. In time, the news filtered into Britain. Portelois who had fled their own country ahead of the German occupation apparently learned about the attack in a French-language broadcast picked up while scanning the wavebands for any news coming through from 'home'.[13]

In the form that *Starkey* took in the end, in the Culminating Phase there was no target of its kind that was more important in the planners' view than *Religion* and *Andante*, those big-gun batteries respectively to the north and south of Le Portel. The Portelois knew of their presence but not, of course, either the codenames that the *Starkey* planners had given them or their relevance to Allied intentions. The bombardment was on such a scale because the planners considered the existence of those guns the greatest threat to the ships heading for the coast between Boulogne and Le Touquet. It was as fierce as it was because the targets were judged – rightly or wrongly – so intimidating and so menacing. The destruction was as intense as it was because so many bombs meant for *Religion* and *Andante*, by day as well as by night, missed the gun emplacements and fell on the town.

Whether or not the destruction was justified in a situation of required realism as opposed to veritable reality, successive steps have to be reviewed to establish what went wrong – and what, if anything, could have been done to avoid the tragedy of Le Portel. The key factors are the locations of *Religion* and *Andante*; the pinpoint references on the Allies' maps for the gun sites and the APs; the position of the town relative to them and its visibility on those maps; the equipment and methods available at that stage of the air war in Europe for finding, marking and bombing targets; and the instructions which came down from on high to the commands, groups, squadrons and crews carrying out those missions.

There is one paramount factor in the bombing of Le Portel that the contemporary War Office maps disclose yet the subsequent reports from the *Starkey* 'top brass' and Bomber Command investigators do not mention. It is the proximity of this built-up area to the gun emplacements.[14] With hindsight, the apparent failure to draw attention to the nearness of these prime targets to a residential district may be regarded as rather disturbing – a blind-spot, perhaps, in the complex planning which this latest research reveals as the fatal flaw.

It will be recalled that the Air Ministry required targets in *Starkey* to be submitted for specific clearance to avoid risk to civilians, and that this requirement was met in the case of both *Religion* (Fort de Couppes) and *Andante* (Cap d'Alprech). That there was concern lest these operations might conflict with War Cabinet rules in respect of bombing activities over occupied territories is indicative that caution was to be exercised when targets were put forward for clearance.

Targets within *Religion* and *Andante* and the selected APs (as with other *Starkey* targets) were given a six-figure grid reference on War Office map GSGS 4040, which used a scale of 1:50,000 (1 inch to 0.79 miles), thus pinpointing each target/AP to within a 100 metre square. Nowadays, with more time for examination and less pressure than in wartime to make a decision, it will seem curious that two targets within the same 100 metre square – one of them nominated for attack by light and medium bombers, the other by heavy bombers – came in for different treatment in the clearance process.[15] Target 8(H)/46 on the list of beach defences that were potential targets for light and medium bombers received clearance for attack by day only, while 9(A)/37 on the list of coastal and railway artillery that were potential targets for heavy bombers received clearance with no such restriction. Although on separate lists, both of these potential targets presumably attracted the same depth of specialist scrutiny at the Air Ministry. Both had the same grid reference, 653525 on War Office map GSGS 4040 Sheet 49, and this pinpointed both potential targets within the same 100 metre square.

Strip aside the 'anonymity' of the numbering system and a perplexing anomaly comes to light. It is this: the biggest guns at Fort de Couppes gained clearance for attack by night while much smaller guns in precisely the same 100 metre square were cleared only for daylight attack. If it was judged a potential risk to civilian life to attack the smaller guns by night, surely it was equally (or more?) risky to attack the larger guns by night when both sites nestled in the identical map reference? Air Ministry having placed no restriction on a night attack on the big guns of Fort de Couppes, the attack proceeded. However, if this more inviting target had been cleared only for daytime attack, two alternatives would have remained: to focus this phase of the night bombing on the only other (and less attractive) gun site in the *Religion* grouping – 9(A)/38, Moulin Bleu, which was further away from the built-up area – or to ignore *Religion* altogether, in either case reducing the likelihood of civilian casualties that night. Was this a slip-up, a misreading of information supplied, a 'one-off' bungle? Strangely, this was not an isolated anomaly: exactly the same discrepancy occurred elsewhere in the Boulogne area (Sheet 49/683554), but this has no bearing on events at Le Portel. It was more distant and neither target (8(H)/47 nor 9(A)/39) was chosen for attack, by day or by night.

As implemented, the single AP picked to achieve the most potent concentration of bombs in each of the two phases was, for *Religion*, between the two sites and, for *Andante*, which encompassed three sites, the one with the biggest guns. On GSGS 4040, these APs are seen to be slightly more than a mile apart, respectively north-east and south-west of the centre of the town. To be more precise, the separation between the two APs is a matter of 1,750 metres (1,914 yards), and the 1,914-yard line straddles a built-up area which is clearly shown on the map, a built-up area annotated 'Le Portel'.

On Bomber Command's own figures, as submitted in a document which was considered by the *Starkey* planners, their average bombing error at that time amounted to ½ mile[16], which virtually merged those target areas. Astonishingly, therefore, civilian casualties must have been a certainty: the northern half of the town could hardly have escaped inclusion within a ½ mile radius of *Religion*, the southern half within a ½ mile radius of *Andante*. If one target alone had been chosen, half of the town might have stood a chance; with both targets chosen, the town itself would seem to have had no escape. With *Religion* and *Andante* confirmed as the APs for Bomber Command (and for the US Air Support Command planes attacking by day), Le Portel was doomed for destruction.

So, with the targets chosen and the purpose of the attacks clear, the key facts can stand reiterating:

The positions of all of the guns and both of the APs were clearly and precisely marked on the War Office map GSGS 4040. Clearly, because of the six-figure reference number based on vertical and horizontal rules on this map and, precisely, because each six-figure grid reference indicated an area no larger than a 100 metre square.

GSGS 4040 shows the built-up area of Le Portel and its proximity to the targets and both APs.

The average bombing error by RAF Bomber Command at that stage of the war was put at ½ mile, and a ½ mile radius of each AP all but overlaps the town, a mere 150 yards or so being a 'bomb-free' zone.

This ½ mile average bombing error was Bomber Command's own figure. A 'half-mile' could not possibly mean precisely 880 yards but an arbitrary ½ mile, and that the ½ mile figure appeared in documentation provided for those planning *Starkey* well before *Religion* and *Andante* were selected for attack.

Given these facts, it is inconceivable that night-time bombing could have been ordered without recognition of the risk to French lives and property, despite the intention to use the most experienced Mosquito crews in Pathfinder Force, carrying out the critical primary target-marking with the benefit of Oboe, the most precise marking aid available.

Furthermore, mustering such a high percentage of crews still under training before joining an operational bomber squadron could only increase the possibility of civilian casualties. With their relative inexperience, surely this could only extend the ½ mile average error range claimed for operational crews – it could hardly reduce it, whatever their personal determination and overall resolution to do their best when, in a sense, competing with squadron crews.

Examination of the squadron records shows that, in one case at least, the presence of a built-up area was remarked on while overhead and formally noted on the return to base.[17] This suggests that in the briefing session before take-off there had been no mention of a built-up area and that its existence therefore came as a surprise to the crew. A Pathfinder Halifax from 405 Squadron, G-George, made one such laconic reference – 'Saw built-up area in light of TI' – when over the target at 2209 hours. The first and only red marker in this phase, concentrated on Fort de Couppes, hung in the night sky at the time. This TI began cascading like a huge blood-red roman candle firework (released by H-Harry, a Mosquito of 109 Squadron). It was visible in the bombsight of this Halifax, flying then at a height of 16,500 feet – more than 3 miles up in the moonlight. This crew was free of the twenty-five or so searchlights that probed that night at one time or another to 'cone' the attacking bombers for the AA guns and for the patrolling night fighters working in conjunction with them.

Boulogne was a built-up area, but that was clear of the APs so would not figure in the plan other than to give its name as a point of reference, for instance when these and other coastal batteries were described as being 'in the Boulogne area'.

Whether or not a built-up area was to be expected, a post-operation report certainly brought its presence to light, although use of the term 'village' to describe the town can be seen as somewhat unfortunate in the circumstances. Some may regard this as an attempt to minimize the consequences of a disclosure that not all of the bombs had hit the proper place. This awareness came about while CIU specialists at RAF Station Medmenham were interpreting the previously mentioned photographic evidence subsequent to the attacks on *Religion* and *Andante*.[18] Their report referred to specific damage to military objectives and several direct hits on a factory, and it included the comment that 'the village of Le Portel has suffered very severely as a result of the attacks', going on to say that 'the property damaged is chiefly residential'.

Perhaps the planners were of the opinion either that the Germans had themselves chosen to move all or most of the civilian population from this part of the Pas de Calais or that British efforts devised in London would be successful in warning the French people who remained there that their lives were at risk if they did not evacuate.* That there was some kind of prebombardment danger signal subsequently and specifically is beyond doubt; it is the form that it took that is in question.

Reports persist among the Portelois that 'several English soldiers with German

---

* The previous summer, prompted by the Political Warfare Executive's propaganda proposals sowing seeds for eventual landings on the Continent by Allied forces large or small, the first steps had been taken to encourage French inhabitants to leave coastal areas between the Belgian frontier in the north and the Pyrenees in the south. The message going out over the air in the BBC French programme and in leaflets dropped by aircraft urged the French to evacuate with the least possible delay: 'Do not wait till the last moment. It will be too late. Go as soon as possible.'[19]

uniforms were going around Le Portel informing people to evacuate' – even up to the day before the bombers began pulverizing the gun sites on the evening of Wednesday 8 September 1943, according to one statement given in writing to the author.[20] So far corroborated only in Le Portel, this enterprising if extreme expedient adds a new dimension to the findings of the respected Boulogne journalist and historian Guy Bataille when he noted (a decade earlier) that there had been advance-warning messages by radio and word of mouth. From mid-1943, London's messages to the French Resistance referred to D-Day being closer than might be anticipated – and, he continued, some families in Le Portel being advised that to remain living there would put them in the greatest danger. This advice, he explained, came from the French Resistance, although naturally they could say nothing more.[21]

There remains to this day an organization dedicated to remembering the victims of the Le Portel bombardment and, by implication, to ensuring that this chapter of the town's history is not allowed to be forgotten. Enquiries within this group produced nothing pointing to an identifiable source that warned specifically of a life-threatening action to engulf the Portelois in that first fortnight of September 1943.

The association's president for many years, M. Charles Merette, who lost an arm during the night attack, insisted that throughout the German occupation there was never any formal warning that lives might be lost if the civilian population remained in the town. However, during a discussion about events leading up to the Anglo-American bombing on 4, 8 and 9 September 1943, evidence emerged which confirms that some inhabitants were urged, on that occasion, to move out of the town for their personal safety.[22] This 'warning' came from a person in his mid-20s, reputedly in the Resistance, who told several people some days before the bombings began that they should leave because Le Portel would be bombed.

Although Merette did not have an opportunity to speak to this person, colleagues indicated to him, at the time, that not only was the young man unable to give a date or to add anything beyond those few words, but also he was frightened that if anyone passed on what he had told them he might be denounced to the Germans.

Merette is not aware of anyone acting on that information, which – assuming it to have been authentic and passed to the young man by underground procedures that have yet to be verified – seems not to have been circulated in any other way (unless credence is given to the 'English soldiers with German uniforms' pronouncement). Arguably, if the warning he mentioned did emanate from London – and especially if it was the only one intended for all or most of the population – then it was entirely haphazard and certainly warranted much better handling in order to minimize the number of casualties. It is Merette's view that it would have been better if Allied aircraft had dropped leaflets during the first daylight attack to give a clear warning that more and heavier bombing was imminent. With positive information like that, issued in the widest possible manner as a formal warning that Le Portel faced total destruction, the Portelois would have left immediately. In such circumstances, he said, the Germans would have been unable to prevent a mass departure, even though the inhabitants needed special documents to leave Le Portel because it was within a restricted zone. In the event, although the population was substantially less than its pre-occupation size, an estimated 5,500 Portelois were left to their fate, virtually trapped with no way out – oblivious, alas, to the Allies' closing moves in *Starkey*.

Target location having been discussed, what about the facilities available and methods open to the target-markers at night and the bomber crews attacking by night and by day? Bombs meant for *Religion* and *Andante* missed not only by night (when the RAF, with the largest number of planes, loaded with the greatest weight of bombs, carried out the two night attacks on 8 September) but also by day (when US Air Force medium bombers carried out two attacks on the evening of 8 September and eight attacks on the morning of 9 September).

Daylight bombing offered greater opportunity for accurate bombing: aerial photographs had been circulated which included the *Religion* and *Andante* gun positions, and the coastline was an unmistakable aid when lining up the target. AA fire from the ground was the big deterrent, proving its effectiveness by bringing down three Marauders (and also damaging one in three of all Marauders that attacked over the course of those two days).[23] Other than that, whether the targets were hit was down to a combination of nervousness, competence and tools – whether or not the sighting mechanism and the bombs performed to the standards that the crews required of them. Reports issued after the bombardment produced aiming-error statistics revealing that, at best, the average 'miss' in the daylight attacks was as much as 500 yards – no better than the achievement by night.[24]

The night raids can be assessed more critically because evidence and comment has been produced which makes it possible to see what went wrong to shift the bombing away from the defended gun positions of German troops and onto the fragile homes of French civilians. The Air Force Commander's choice of words in his report on *Starkey* may raise a few eyebrows when read in the context of the damage inflicted not on enemy territory but on a town in an occupied country. Referring to the attacks on the coastal batteries the night before the convoys sailed, he recalled that RAF Bomber Command had been requested to put its entire allocated night effort 'to the area bombing' of *Religion* and *Andante*.[25] In post-war times, 'area bombing' has become an emotive phrase generally regarded as being a form of attack in which the bombing is directed against an entire area instead of on particular targets inside it. Although the effect on Le Portel may have resembled the aftermath of area bombing on somewhere in Germany, precision was certainly the aspiration, if not the outcome, in respect of the choice, marking and bombing of both targets.*

---

* It can be argued that Air Vice Marshal Saunders' use of the term 'area' bombing when summarizing the Anglo-American air forces' contribution to *Operation Starkey* confirms that the devastation of this French town was the result of the RAF having to resort to this tactic because individual gun emplacements presented impossible targets. *Religion* embraced two separate gun positions ½ mile apart; and *Andante* was a grouping of three which spanned over a mile. Various contemporary RAF documents refer to 'Area 1' and 'Area 2' (instead of Phase I and Phase II), but the most unequivocal statement comes in a previously quoted Bomber Command summary of operations (see p. 129). This referred to the bomber force that night being 'divided to carry out two area attacks in the vicinity of Boulogne', the APs being selected 'to cover predetermined areas in which enemy coastal defences were sited'. Interestingly, if area bombing was in mind, there was a bonus in prospect: the potential destruction of two large radar sites, one some 700 metres to the south-east of Le Portel, the other at Cap d'Alprech. Prof. R.V. Jones regarded these coastal radars as key objectives in the campaign to neutralize the German fighter force, so these sites especially would have constituted further important targets, albeit secondary to the five gun-battery positions pinpointed in the *Starkey* documentation (see Appendix I).[26]

That precision was the intention is clear from the pinpointing, marking and bombing procedures documented in the plan of attack. To find and mark the targets in both raids, RAF Bomber Command put its trust implicitly into the tried and proven techniques of Pathfinder Force, whose fast, high-flying Mosquitoes with their two-man crews had apparently done so well already in leading attacks on targets hidden in the forests of northern France in the earlier stages of *Starkey*.[27] With the benefit of Oboe, a navigational method so advanced that it not only directed the Mosquitoes to their target but even indicated the marker-release point through the navigator's headset, accuracy of the highest degree currently achievable by Bomber Command was in prospect. However, it transpired that there were two problems before the Pathfinders were in the air: first, *Religion* and *Andante* were not best placed for an Oboe attack – the geography of the target area halved the number of planes that could use Oboe;[28] second, the only alternative radio-direction device was the Baillie beam – an earlier and less popular system which was the 'fall-back' for the other half.[29]

What happened was a classic example of Pilot Officer Murphy's Law in that something was bound to go wrong – it just couldn't be helped. It was not so much 'something' going wrong on this occasion – more a case of everything going wrong. The result was that not only were there equipment failures among key aircraft – for example, the first to go in, which also had the most experienced crew on board – but additionally the reserve aircraft were unable to act as stand-ins and had to return to base with their markers. Consequently just half of the number of target-indicating flares carried by the Mosquitoes was dropped; and none of them was sufficiently close to the gun-emplacement objective for either of the two raids to stand much chance of success. *Religion* and *Andante* being situated in a part of the Continent that was 'very poor' for using Oboe, supplementing with the Baillie beam to guide the primary markers to the APs served only to reduce the prospects for acceptable marking.

Back-up marking was down to the remaining Pathfinder crews, those flying four-engined Halifaxes carrying high explosives as well as TIs. They had no sophisticated equipment to help them, simply human eyes to see the Mosquitoes' TIs going down and the use of bomb-sights to position their own TIs on top of those of the Mosquitoes.

The Halifax crews would have to rely on their considerable operational experience and drop their TIs as close as possible to those of the Mosquitoes which appeared to be the most accurate, or hold back if it seemed that the Mosquitoes' TIs were wrongly placed. It was normal procedure, these Pathfinder squadrons having worked together routinely before and during *Starkey*. Oboe-marking was the most accurate method available and markers that were obviously misplaced were simply ignored: for instance, a faulty release 7 miles west of the target in the Forêt de Raismes on 3 September, which was the last time the Pathfinders had spearheaded a *Starkey* mission.[30] The bombers, as well as the back-up marking Pathfinders, recognized this as being a misplaced marker, so it attracted no bombing. Exceptions like this aside, to all intents and purposes, Mosquito marking was 'spot on'.

In the raids on *Religion* and *Andante* the positioning of the earliest TIs was critical because the first Halifax would be going in after the first Mosquito. Then the first of the Main Force bombers would arrive – and all crews, whether with squadron experience or in the final stages of operational training, had to aim their bombs at the TIs. If no TIs were visible, they would go back home with their bombs still on board. The safety factor was implicit in the teleprinted orders passed down the chain of command. It was the Pathfinders' responsibility to place those bright-burning coloured flares which all the bombers would use as their markers. No Pathfinders' TIs: no bombing, and Main Force planes returned to base with all bombs safe in the bomb-bays.

The truth of the matter is that the Pathfinders' marking was regrettably much less accurate than on other not-so-critical occasions, for instance the *Starkey* attacks on ammunition dumps inside French forests when the 'estimated impact points' indicated an average error as small as 66¼ yards. This time, however, Main Force, following orders, largely bombed markers which were as much as some 960 and 1,200 yards from the AP for *Religion* and straddling a full mile in the case of *Andante*.[31] Unexpectedly having fallen in three parts, even this marker was some 350 yards off-target at its closest point. The plate section contains a detailed map that shows just how close Le Portel was to both target areas, leaving no doubt as to why the town and its people suffered more that night than in the daylight bombing.

In the attack on the northern target, the first TI green at 2202 hours and the back-up green at 2205 hours attracted two in three bombers; but as both markers were more than ½ mile from the AP, effectively this shifted the bomb-aimers' target to the built-up residential area. Against the southern target, three in four bombers centred on the three parts of the TI red dropped at 2243 hours, the middle part falling on the southern edge of the town and another on the northern edge. By chance this was scarcely more than the length of a rugby pitch from the most powerful guns in the previous (Phase I) target area! The remaining one-third performed best in serving Bomber Command's purposes although, as already noted, it was still 350 yards off a bull's-eye.

Bomber Command was following custom by putting Mosquito marker planes in the lead, the crews having the benefit of highly advanced equipment to minimize human error; and it was following custom by using Halifax squadrons, dedicated to these duties and experienced in them, to drop further markers on a visual sighting. It was like a gigantic 'follow-my-leader' in the bright moonlight over Le Portel, with Halifax crews releasing their TIs on those subsequently shown to have been dropped out of position by the Mosquitoes. The Halifaxes, having compounded the error by doing as they were told and aiming for the Mosquitoes' TIs, found that the Stirlings and Wellingtons of Main Force were doing as they too were told, and aiming on markers since known to have been incorrectly placed. Main Force, in the mistaken belief that its entire bombing effort was concentrated on the successive APs, *Religion* and then *Andante*, managed to kill far more of the Allies' friends that night than its enemies. Also, as aerial photography was later to show, the bombers succeeded in wreaking far more havoc among French homes than among the German gun positions. Some seventy-nine hits were reportedly scored by Bomber Command on the sites of the two groups of targets that night,[32] yet its planes (including the American Fortresses) dropped some 2,243 bombs in the two phases of that night attack.

A Bomber Command report commented on the Pathfinders' role, first explaining how the Mosquitoes were directed to their targets and then recording the positions of their markers relative to the APs. It went on to state that the pattern of Main Force bombing followed that of the Pathfinders' marking.[33] With those facts on record, the bombing of Le Portel by night, which was by far the most devastating of the series, came as a result of successive errors – the accidental total destruction of a town the size of a Caernarvon, a Lichfield or a Prestwick of its day. A French town – with many lives lost; men, women and children maimed – and all for the sake of what RAF Bomber Command's chief – arguing against *Starkey* – described in advance as being at best 'a piece of harmless play-acting'.[34] Play-acting it was; harmless it was not. . . .

Targeting, target-marking and bomb-aiming having been discussed, what vindication can be found for the bombardment and consequent destruction of Le Portel? It was, after all, one small move in a board-game that had pretence as its purpose; reality was missing, realism the overriding intention among the players in *Starkey*.

The deception plan hatched in early 1943 called for strenuous efforts, albeit reduced over the months, to convince the enemy that the Allies were about to put their troops into Europe, astride Boulogne, and that this was not just a landing but a large-scale bid to liberate the occupied countries, starting with France and pushing far and deep into Nazi-run territory.

Pressure was mounting for a 'Second Front', especially from Russia but also within Britain, where *The Times* reported the criticism in a Soviet fortnightly review that bombing operations in Europe were not taking the place of a second front, 'with regard to which the obligations of our allies are still awaiting fulfilment'.[35] Mrs Churchill, wife of the British premier, on the eve of her Aid to Russia Fund flag day, reminded people in Britain that 220 enemy divisions had been pinned down on the vast Russian front. Russian troops, she declared, were no longer on the defensive, having wrested the initiative from the enemy.[36]

There was no possibility of an invasion of northern Europe in 1943, but the Germans had to be made to take the opposite view. If the ruse was a success, a substantial part of the German air force would have been eliminated in the process and enemy influence eased on Allied moves in the Russian and Mediterranean theatres of war. It was evident at the time that it did not achieve the desired effect: the Germans, for whatever reason, just refused to take the bait.

Following *Operation Starkey*, two hypotheses were considered among the military planners in the armed services. One was that the enemy may have had information that the extent of the Army participation in this operation amounted to little more than an administrative exercise. The other was that the enemy were firmly convinced that there could be no serious threat from Britain at that time – that, therefore, a full-scale landing on the beaches of the Pas de Calais was not intended. It is particularly interesting, therefore, to find now that a typewritten manuscript produced as an 'historical record of deception in the war against Germany and Italy' claims the *Cockade* episode to have been 'extremely successful'. (It will be remembered that *Cockade* was the umbrella designation for the three concurrent but separate operations of that era: *Starkey* and the two purely deception activities known as *Wadham* and *Tindall* – see p. 5).

That verdict appears in a London Controlling Section file held in the Public Record Office at Kew (CAB 154/100), in the course of which it calls into question the undue emphasis placed on bringing the German Air Force to battle in anticipation of an 'Armageddon-of-the-Air' – its 'unfortunate prominence' causing the nomination of RAF Fighter Command's top man to run *Starkey* and the main issue – deceiving the enemy – to be obscured. This was a view from outside the armed services, LCS being a planning section set up in October 1941 under the Chiefs of Staff.

It is apparent from this source that the now much-publicized double-agent *Garbo* had a significant responsibility within *Starkey*: it was his job, for a period of some two months, to persuade the German Secret Service (who obviously considered him to be '*their*' man!) that the Allies intended an assault on the Pas de Calais. Then, when the Culminating Phase came and went without a single landing craft nosing closer than 10 miles off the Boulogne–Le Touquet coastline, he had to retrieve the situation and maintain credibility by convincing those same people that the Allies' explanation was typically a pack of lies. The LCS manuscript tells how he did it . . . it was, he told his German 'masters', British propaganda designed to cover incompetence and muddle before and during embarkation.

With the benefit of authenticated post-war information, LCS asserts that the Germans considered an Allied assault on France to have been much more of a possibility than the Allies thought at the time of *Starkey*. To high-ranking German officers it was a 'strong possibility' although they were 'far from sure' that the assault would take place in the Pas de Calais. So, if *Starkey* is now accepted as being *primarily* an integral part of the overall deception strategy in that phase of the war against Germany and Italy, with the demolition of the GAF *secondary* in intent, *Starkey* stands revealed as having exerted a more effective influence on the Allies' fortunes than its military commanders conceded in their post-*Starkey* reports. Certainly this operation is entitled to a share of the credit in one aspect where the LCS history is quite explicit: that the deception strategy succeeded in its objective to hold, in France, during the summer and autumn of 1943, some 40 German divisions 'which could profitably have been used elsewhere'.

Garbo's activities on a wider scale are described in a published post-war history, *British Intelligence in the Second World War*, vol. 5; where Sir Michael Howard deals with Strategic Deception, it is noted that while the deception staffs failed to persuade the Germans that the feint attack across the Channel on 9 September 1943 was a serious venture, deception activities in the UK 'had convinced at least von Rundstedt of the probability, even the imminence, of an invasion attempt, and he remained so convinced until late November'.

In that late summer of 1943, even if bad weather curbed German aerial reconnaissance which would have substantiated what *Garbo* was meant to be passing on (also, presumably, via organized 'leaks' in neutral countries), it may still have looked as though preparations were well advanced for an Allied landing in France, for a number of reasons including that of timing. The Quebec Conference was taking place during August, its chief purpose to intensify the war in all theatres where British, American and Dominion services were engaged; all enemy resistance in Sicily was at an end; and, openly and boldly, areas on the English coast closest to

France had been declared restricted to visitors. As people say these days, 'it was all happening' while *Starkey* gathered momentum.

It is the deception element at the root of the Le Portel bombardment that makes the calamity all the more hard to accept. Even with such a heavy toll, discovering that this was the 'real thing' would have made their anguish a touch more palatable. In Normandy, when eventually the Allies did set foot on the Continent in strength sufficient to link with the Russians forging forward from the east, French civilians were killed and their property destroyed. It could not be helped; it was war. Lives had been laid down for a reason – a reason that was there for all to see now that the jackboots were gone, now that the laughter was back.

Searching for some justification for the tragedy of Le Portel, no parallel appears to exist between the suffering sustained in Normandy and that in Le Portel. The landings on 6 June 1944 were announced while in progress, and the Allies' intentions were plain, so there should have been no doubts among the French that German positions would be attacked on land and from the air. Short of a reversal of fortune, the Allies would advance and the Germans would retreat. The landings were the beginning of the end, with liberation a virtual certainty, village by village, town by town, right through France and the rest of occupied Europe. Obviously there were risks to French lives – they could find themselves in the firing line twice over, facing both the Allies and the Germans, despite the euphoria of fast-approaching freedom after four years of oppression.

In Le Portel, nine months before the invasion of Normandy, the situation bore no similarity with what their countrymen would experience as the first gliders swished overhead, the first paratroops arrived, the first landing craft neared the beaches and the first bombs fell on German coastal defence positions. Families in Normandy knew what was happening; families in Le Portel were totally unaware what was going on other than that bombs from Allied aircraft were destroying their homes, and killing and injuring relatives and friends. The information gap was as wide as the English Channel – if the English knew what was going on, they certainly were not channelling the facts! Throughout *Starkey*, none of the leaflet-dropping missions carried out by the RAF was even remotely close to the Boulogne region.[37] If any indication went to a unit of the French Resistance which could have been relayed in part to any of the Portelois, it is highly questionable whether that version of the truth would have satisfied the Portelois, let alone pacified them in their night of terror when the bombs screamed down. Why did it begin, when would it end?

There was nothing to be done but to stay put in the shelters or carry on with the civil defence duties. There was no indication as to the purpose of the aerial assault or its length. No one knew when the bombers would be gone; and, once everything was comparatively quiet again, no one knew if another wave would be on its way. If some thought that an Allied landing was in prospect, or were aware that underground organizations must 'stay their hand' until London told them what to do, they were completely in the dark about timescales and locations. If the port facilities in the greater Boulogne area were thought to be the bombers' targets, this suggested that this was not where the landings would take place – the Allies would surely want to safeguard docks as important as Boulogne rather than smash them to pieces!

Some Portelois guessed that the bombing could well be the prelude to a landing, a landing somewhere else in the Pas de Calais perhaps. Anyone seeing evidence of an armada approaching the French coast on the morning after the night of bombing could have been forgiven for assuming a landing was in progress. They could not have known that it was 'play-acting' and that already the enemy had seen through the deception, the prime objectives of *Starkey* thus unachieved.

By then, however, Le Portel was in the throes of total evacuation, so the worst was over for the townspeople. If the Allies were coming, the Portelois would learn about it all in good time; just as they would learn precisely why their friends across the water had destroyed so many of their number – destroyed in body, yes, but not, fortunately, in spirit.

To blame was the British-led *Operation Starkey*, an ambitious move to hoax the enemy at a time when the Allies were too weak to mount a real assault against the heavily defended coast of northern France. In southern England, many thousands of British and Canadian soldiers assembled; the British and American air forces flew record numbers of sorties across the Channel; and the Royal Navy masterminded convoys comprising a remarkable assortment of vessels from motor launches to ocean-going merchant ships, heading as if to disgorge an army on the beaches south of Boulogne. In the midst of all these multifarious activities, Le Portel became an unexpected focus for just two reasons: its geographical location and its adjacent armament.

The nearby gun batteries at Fort de Couppes and Cap d'Alprech had been targeted as menacing an invasion fleet that carried no invaders; the planes sent to attack those guns dropped far more high-explosive bombs on civilian property than on military fortifications; and for every casualty among the occupying German forces, the French population suffered more than a hundredfold[38] – accidental obliteration, needless slaughter. For while pretence spawned the circumstances that led to the bombardment, the consequential death and destruction was real enough.

In the time since Prof. Jones dismissed any suggestion that the bombardment of Le Portel was a deliberate act, the considerable weight of material assembled for the foregoing pages has clarified its purpose and its implementation. Nevertheless, the professor's concluding words to the Portelois remain as fitting a tribute to the victims today as they did when they were published in the commemorative booklet that Mayor Barbarin initiated for the fortieth anniversary back in 1983.

Jones indicated that the Allied Air Forces learned from what he described as 'the mistake' and 'were thus led to improve their techniques to the stage where they contributed so effectively to the D-Day landings'. So, in a sense, he wrote, 'we should remember the citizens of Le Portel as among those whose sacrifice helped ensure the success of the invasion when it came'.

When the invasion did come, early on the morning of 6 June 1944, on the beaches of Normandy, it was as if *Starkey* had turned full circle. There was another deception operation, again involving Boulogne. The Mosquitoes of 109 and 105 Squadrons were in action, target-marking again; their targets and those of Main Force were coastal gun batteries, again; and, just as before, there was Oboe.

First came the fresh deception which centred on Boulogne. Coincidentally, it involved one of the very squadrons, 218 (Gold Coast) Squadron,[39] which took part both in Phase I and Phase II of Bomber Command's night-time assaults aimed at *Religion* and *Andante*. Then, 11 Stirlings participated. This time, starting at 2339 hours on 5 June, 8 Stirlings were airborne – not for bombing but for a more peaceful mission intended (shades of *Starkey!*) to make the Germans believe that Boulogne would provide the invasion beaches for the Allies already packed in the landing craft.

Operation Glimmer was the codename for this deception plan, which required 6 Stirlings (with 2 in reserve) to fly precise patterns in the night sky, the crews dropping huge quantities of aluminium foil when following a series of predetermined rectangular courses, each one taking the aircraft closer to the French coast. Below them, motor launches towed barrage balloons, each fitted with a radar-reflector device, the combined air-sea activities contributing to this deception. Planned to tolerances of seconds in time and to yards in distance, this ingenious scheme aimed to make the enemy radar system believe that a large convoy of ships was approaching Boulogne, steaming surely and steadily forward at an appropriately credible speed, and obviously crammed full with battle-ready soldiers making for the shore.

For a bombing mission, Stirlings carried a crew of seven; for this operation, 218 Squadron mustered as many as thirteen in each plane, the additional crew members including a second pilot plus second and third navigators. *Glimmer* demanded an exceptionally high degree of accuracy to achieve the intricate manoeuvring, and following the navigators' instructions placed unusually heavy demands on the 'man in the driving seat'. As well as the two pilots, the three navigators, flight engineer, wireless operator/air gunner, mid-upper gunner and rear gunner, there were four extra crew members on board each aircraft, all dedicated to the timed release of the foil, which went by the name of Window.

Three Stirlings – N-Nuts, K-King and A-Apple – were airborne within the space of 5 minutes, followed by two reserve aircraft – U-Uncle and E-Edward – taking off together at 2350 hours. Just an hour after the first Stirlings had achieved 'wheels-up', the first of the remaining trio was off – I-Ink at 0039 hours, then G-George at 0042 hours and F-Freddie at 0043 hours. It would be gone 0500 hours (when the first troops were becoming established on Normandy soil) before the Stirlings were all back home again, their mission completed 'without incident', according to the squadron's operations record book.

The commissioned and non-commissioned officers of 218 Squadron provided an interesting international blend: there were five Australians and three New Zealanders among the sixteen pilots and second pilots that night; and in U-Uncle the New Zealand pilot had an Australian second pilot, plus another Australian and three Canadians in his crew. Most of the pilots and most of the second pilots had captained aircraft which were more lethally operational the previous month: some took Stirlings on mine-laying flights; some bombed Chambly, the main railway stores and repair depot for the northern France system; and at least one pilot separately laid mines and bombed. The Chambly raid, which Pathfinder Force's 'Master of Ceremonies' was heard to describe as 'Wizard bombing', put the depot completely out of action for ten days. After sea mines and high-explosive bombs, carrying and releasing aluminium foil must have seemed odd to say the least!

Glimmer did more than produce a mere ray of hope to safeguard the Allies' fortunes in Normandy that morning of 6 June 1944; it confused the enemy exactly as had been intended. The ghost fleet prompted the Germans to despatch reconnaissance sorties by air and sea without, not surprisingly, signs of any Boulogne-bound boats.[40] From German records it appears that daylight arrived before the invasion threat to Boulogne was dismissed, by which time real convoys of troop-carrying vessels were off Normandy.

While 218 Squadron was performing so patiently over the Channel, edging ever-nearer to Boulogne (and 617 Squadron's Lancasters were doing much the same near Le Havre in *Operation Taxable*), 109 and 105 Squadrons were despatching a record number of their Pathfinder Mosquitoes to mark ten coastal gun batteries threatening the oncoming invasion convoys – an echo of these squadrons' activities in *Starkey* nine months previously. Only two of those ten targets for Bomber Command were free of cloud that night – La Pernelle and Ouistreham – all other bombing being entirely based on Oboe-marking. Some 946 bombers dropped at least 5,000 tons – a record tonnage in a single night at that stage of the war.[41]

A message to participating crews from 'Bomber' Harris, through the Air Officer Commanding, Pathfinder Force, and retained for posterity in 105 Squadron's operations record book, noted: 'You did famously last night in the face of no mean difficulties.' Fire from the coastal batteries 'which were your targets' was reported to have been 'virtually negligible'. He did not mention that one of the gun positions, Merville, 7 miles from Caen, called for additional treatment beyond that of his bombers. It was known to menace the entire eastern flank of the Normandy beaches, where the British and Canadians were due to go ashore, so parachute and glider-borne troops were sent in post-bombardment to ensure that this threat no longer existed.

The D-Day landings have been well documented so, finally, back to the people of Le Portel and their sacrifice of fifty-plus years ago. For sacrificed they were, sacrificed to subterfuge, sacrificed in a tragic yet ironically ineffectual milestone down the long, long road to peace in Europe and victory for the Allies in the Second World War.

It surely was a sacrifice – sacrificed to *Starkey* – that 'comparatively futile operation', that 'piece of harmless play-acting' in the 'D-Day that never was' in the late summer of 1943.

APPENDICES

Appendix I: Key targets on map GSGS 4040 Sheet 49

Religion

9(A)/37	Boulogne/Le Portel	653525*	3 x 21 cm guns in turrets on open concrete platforms; range about 35,000 yards (20 miles); site about 350 yards square. Estimated bomb hits: 32 by day and 20 by night.
9(A)/38	Boulogne/Moulin Bleu	659529	6 x 8.8 cm AA/CD dual-purpose guns on roofs of concrete shelters; range probably 16,000 yards (10 miles); site about 200 yards square. Estimated bomb hits: 25 by day and 11 by night.
8(H)/46	Le Portel	653525*	Subsidiary gun positions – size, type and quantity unspecified in *Starkey* documentation.

*Identical pinpoints
Aiming point for night attack: 657528   Primary target: 653525

Andante

9(A)/34	Boulogne/Cap d'Alprech	650512	4 x 15 cm guns in open concrete circular emplacements; range about 25,000 yards (14 miles); site about 400 yards square. Estimated bomb hits: 14 by day and 17 by night.
9(A)/35	Boulogne/Mont Soleil	660515*	6 x 8.8 cm AA/CD dual-purpose guns in open square emplacements; range about 17,600 yards (10 miles); site about 200 yards square. Estimated bomb hits: 29 by day and 23 by night.
8(H)/43	Boulogne (S)	665507	Six-gun battery, size and type unspecified in *Starkey* documentation; site about 370 yards square. Estimated bomb hits: 2 by day and 8 by night.
8(H)/45	Le Portel	660515*	Six-gun battery, size and type unspecified in *Starkey* documentation.

*Identical pinpoints
Aiming point and primary target for night attack: 650512

Notes: 1. Targets with a serial number commencing with the figure '9' were on list 9, coastal and railway artillery for attack by US heavy bombers by day and by RAF heavy bombers by night. Targets with a serial number commencing with the figure '8' were on list 8, enemy beach defences for attack by RAF light and medium bombers and US medium bombers. 2. Air Ministry clearance was given for all of the above targets from lists 8 and 9 except that 8(H)/43 in *Andante* and 8(H)/46 in *Religion* 'should be attacked by day only'.

Appendix II: Operation Starkey *timetable of key events*

14.1.43 Churchill and Roosevelt open Casablanca Conference; decision taken to carry out deception scheme to pin enemy in West and keep alive expectations of large-scale cross-Channel operations in 1943.

26.4.43 Directive to Lt-Gen. Frederick Morgan (COSSAC) to plan (a) amphibious feint to bring air battle with German air force, (b) return to Continent in event of German disintegration at any time; and (c) full-scale assault against Continent in 1944.

24.5.43 Combining first two objectives, Morgan presents plan for August/September operation involving Army, Navy, RAF and US Air Force in preparations consistent with assault on Boulogne.

17.6.43 Codenamed *Starkey*, this ambitious operation is now limited by War Cabinet Joint Planning Staff to purely deceptive measures involving no plans for a re-entry into the Continent.

26.6.43 Morgan issues document detailing background, purpose and implementation stages to *Starkey*, envisaging largest possible number of landing craft in Channel by 1 September.

7.7.43 Air Marshal Sir Trafford Leigh-Mallory, AOC-in-C Fighter Command, chairs first *Starkey* conference, to which Air Chief Marshal Sir Arthur T. Harris, having earlier assumed no active part for his bombers, sends wing commander to liaise.

16.7.43 *Starkey* muscle power diminishes when Morgan told to assume no battleships available, and not to count on large diversion of bomber effort from air offensive against Germany.

11.8.43 Bomber Command examination of prospective *Starkey* targets among coastal artillery between Calais and Boulogne shows 11,000 bombing sorties needed to neutralize all but four batteries that are judged invulnerable to attack from the air.

16.8.43 Preliminary Phase begins, ending 24.8.43, with troop movements, landing craft assembling, glider fleets visible on airfields and restrictions on civilians in south/south-east coastal areas.

24.8.43 Air Ministry issues *Starkey* orders to 'Bomber' Harris, who protests that this operation is play-acting and comparatively futile – an intolerable diversion at peak of bombing offensive.

25.8.43 Preparatory Phase begins, ending 8.9.43, with disappointingly few air attacks possible due to unsuitable weather – while enemy reaction ranges from nil to cautious.

27.8.43 As result of further examination of *Starkey* plan, Air Ministry revises earlier orders to Bomber Command, reducing effort from Harris's heavies against enemy coastal batteries. Bombardment policy against objectives in occupied territories having been drawn to attention of *Starkey* participants – policy to avoid undue civilian casualties – 11 lists of potential targets sent to Air Ministry for clearance.

28.8.43 Morgan queries justification for continuing *Starkey*; unfavourable weather hampering both sides – puts limit on air reconnaissance which would alert enemy to Allied intentions.

1.9.43 British minesweepers under fire from enemy's long-range guns; first *Starkey* death at sea.

4.9.43 German intelligence service said to have reported operation about to be launched from UK, probably against Channel ports. Chiefs of Staff decide against abandoning *Starkey*; Churchill, out of Britain seeing US President again, receives this news and sends them good-luck message.

6.9.43 RAF Mission in Moscow instructed to let Russians into secret of *Operation Starkey* deception scheme and to warn them against being taken in by German propaganda of failed landings.

7.9.43 'D-Day' for *Starkey* postponed from 8.9.43 to 9.9.43 because of unsuitable weather. As on previous night, Bomber Command cancels plans for heavy bomber assault on coastal guns.

8.9.43 Weather shows improvement so Culminating Phase sees RAF/USAAF bombers begin attacks against seven big-gun batteries most likely to engage assault convoy sailing towards French coast next morning. Among them are two close to Le Portel, judged 'most dangerous' guns.

9.9.43 Convoy comprising 355 ships sails in daylight to within 10 miles of coast between Boulogne and Le Touquet; turns back as planned. No reaction from enemy planes, ships or guns. *Starkey* ends.

Appendix III: Starkey *bombing operations in the three phases*

Preliminary Phase, 16 to 24 August

Date	US aircraft	tons	RAF aircraft	tons	Target
16.8.43	297	551	28	18	airfields
			36	36	various
17.8.43	64	75	24	12	airfields
			9	10	various
18.8.43	50	69			airfields
19.8.43	126	238	12	24	airfields
			23	35	various
20.8.43	35	51			airfields
			24	48	various
24.8.43	108	287			airfields
Totals:	680	1,271	156	183	

Airfields were attacked by 680 US aircraft, dropping 1,271 tons of bombs, and by 64 RAF aircraft, dropping 54 tons, a total of 744 aircraft dropping 1,325 tons. Transportation, industrial and other targets were attacked by 92 RAF aircraft, dropping 129 tons.

Preparatory Phase, 25 August to 8 September

Date	US aircraft	tons	RAF aircraft	tons	Target
25.8.43	31	44	36	47	airfields
	21	31			various
26.8.43	36	46			airfields
27.8.43	35	51			airfields
	183	368	5	5	various
30.8.43	34	48	41	61	various
31.8.43	141	364	24	35	airfields
	33	43			various
1.9.43			10	10	various
2.9.43	35	104			airfields
	105	133	56	60	various
3.9.43	311	773			airfields
	20	60	42	58	various
4.9.43	125	164	126	182	various
5.9.43			26	15	airfields
	63	83			various
6.9.43	201	297	56	86	various
7.9.43	104	311	8	2	airfields
	140	295	26	36	various
8.9.43	136	200	24	39	airfields
			17	21	various
4 nights			143	272	forest dumps
Totals:	1,754	3,415	640	929	

Airfields were attacked by 829 US aircraft, dropping 1,893 tons of bombs, and by 118 RAF aircraft, dropping 138 tons, a total of 947 aircraft dropping 2,031 tons. Transportation, industrial and other targets were attacked by 925 US aircraft, dropping 1,522 tons, and by 522 RAF aircraft, dropping 791 tons, a total of 1,447 aircraft dropping 2,313 tons.

Culminating Phase, 8 and 9 September

Date	US aircraft	tons	RAF aircraft	tons	Target
8.9.43	68	90	32	35	gun sites (day)
8.9.43	5	10	244	668	gun sites (night)
9.9.43	202	300	70	79	gun sites (day)
9.9.43	331	611	70	65	airfields (day)
Totals:	606	1,011	416	847	

Airfields were attacked by 331 US aircraft, dropping 611 tons of bombs, and by 70 RAF aircraft, dropping 65 tons, a total of 401 aircraft dropping 676 tons. Gun sites were attacked by 275 US aircraft, dropping 400 tons of bombs, and by 346 RAF aircraft, dropping 782 tons, a total of 621 aircraft dropping 1,182 tons.

Grand Totals: 3,040 US aircraft, dropping 5,697 tons of bombs; and 1,212 RAF aircraft, dropping 1,959 tons; a total of 4,252 aircraft dropping 7,656 tons during the three phases of *Operation Starkey*.

Appendix IV: *USAAF attacks by day on coastal guns/beach defences*

8 September 1943

1715	18 Marauders	323 Group	107 x 500 lb	*Religion*
1800	18 Marauders	387 Group	108 x 500 lb	*Andante*
1804	14 Marauders	322 Group	79 x 500 lb	*Pomeranian*
1813	18 Marauders	386 Group	108 x 500 lb	*Pomeranian*

9 September 1943

0745	18 Marauders	322 Group	108 x 500 lb	*Religion*
0747	17 Marauders	322 Group	96 x 500 lb; 6 x 600 lb	*Andante*
0800	17 Marauders	322 Group	78 x 600 lb; 24 x 500 lb	*Millstone*
0800	15 Marauders	323 Group	90 x 600 lb	*Pomeranian*
0815	16 Marauders	323 Group	88 x 600 lb; 6 x 500 lb	*Religion*
0815	18 Marauders	323 Group	108 x 600 lb	*Andante*
0829	18 Marauders	386 Group	96 x 500 lb; 12 x 600 lb	*Pomeranian*
0845	18 Marauders	387 Group	102 x 600 lb; 6 x 500 lb	*Millstone*
0846	18 Marauders	386 Group	90 x 500 lb; 12 x 600 lb	*Religion*
0846	17 Marauders	386 Group	87 x 500 lb; 18 x 600 lb	*Andante*
0915	13 Marauders	387 Group	72 x 600 lb; 6 x 500 lb	*Religion*
0915	17 Marauders	387 Group	96 x 600 lb; 6 x 500 lb	*Andante*

Notes: 1. A combined total of 547,000 lb of high explosives (1,014 bombs/244.20 tons) was dropped by day against *Religion* and *Andante* on 8 and 9 September; it compares with 2,243 bombs (678.10 tons) dropped by night on 8/9 September and gives a 'grand total' of 3,257 HE bombs (922.30 tons) unleashed against these two targets either side of Le Portel. 2. A further quantity of HE landed in the town on 4 September, but the number and weight must stay unrecorded – this bombing was not intended for the Le Portel area. It is not unreasonable to determine that some 1,000 tons of HE devastated this seaside resort on 4, 8 and 9 September 1943.

Appendix V: *RAF attacks by day on coastal guns/beach defences*

8 September 1943

1742	7 Whirlwinds	263 Squadron	14 × 250 lb	*Menagerie*
1745	12 Mitchells	98 Squadron	45 x 1,000 lb	*Pumicestone*
1745	6 Mitchells	180 Squadron	24 x 1,000 lb	*Millstone*
1802	7 Typhoons	181 Squadron	14 x 500 lb	*Menagerie*

9 September 1943

0726	6 Mitchells	98 Squadron	24 x 1,000 lb	*Pumicestone*
0730	6 Venturas	21 Squadron	36 x 500 lb	*Pumicestone*
0730	6 Mitchells	180 Squadron	23 x 1,000 lb	*Millstone*
0730	6 Mitchells	320 Squadron	24 x 1,000 lb	*Pomeranian*
0738	6 Mitchells	98 Squadron	17 x 500 lb; 17 x 500 lb/30 minute delay	*Pumicestone*
0740	6 Venturas	21 Squadron	24 x 250 lb; 24 x 250 lb/30 minute delay	*Pumicestone*
0745	5 Mitchells	180 Squadron	20 x 500 lb; 20 x 500 lb/30 minute delay	*Millstone*
0745	6 Mitchells	320 Squadron	45 x 500 lb	*Pomeranian*
0831	11 Whirlwinds	263 Squadron	20 x 250 lb	*Menagerie*
0900	12 Typhoons	3 Squadron	23 x 500 lb	*Menagerie*

Note: Combined RAF and USAAF bomb loads dropped on *Pomeranian* (111.25 tons), *Millstone* (84.82 tons), *Pumicestone* (51.79 tons) and *Menagerie* (12.05 tons) amounted to 582,200 lb (259.91 tons); this compares with 922.30 tons on *Religion* and *Andante*.

Appendix VI: RAF attacks by night on coastal guns

Bomber Command and the target-marking by its Pathfinder planes on 8 September 1943:
Phase I (*Religion*), zero hour 2200 hours (Time, Squadron, Aircraft Type + Letter, TI colour)

Time	Intended marking (15 planes)	Actual marking (9 planes)
2158	109 Mosquito Red	
2159		
2200	109 Mosquito Green	
2201	35 Halifax Green	
2202	405 Halifax Green	109 Mosquito 'W' Green
2203	35 Halifax Green	
2204	105 Mosquito Green	
2205	35 Halifax Green	405 Halifax 'K' Green
2206	405 Halifax Green	
2207	35 Halifax Green	
2208	109 Mosquito Red	109 Mosquito 'H' Red
		35 Halifax 'R' Green
2209	35 Halifax Green	405 Halifax 'G' Green
		35 Halifax 'E' Green
2210		
2211	405 Halifax Green	405 Halifax 'N' Green
		35 Halifax 'X' Green
2212	109 Mosquito Green	
2213	35 Halifax Green	109 Mosquito 'V' Green
2214	35 Halifax Green	
2215	End of Phase I	

Bomber Command and the target-marking by its Pathfinder planes on 8 September 1943:
Phase II (*Andante*), zero hour 2245 hours (Time, Squadron, Aircraft Type + Letter, TI colour)

Time	Intended marking (15 planes)	Actual marking (11 planes)
2243	109 Mosquito Red	109 Mosquito 'S' Green
		109 Mosquito 'E' Red
2244		
2245	109 Mosquito Green	
2246	35 Halifax Green	35 Halifax 'R' Green
		35 Halifax 'M' Green
2247	405 Halifax Green	35 Halifax 'Z' Green
2248	35 Halifax Green	
2249	105 Mosquito Green	
2250	35 Halifax Green	
2251	405 Halifax Green	405 Halifax 'G' Green
2252	35 Halifax Green	35 Halifax 'G' Green
2253	109 Mosquito Red	35 Halifax 'E' Green
2254	35 Halifax Green	109 Mosquito 'R' Green
2255		405 Halifax 'N' Green
2256	405 Halifax Green	
2257	109 Mosquito Green	
2258	35 Halifax Green	
2259	35 Halifax Green	35 Halifax 'A' Green
2300	End of Phase II	

Appendix VII: RAF attacks by night on coastal guns, Phase I

Bomber Command and the contribution of participating Groups on 8 September 1943:
Phase I (*Religion*), 2200–2215 hours (Units, Location, Aircraft, Bombs Dropped)

3 Group

57 Stirlings (53 effective)   225.9 tons   378 x 1,000 lb + 256 x 500 lb = 506,000 lb   Phase I

15 Squadron: 8 Stirlings effective from Mildenhall, Suffolk   Phase I
75 Squadron: 8 Stirlings effective from Mepal, Cambridgeshire   Phase I
90 Squadron: 10 Stirlings effective from Wratting Common, Cambridgeshire   Phase I
196 Squadron: 4 Stirlings effective from Witchford, Cambridgeshire   Phase I
199 Squadron: 8 Stirlings effective from Lakenheath, Suffolk   Phase I
218 Squadron: 7 Stirlings effective from Downham Market, Norfolk   Phase I
620 Squadron: 8 Stirlings effective from Chedburgh, Suffolk   Phase I

8 Group, Pathfinders

10 Halifaxes (9 effective)   18.3 tons   31 x 1,000 lb + 20 x 500 lb = 41,000 lb   Phase I
                               1.3 tons (TIs – incendiaries)   12 x 250 lb   Phase I
6 Mosquitoes (3 effective)   1.3 tons (TIs – incendiaries)   12 x 250 lb   Phase I

35 Squadron: 6 Halifaxes effective from Graveley, Huntingdonshire (3 for target-marking; 6 for bombing)   Phase I
105 Squadron: Nil Mosquitoes effective from Marham, Norfolk   Phase I
109 Squadron: 3 Mosquitoes effective from Marham, Norfolk (all for target-marking)   Phase I
405 Squadron: 3 Halifaxes effective from Gransden Lodge, Bedfordshire (3 for target-marking; 3 for bombing)   Phase I

91 Group

22 Wellingtons (19 effective)   29.0 tons   130 x 500 lb = 65,000 lb

15 OTU: 2 Wellingtons effective from Harwell, Berkshire   Phase I
22 OTU: 8 Wellingtons effective from Wellesbourne, Warwickshire   Phase I
23 OTU: 9 Wellingtons effective from Stratford and Pershore, Worcestershire   Phase I

93 Group

39 Wellingtons (35 effective)   57.8 tons   259 x 500 lb = 129,500 lb

18 OTU: 9 Wellingtons effective from Finningley, Nottinghamshire   Phase I
27 OTU: 8 Wellingtons effective from Lichfield, Staffordshire   Phase I
28 OTU: 7 Wellingtons effective from Castle Donnington and Wymeswold, Leicestershire   Phase I
30 OTU: 2 Wellingtons effective from Hixon, Staffordshire   Phase I
82 OTU: 9 Wellingtons effective from Ossington and Bircotes, Nottinghamshire   Phase I

Combined force of operational squadrons and operational training units

Halifaxes*	10 detailed	9 effective	18.3 tons + 1.3 tons (TIs)	Phase I
Mosquitoes	6 detailed	3 effective	1.3 tons (TIs)	Phase I

*The same 10 Halifaxes were also detailed for Phase II

Wellingtons	61 detailed	54 effective	86.8 tons	Phase I
Stirlings	57 detailed	53 effective	225.9 tons	Phase I
USAAF				
Fortresses	5 detailed	5 effective	9.6 tons	Phase I

Totals:	139 planes	124 sorties	340.6 tons (HE)	Phase I

Appendix VIII: RAF attacks by night on coastal guns, Phase II

Bomber Command and the contribution of participating Groups on 8 September 1943:
Phase II (*Andante*), 2245–2300 hours (Units, Location, Aircraft, Bombs Dropped)

1 Group
24 Wellingtons (23 effective)   45.5 tons   2 x 4,000 lb + 188 x 500 lb = 102,000 lb

166 Squadron: 10 Wellingtons effective from Kirmington, Lincolnshire   Phase II
300 Squadron: 13 Wellingtons effective from Ingham, Lincolnshire   Phase II

3 Group
55 Stirlings (51 effective)   219.7 tons   355 x 1,000 lb + 274 x 500 lb = 492,000 lb   Phase II

15 Squadron: 2 Stirlings effective from Mildenhall, Suffolk   Phase II
75 Squadron: 7 Stirlings effective from Mepal, Cambridgeshire   Phase II
90 Squadron: 10 Stirlings effective from Wratting Common, Cambridgeshire   Phase II
149 Squadron: 9 Stirlings effective from Lakenheath, Suffolk   Phase II
196 Squadron: 3 Stirlings effective from Witchford, Cambridgeshire   Phase II
214 Squadron: 8 Stirlings effective from Chedburgh, Suffolk   Phase II
218 Squadron: 4 Stirlings effective from Downham Market, Norfolk   Phase II
622 Squadron: 5 Stirlings effective from Mildenhall, Suffolk   Phase II
623 Squadron: 3 Stirlings effective from Downham Market, Norfolk   Phase II

6 Group
12 Wellingtons (12 effective)   23.2 tons   104 x 500 lb = 52,000 lb

432 Squadron: 12 Wellingtons effective from Skipton-on-Swale, Yorkshire   Phase II

8 Group, Pathfinders
10 Halifaxes (10 effective)   17.4 tons   19 x 1,000 lb + 40 x 500 lb = 39,000 lb   Phase II
                              2.0 tons (TIs – incendiaries)   18 x 250 lb   Phase II
10 Mosquitoes (7 effective)   3.1 tons   12 x 500 + 4 x 250 lb = 7,000 lb   Phase II
                              1.3 tons (TIs – incendiaries)   12 x 250 lb   Phase II

35 Squadron: 7 Halifaxes effective from Graveley, Huntingdonshire (6 for target-marking;   Phase II
7 for bombing)
105 Squadron: 4 Mosquitoes effective from Marham, Norfolk (all for bombing)   Phase II
109 Squadron: 3 Mosquitoes effective from Marham, Norfolk (all for target-marking)   Phase II
405 Squadron: 3 Halifaxes effective from Gransden Lodge, Bedfordshire (2 for target-   Phase II
marking; 3 for bombing)

92 Group
23 Wellingtons (22 effective)   28.6 tons   128 x 500 lb = 64,000 lb

12 OTU: 5 Wellingtons effective from Chipping Warden, Oxfordshire   Phase II
16 OTU: 4 Wellingtons effective from Upper Heyford, Oxfordshire   Phase II
17 OTU: 5 Wellingtons effective from Upwood, Huntingdonshire   Phase II
26 OTU: 4 Wellingtons effective from Wing, Buckinghamshire   Phase II
29 OTU: 4 Wellingtons effective from Bruntingthorpe, Leicestershire   Phase II

Combined force of operational squadrons and operational training units

Halifaxes	10 detailed	10 effective	17.4 tons + 2.0 tons (TIs)	Phase II
Mosquitoes	10 detailed	7 effective	3.1 tons + 1.3 tons (TIs)	Phase II
Wellingtons	59 detailed	57 effective	97.3 tons	Phase II
Stirlings	55 detailed	51 effective	219.7 tons	Phase II
Totals:	134 planes	125 sorties	337.5 tons (HE)	Phase II

Appendix IX: Starkey *bombing operations – targets and tonnages*

(During *Operation Starkey*, 16 August to 9 September 1943, the total tonnage of bombs dropped on all targets amounted to half as much again as RAF Bomber Command's record-breaking 5,000 tons in a single night – that of 5/6 June 1944, the eve of the 'D-Day' landings in Normandy.)

Proportion of bomb tonnage dropped by target type (7,656 tons overall)

Airfields received 4,032 tons

Transportation, industrial and other targets received 2,442 tons

Coastal guns and beach defences received 1,182 tons, more than three-quarters of this directed on the two sites closest to Le Portel, which were codenamed *Religion* and *Andante*

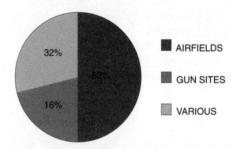

Proportion of bomb tonnage dropped by gun location (1,182 tons overall)

Religion and *Andante* received 678 tons by night

Religion and *Andante* received 244 tons by day

Pomeranian, Pumicestone, Millstone and *Menagerie* received a combined 260 tons, *Religion* and *Andante* together attracting 922 tons – an amount, within some 16 hours, equating to some 12 per cent of the total tonnage dropped throughout the entire *Starkey* bombing operations

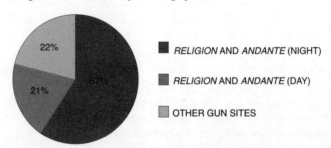

Bombs dropped by Pathfinders and Main Force by night on *Religion* and *Andante*

2 x 4000 lb	(3.6 tons)	783 x 1,000 lb	(349.5 tons)
1,411 x 500 lb	(314.9 tons)	4 x 250 lb	(0.5 tons)
TIs/incendiaries		54 x 250 lb	(5.9 tons)
US 8th Air Force		43 x 500 lb	(9.6 tons)

SOURCES

Chapter One

1 Archives at Le Portel Town Hall: Statistics 2.6.43, supplied in response to request by Boulogne-sur-Mer *Sous-Préfecture*.
2 PRO WO 106/4147 Encl 62A Personal Minute No. 271/3 dated 15.4.43 from Prime Minister to Chiefs of Staff.
3 PRO WO 106/4223 Encl 18A Annex to COS (43) 215 (0) dated 26.4.43 includes Directive issued to COSSAC.
4 Ibid.
5 PRO WO 106/4223 Encl 29A COSSAC (43) 5 dated 24.5.43, Para 2(ii).
6 PRO WO 106/4223 Encl 34B Joint Planning Staff Paper JP (43) 209 (Final) dated 17.6.43 details their objectives; and *Deception in World War II*, Charles Cruickshank, studies them.
7 PRO WO 106/4223 Encl. 29A COSSAC (43) 5 dated 24.5.43, Para 5.
8 PRO AIR 8/1202 COSSAC (43) 4 (Final) dated 26.6.43, Appreciation for Outline Plan, a 13-page, 91-paragraph document with 12 appendices and 5 maps, Outline Plan commencing Para 64; Assault Phase refers to potential commando attack against Le Portel. Distribution list indicates initial issue no more than 85 copies, such was need for secrecy.
9 PRO CAB 121/109 Encl 52A, also 52C where Ismay, referring to Churchill's memo dated 8.8.43, admits to colleague that 'the Prime Minister makes out a good case and we must do everything possible to fall in with his wishes'.
10 PRO DEFE 2/565 Annex II to COS (43) 337 (0) dated 23.6.43; Operation A was *Starkey*, B was *Wadham* and C was *Tindall*.
11 PRO AIR 8/1202 Appreciation for Outline Plan, Para 30.
12 Ibid, Appendix G, concentrating on beach surveys, notes that in general those north of Boulogne are shorter and have steeper gradients than those to south.
13 Ibid, Para 34.
14 Ibid, Para 53.
15 Ibid, Para 70.
16 Ibid, Para 3.

Chapter Two

1 PRO WO 106/4223 Encl 10A GHQ Home Forces letter HF/00/136/G (Plans) and reply from DDMO (H) War Office, both dated 31.3.43.
2 Ibid, Encl 32B COSSAC Paper (43) 15 (Final) dated 3.6.43 to Chiefs of Staff Committee, Para 7.
3 Ibid, Para 9.
4 Ibid, Encl 34B Joint Planning Staff Paper JP (43) 209 (Final) dated 17.6.43, Paras 10, 11 and 12.
5 Ibid, Para 43.
6 Ibid, Annex II.
7 Ibid, Para 40.
8 PRO CAB 122/1293 COS (43) 337 (0) dated 23.6.43 Annex I.
9 PRO WO 106/4223 Encl 34A Minutes of Chiefs of Staff Committee Meeting held 21.6.43, Para 9.
10 PRO AIR 8/1202 COSSAC (43) 4 (Final) dated 26.6.43 Appreciation for Outline Plan.
11 PRO WO 106/4223 Encl 33A Extract from Chiefs of Staff Committee Meeting held 17.6.43.
12 PRO AIR 20/4801 DDB Ops Note under cover of COSSAC/RAF/363 dated 30.6.43 recording

discussions involving RAF DB Ops and COSSAC HQ RAF Branch staff.

13 PRO AIR 9/187 Bombardment Policy contained in letter CS15803/ASP1 dated 29.10.42.

14 PRO AIR 8/1202 AOC-in-C Bomber Command Signal A201 to VCAS sent 25.8.43, Part I Para 1.

Chapter Three

1 PRO DEFE 2/458 Minutes of 1st *Starkey* Conference held 7.7.43.

2 *Overture to Overlord*, Lt-Gen. Sir Frederick Morgan KCB (COSSAC).

3 PRO DEFE 2/458 Minutes of 1st *Starkey* Conference.

4 PRO AIR 8/1202 Signal A201 to Air Ministry for attention VCAS sent 25.8.43 (1215 hours), Part I Paras 1 and 2.

5 PRO WO 106/4241 Encl 22C Letter BC/S30324/Ops to COSSAC dated 11.8.43.

6 PRO AIR 8/1202 Letter ATH/DO/4 to Portal dated 9.7.43 and 'Most Secret and Personal' letter to Harris dated 10.7.43.

7 PRO AIR 20/4801 Note from ACAS (Ops) to CAS, Ops 1/276 dated 7.7.43, reporting discussions with AOC-in-C Fighter Command, Norfolk House Planning Staff and Gen. Candee regarding diversion of bomber effort.

8 PRO DEFE 2/458 Memorandum by COSSAC to Chiefs of Staff Committee dated 19.8.43, Para 4 .

9 Ibid, Para 6.

10 PRO AIR 8/1202 Signal AX695 to AOC-in-C Bomber Command sent 24.8.43.

11 Ibid, Signal A201 sent 25.8.43 (1217 hours) to VCAS, Part II Paras 4 and 5.

12 Ibid, Signal A202 sent 25.8.43 (1701 hours) to Air Ministry.

13 PRO DEFE 2/458 Note by VCAS to Chiefs of Staff Committee dated 26.8.43.

14 PRO AIR 8/1202 Extract from Chiefs of Staff Committee Meeting held 27.8.43.

15 Ibid, Signal AX944 sent 27.8.43.

16 PRO DEFE 2/458 Extract from Chiefs of Staff Committee Meeting held 28.8.43.

17 Ibid, Air Ministry Signal AX694 sent 24.8.43; confirmation followed in AOC-in-C Fighter Command response signal AO785 sent 26.8.43.

18 PRO AIR 20/4201 File on warnings issued to civilian population includes authorization by Air Ministry to USAAF on 22.6.43 to commence 'precise attack by day' on targets in France and, later, Belgium and Holland.

19 PRO AIR 20/4801 Letter FC/KG/F27 dated 27.8.43 to Under Secretary of State, Air Ministry, copied to AOC No. 11 Group, requesting 'as early as possible' confirmation of clearance to attack.

20 PRO WO 205/447 GHQ Home Forces' letter A.Gp. 00/60/Ops dated 20.7.43 shows that choosing targets for *Starkey* bombers was 'greatly complicated' by these 'conflicting requirements'.

21 PRO AIR 20/4801 Air Ministry signal AX993 sent 27.8.43 (1859 hours); same-day response to above request.

22 PRO AIR 16/766 Report by Chief of Combined Operations to COSSAC dated 14.8.43.

23 PRO WO 106/4223 Encl 39C PWE Plan dated 8.7.43, PWP/C1.

24 Ibid.

Chapter Four

1 *The Times*, 16.8.43.

2 PRO CAB 122/1293 COS (43) 389 (0) dated 20.7.43.

3 PRO WO 106/4241 Encl 16A Combined Plan for *Operation Starkey*, Para 9.

4 PRO AIR 8/1202 Extract from Chiefs of Staff Committee Meeting held 28.7.43.

5 Ibid, Extract from Chiefs of Staff Committee Meeting held 12.8.43.

6 PRO ADM 179/275 J-Force Commanding Commodore Document No. 0850/5/1 dated 14.8.43.

7 PRO FO 898/373 COSSAC/00/2/2/Ops dated 6.8.43, Appendix E details construction of camps in assembly areas of Southern and South Eastern Commands for *Operation Starkey*.

8 *The Times*, 16.8.43.

9 PRO ADM 179/264 Post-*Starkey* Report by Officer Commanding, Dover.

10 PRO WO 106/4223 Encl 32A Minutes of Chiefs of Staff Committee Meeting held 8.6.43, Para 7

refers to expectation of heavy air attacks on assembly ports.

11 PRO FO 898/373 AOC-in-C Fighter Command's Weekly Progress Report No. 5 dated 2.9.43.

12 PRO ADM 179/271 Summary Report of Wireless Simulation, issued 9.9.43 to C-in-C Portsmouth (through Staff Signal Officer).

13 PRO CAB 80/73 COS (43) 470 (0) dated 16.8.43, Para 1(i), COSSAC reported enemy bomber effort over south coast unfortunately unavoidably cause of casualties and damage.

14 PRO FO 898/373 AOC-in-C Fighter Command's Weekly Progress Report No. 4 dated 26.8.43.

15 PRO AIR 20/4801 Air Force Commander's Report, 11G/S500/111/Ops dated 16.9.43, Paras 32 to 35 incl.

16 Ibid, Para 25.

17 PRO ADM 179/264 report by Lt-Cdr in command of minesweeper *Hydra*.

18 Ibid, report by RNVR Lt in command of attendant ship *Qualicum*.

19 PRO AIR 8/1202 Appreciation for Outline Plan, Appendix H concentrates on long-range coastal batteries in Pas de Calais.

Chapter Five

1 PRO AIR 8/1202 Extract from Chiefs of Staff Committee Meeting held 28.8.43.

2 Ibid, Extracts from Chiefs of Staff Committee Meeting held 4.9.43.

3 Ibid.

4 PRO WO 219/1856 COSSAC Army Intelligence Section Report on enemy reactions to Starkey over period August/October 1943.

5 PRO AIR 8/1202 Most Secret cypher telegram Concrete No. 736 sent 4.9.43 (1750 hours) from Chiefs of Staff to Prime Minister (attending Quebec Conference).

6 Ibid, Response message Welfare No. 616 sent 5.9.43 (0425 hours).

7 PRO AIR 20/4801 Air Force Commander's Report, 11G/S500/111/Ops dated 16.9.43, Para 67.

8 PRO DEFE 2/565 Naval Operation Order No. 1 dated 21.8.43, Appendix D gives names and meaning of signals to execute *Starkey*.

9 PRO AIR 20/4801 Target List, accompanying Air Commodore Strafford's letter FC/KG/F27 dated 27.8.43, includes dates and references in respect of existing photographic cover.

10 Ibid, Air Ministry signal AX993, same-day response (27.8.43) to above request for clearance to attack listed targets.

11 PRO ADM 223/8 Special Intelligence Summary from DDIC dated 8.9.43 citing some German naval movements as being 'possible reactions to *Operation Starkey*'.

12 PRO AIR 24/259 Bomber Command Intelligence Reports 3677 dated 5.9.43 and 3682 dated 7.9.43 as well as Photo-Interpretation Report SA561 dated 13.9.43; and PRO AIR 20/4801 Air Force Commander's Report, Appendix D summarizing air effort dedicated to *Starkey*.

13 PRO AIR 8/1202 HQ No. 11 Group signal A322 sent 7.9.43 (1500 hours); and PRO AIR 20/4801 Air Force Commander's Report Para 26.

14 PRO WO 106/4241 Encl 37A War Cabinet Minute 4 dated 6.9.43.

15 PRO AIR 8/1202 Air Ministry signal sent 6.9.43 (1635 hours), 'Most Secret and Personal' for No. 30 Mission from Chiefs of Staff.

16 PRO AIR 25/129 HQ No. 6 Group ORB.

17   PRO AIR 29/687 No. 82 OTU ORB.

18 PRO AIR 20/4801 HQ No. 11 Group Signal A366 sent 8.9.43.

19 Ibid, Air Force Commander's Report Paras 67 and 68.

Chapter Six

1 Archives at Le Portel Town Hall: Statistics, 2.6.43, supplied in response to request by Boulogne-sur-Mer *Sous-Préfecture*.

2 PRO AIR 20/4801 Air Force Commander's Report, 11G/S500/111/Ops dated 16.9.43, Appendix D, Ramrod operations S30 and S32, 4.9.43; also PRO AIR 24/259 Bomber Command Intelligence Report No. 3677 dated 5.9.43 and Photo-Interpretation Reports SA 524 dated 7.9.43 and SA 561

dated 13.9.43.

3 Ibid.

4 PRO AIR 27/1131 No. 180 Squadron ORB describes flak as 'moderate accuracy and intensity' in the afternoon, and 'intense heavy flak' in the evening.

5 *Histoire du Portel et des Portelois*, André Verley.

6 Ibid.

7 Interview with Gabriel Duval – Père Césaire of the Franciscan Order, specialist in local history and genealogy with number of books to his credit.

8 *Histoire du Portel et des Portelois*, André Verley.

9 *Notes et Documents du Cercle Historique Portelois*, July 1988, article recalling air-raids in 1917/18.

10 Ibid, July 1989, article tracing history of Boulogne airport.

11 Archives at Le Portel Town Hall: Definitive document produced for French Government, 24.5.48, states that about 5,500 of pre-war total of 8,500 inhabitants remained at time of bombardment.

12 Interview with members of Duval family.

13 *L'aube de la libération*, Guy Bataille, notes Boulogne under German occupation 1582 days until 1100 hours 23.9.44 when Canadian army made official announcement of surrender (previous afternoon) of what Germans called *Festung Boulogne*.

14 *CHP Notes et Documents*, July 1990, 50th anniversary series of articles recalling exodus around time Germans entered France in May 1940.

15 Ibid, July 1992, feature recalling early days of Second World War and life under enemy occupation.

Chapter Seven

1 *CHP Notes et Documents*, July 1990, 50th anniversary series of articles recalling exodus around time Germans entered France in May 1940.

2 Ibid.

3 Ibid.

4 Ibid.

5 Interview with members of Duval family.

6 *CHP Notes et Documents*, July 1991, article signed M. Bourgain.

7 Interview with Père Césaire.

8 *CHP Notes et Documents*, July 1992, feature recalling early days of Second World War and life under enemy occupation. Definitive document produced at Le Portel Town Hall for French Government, 24.5.48, states that numbers of Portelois were deported or interned following acts against enemy; others were killed while carrying out acts of resistance; and many were deported to Germany as STO conscripts.

9 Ibid.

10 Ibid.

11 Ibid.

12 Ibid.

13 Interview with Ernest MacKenna.

14 *CHP Notes et Documents*, July 1992, feature recalling the early days of the Second World War.

15 Archives at Le Portel Town Hall: Statistics, 2.6.43, supplied in response to request by Boulogne-sur-Mer *Sous-Préfecture*.

16 *CHP Notes et Documents*, July 1992, feature recalling the early days of the Second World War.

17 Archives at Le Portel Town Hall: Statistics, 2.6.43.

18 Ibid.

19 Ibid.

20 Archives at Le Portel Town Hall: Definitive document, 24.5.48, states that when Le Portel was liberated, 23.9.44, about 1,500 of prewar total of 1,800 dwellings found to be totally destroyed and none of remaining 300 dwellings habitable. Other sources put destruction of town itself between 90 and 95 per cent – '93 per cent destroyed', according to Mayor Paul Barbarin in Preface to 40th anniversary commemorative booklet, *La tragédie du Portel, 4, 8, 9 septembre 1943*.

21 See Chapter Three for nomination and clearance of coastal/beach defence gun-position targets.

Chapter Eight

1 PRO documents contain discrepancies in number of aircraft detailed and effective in Bomber Command raids on night of 8.9.43. The author offers statistics that rely on squadron and unit documents as now being definitive account (Appendices VII and VIII).

2 Described later in chapter, Oboe was British 'blind bombing control' invention using radio beams from pair of ground stations whose signals were received in bomber crew's headphones, intersection of those beams pinpointing target for bombing or marking. Appendix II, page 125, *The History of Oboe*, compiled by HQ No. 60 Group (PRO AIR 16/917) indicates a 62 per cent success in the 9,624 Oboe sorties carried out from December 1942 to May 1945. This history calls Oboe 'one of the most important of Britain's secret weapons'.

3 PRO AIR 41/41 First draft of RAF Air Historical Branch narrative on bombing offensive June 1941 to February 1942 also shows in Para 7(i) that in 100 raids studied in first scientific analysis of night bombing, only 20 per cent of sorties despatched arrived within 5 miles of target, yet rarely fewer than 75 per cent claimed to have found objective. Only one in three who claimed to have attacked was within 5 miles.

4 PRO AIR 14/1804 Memo from Officer i/c ORS to Deputy C-in-C BC dated 20.4.43 assessing estimated effectiveness of PFF for period January/March 1943.

5 PRO AIR 41/41 First draft of above narrative includes Para 7(iii) comment that best claimed for this device was that one bomb fell between target battle-cruiser and quay.

6 Interview with J.E.N. Hooper.

7 *The Challenge of War*, Guy Hartcup.

8 Interview with J.E.N. Hooper.

9 PRO AIR 20/4736 ORS Report No. S102 dated 31.8.43 on operational use of Oboe from introduction 20/21.12.42 to introduction of K-Oboe mid-June 1943.

10 Ibid.

11 Ibid.

12 PRO AIR 16/917 Guarantee came from Officer Commanding 109 Squadron according to 20 August 1943 decision given in *The History of Oboe, 1940 to 1943*, Chapter 7, page 42.

13 PRO AIR 27/853 109 Squadron ORB shows four Mosquito IV and one Mosquito IX detailed for each of these two targets, total of ten Oboe-equipped aircraft, each with two-man crew.

14 PRO AIR 20/4776 reports on target-marking performance by PFF Oboe-equipped Mosquitoes on various nights between 5.3.43 and 4.9.43.

15 PRO AIR 20/4736 Minute Sheet from DD Radar 1 to DB Ops dated 14.8.43, Air Ministry file CMS 114/R3(a).

16 Ibid, Attachment, CMS 114/Radar 3A dated 16.8.43, to above Minute Sheet.

17 PRO AIR 14/3106 Teleprinted Plan of Attack called for four Mosquitoes of 109 Squadron to 'mark the exact aiming point with TI red' at Z-2 (Z = zero hour) and Z+8, Northern Target, Z+43 and Z+53, Southern Target.

18 *The Bomber Command War Diaries*, Martin Middlebrook and Chris Everitt.

19 *History of the Second World War, The Strategic Air Offensive Against Germany 1939–1945*, Sir Charles Webster and Noble Frankland.

20 PRO AIR 29/169 and PRO AIR 29/168 contain the timing sheets for this 'unsuccessful run', respectively the operational files of Air Ministry Experimental Stations Worth Matravers (tracking) and Trimingham (releasing).

21 PRO AIR 29/145 Hawkshill Down I Operational files of Hawkshill Down I cite two separate occasions, 22.10.42 and 31.10.42, when ground defences opened fire on enemy aircraft; and when describing 8.9.43 operations refer specifically to the two targets (at Le Portel) as being 'only a mile apart'.

22 PRO AIR 27/853 109 Squadron ORB contains personnel movements as well as flying duties.

23 PRO AIR 14/3020 provides handwritten Oboe details for 105 Squadron operations on 8.9.43.

24 *Bomber Squadrons of the RAF and their Aircraft*, Philip J.R. Moyes.

25 *The RCAF Overseas – The First Four Years*.

26 PRO AIR 14/3106 Signal P1455 from SASO HQ No. 3 Group to its bases and stations, also to USAAF 422nd Squadron, repeated to HQ Bomber Command.

27 Interview with aircrew member of 35 Squadron.
28 Ibid.

Chapter Nine

1 *The Bomber Command War Diaries*, Martin Middlebrook and Chris Everitt.
2 PRO AIR 25/152 No. 8 Group ORB entry for 8.9.43.
3 PRO AIR 25/136 Teleprinted orders detailed Nos 1, 3, 4, 5 and 6 Groups for this 12 minute attack; it envisaged releasing 40 tons of high explosives every minute on German capital (roughly twice rate inflicted during Le Portel night attack).
4 PRO AIR 29/670 No. 27 OTU ORB includes first operational order, 30.6.41, describing execution of 'Nickelling' and stating that 'in the course of training at the OTU it is desirable that all crews complete one nickelling operation'.
5 Ibid, No. 28 OTU ORB entry for 8.9.43.
6 PRO AIR 25/753 Letter from AOC No. 91 Group, 91G/1402/3/P1 dated 5.9.43.
7 PRO AIR 29/654 No. 15 OTU ORB reports that two aircraft from 102 Squadron, two from 77 Squadron and one from 78 Squadron landed at Harwell when returning from operational sortie to Milan night of 12.8.43.
8 PRO AIR 29/666 No. 22 OTU ORB reported that guns in rear turret of this Wellington X 'could not be fired'; like Wellington III with engine on fire, it returned safely with full bomb load.
9 PRO AIR 14/2677, AIR 25/52, AIR 27/646 and AIR 28/532 Respectively Bomber Command Bomb Raid Sheet No. 1836(A) and ORBs of HQ No. 3 Group, 75 (NZ) Squadron and RAF Station Mepal, all carrying reports on this fatal crash at 2130 hours 8.9.43.
10 PRO AIR 28/532 RAF Station Mepal ORB reports crash-landing as following attack against Berlin 23.8.43.
11 PRO AIR 14/526 No. 3 Group Summary of Events 1.9.43 to 30.9.43 also notes that the 30 sorties by USAAF 422nd Squadron spread over six nights that month provided 'a welcome addition to the weight and accuracy of Bomber Command's night attacks'.
12 *Only owls and bloody fools fly at night*, Group Captain Tom Sawyer DFC.
13 PRO AIR 14/2991 Documents accompanying special target plot of night photographs provide this information, each photograph processed showing time it was taken.
14 PRO AIR 29/667 No. 23 OTU ORB gives no further explanation for this single failure to bomb; the ten Wellingtons were from Stratford (six) and Pershore (four).
15 PRO AIR 27/1172 199 Squadron ORB provides this comment from first of the eight crews back at base – its sortie completed in squadron record time, 2 hours 15 minutes.
16 PRO AIR 14/526 No. 3 Group Summary of Events 1.9.43 to 30.9.43 made point of reporting there was 'much speculation at Station' as to reason for heavy attack on targets near Boulogne night of 8.9.43 (a reference in print that possibly merely fuelled conjecture!).
17 Ibid, reports four-man Soviet Military Mission visit to Little Snoring, Norfolk, home of group's first Lancaster squadron, 115, which began operations from this airfield 10.8.43 – losing one plane and crew in crash on farm 5 miles from Maidstone, Kent, on way home from Nuremburg (PRO AIR 27/890, 115 Squadron ORB). Night of visit, four crews on standby for Berlin but operations were cancelled.
18 Appendix VII lists units and location of all participating aircraft in Phase I with numbers and weights of bombs dropped against Northern Target.
19 PRO AIR 24/259 Teleprinted orders called for maximum number of 500 lb GP and/or 1,000 lb GP bombs fused with 0.025 seconds time delay, except Wellington 423s which were to carry 4,000 lb HC bombs, adding that 'as few Wellington 423s as possible are to be employed'.
20 PRO AIR 27/1657 300 Squadron ORB shows that besides E-Edward, O-Orange also encountered an engine problem and, when engine caught fire crossing English coast, turned back to make safe landing at Marham (coincidentally, PFF Mosquitoes' base).
21 Ibid.
22 PRO AIR 27/1089 166 Squadron ORB shows that all ten Wellingtons 'successfully bombed the target' and 'no aircraft experienced any difficulties'.
23 PRO AIR 24/259 HQBC Interceptions/Tactics Report No. 188/43 issued 16.9.43 describes

encounters by six of No. 3 Group's Stirlings; in no other cases were strikes claimed. Two Wellingtons also logged hits – one from No. 1 Group on FW 190, other from No. 6 Group on believed Me 109.

24 PRO AIR 25/70 Entry in Appendix to No. 3 Group ORB; PRO AIR 27/1322 214 Squadron ORB shows all eight aircraft bombing in 8 minutes from 2241 hours.

25 PRO AIR 14/526 No. 3 Group Summary of Events 1.9.43 to 30.9.43 noted that fifty-nine photographs taken by its bombers that night showed aiming point and 85 per cent (of all photographs taken by its 104 Stirlings) were plotted within 3 miles.

26 PRO AIR 27/1860 No. 432 (RCAF) Squadron ORB discloses an unfortunate sequel: pilot, co-pilot, navigator, air bomber and wireless operator/air gunner in D-Dog all failed to return from attack on Hannover night of 27.9.43 – this pilot's twenty-fifth operational mission.

27 PRO AIR 29/641 No. 12 OTU ORB Appendices with entries for months August and September 1943.

28 Ibid.

29 PRO AIR 29/656 No. 16 OTU ORB adds that besides this pupil pilot being commended on his performance, 'a green endorsement was made in his log book'.

30 PRO AIR 25/762 No. 92 Group ORB also refers to 8.9.43 attacks as 'a grand finale' in series of special operations against targets in Pas de Calais.

31 PRO AIR 24/259 Form G for 1800 hours 8.9.43 shows following aircraft, with crews, available for operations: No. 1 Group, 94 Lancasters and 25 Wellingtons; No. 3 Group, 4 Lancasters and 126 Stirlings; No. 4 Group, 99 Halifaxes; No. 5 Group, 116 Lancasters; No. 6 Group, 3 Lancasters, 48 Halifaxes and 15 Wellingtons; and No. 8 Group, 75 Lancasters, 25 Halifaxes and 36 Mosquitoes; total of 666 front-line bombers (in operational squadrons, excluding OTU Groups).

32 PRO WO 205/1A Intelligence Summary No. 6 by 21 Army Group covering 24 hours to 1700 on 9.9.43 names Hastings and these East Anglian locations as receiving bombs that night: Snailwell, Thetford, Stanton, Hepworth, East Winch and Palling.

33 PRO AIR 24/259 HQBC Interceptions/Tactics Report No. 188/43 adds that there was some heavy flak from Gravelines, Dunkirk and Calais, also from batteries in St Omer area where accuracy 'usually greater than elsewhere'.

Chapter Ten

1 *CHP Notes et Documents*, July 1983, article signed Marcel Cartailler.

2 Ibid, article signed Louis Justin.

3 *CHP Notes et Documents*, July 1993, article signed Paul Justin.

4 *Sous la botte allemande*, Guy Bataille.

5 *CHP Notes et Documents*, July 1983, Paul Justin interview with l'Abbé Boidin.

6 Ibid, July 1983, article signed Marcel Cartailler.

7 *Sous la botte allemande*, Guy Bataille.

8 *Nos villes dans la tourmente* (illustrated booklet series published 1944).

9 Ibid.

10 *CHP Notes et Documents*, July 1983, article signed Mlle Moisson.

11 *Nos villes dans la tourmente*: montage of memorial columns.

12 *CHP Notes et Documents*, July 1983, article signed A. Dumont, Note (3).

13 *La tragédie du Portel, 4, 8, 9 septembre 1943*, 40th anniversary booklet: see Preface by Mayor.

Chapter Eleven

1 *Rapport général sur l'évacuation des réfugiés du Pas de Calais dans la Marne, septembre 1943/mai 1946.*

2 *Nos villes dans la tourmente* (illustrated booklet published 1944).

3 *Sous la botte allemande*, Guy Bataille.

4 *Nos villes dans la tourmente*, which credits unnamed Porteloise, benefiting from one of its 5,000 meals, with use of term 'miracle train'.

5 *CHP Notes et Documents*, July 1984, series of articles on post-bombardment evacuation.

6 *CHP Notes et Documents*, July 1983, article signed Mlle Moisson.

7 *Rapport général sur l'évacuation des réfugiés du Pas de Calais dans la Marne, septembre 1943/mai 1946.*
8 PRO CAB 80/72 COS (43) 32 (Final) dated 27.7.43, Appendix C, Para 29.
9 *CHP Notes et Documents*, July 1992, Lucien Vasseur article on German fortifications, Le Portel, 1940/4.
10 *CHP Notes et Documents*, July 1983, Paul Justin interview with l'Abbé Boidin.
11 *CHP Notes et Documents*, July 1984, article signed Mme Louise Gournay-Libert.
12 *CHP Notes et Documents*, July 1993, article signed Joseph Germe.
13 *CHP Notes et Documents*, July 1984, article signed Famille Gournay-Lamirand.
14 *Sous la botte allemande*, Guy Bataille.
15 *CHP Notes et Documents*, July 1984, article signed Louis Coppin.
16 Ibid, article signed Paul Justin, Note (2).
17 Ibid, article signed Marie Robert.
18 Ibid, article signed P.J.
19 Ibid, article signed Mme Louise Gournay-Libert.
20 Ibid, photo taken at Rheims shows 'more than 300 Portelois' attending reunion of *émigrés* scattered throughout Marne.
21 Ibid, article signed Marie Robert.
22 Ibid.
23 *CHP Notes et Documents*, July 1994, *CHP* interview with Louis Bourgain.
24 *CHP Notes et Documents*, July 1983, article signed Jean Bouveur.
25 *CHP Notes et Documents*, July 1994, *CHP* interview with Louis Bourgain.
26 *Sous la botte allemande*, Guy Bataille.
27 *Croix de Guerre* citation, see plate section.
28 *CHP Notes et Documents*, July 1983, article signed Mlle Moisson.
29 *CHP Notes et Documents*, July 1984, article signed Paul Justin cites Desvres, Bapaume, Arras, Campagne-lès-Hesdin, Rheims and Paris hospitals as receiving injured Portelois. Definitive document produced at Le Portel Town Hall for French Government, 24.5.48, states 250 injured; and *CHP Notes et Documents*, July 1983, article signed A. Dumont, gives 1,200 injured, 400 of them seriously.
30 *CHP Notes et documents*, July 1983, article signed Louis Robert.

Chapter Twelve

1 PRO AIR 20/4801 Air Force Commander's Report, 11G/S500/111/Ops dated 16.9.43, Para 42.
2 Ibid, Paras 67 and 68.
3 PRO AIR 20/4801 Air Ministry signal AX993 sent 27.8.43 restricted attack on gun emplacement targets at Le Touquet, 9(A)/29, limiting to daytime only.
4 PRO AIR 20/4801 Letter FC/KG/F27 dated 27.8.43 from Air Commodore Strafford to Under Secretary of State, Air Ministry.
5 PRO AIR 20/4801 Air Force Commander's Report, Appendix D refers to 15 Venturas, 19 Bostons and 34 Mitchells attacking E-boats and port installations; and PRO AIR 24/259 Bomber Command Intelligence Report No. 3677 dated 5.9.43 to 141 Spitfires and 29 Typhoons providing escort and support for attacks, in course of which 1 FW 190 destroyed and 1 damaged without loss.
6 PRO AIR 24/259 Bomber Command Intelligence Report No. 3687 dated 9.9.43.
7 PRO AIR 14/2692 Combined BC ORS Report No. S126 and AWAS Report 52 dated 17.3.44, contains Appendix A, Diary of attacks on Boulogne area 8.9.43/9.9.43, sometimes conflicting with Squadron ORBs.
8 Appendix IV.
9 PRO AIR 40/904 Reports by USAAF Bombardment Groups carrying out Mission 54 on 8.9.43.
10 PRO DEFE 2/458 Note by VCAS to Chiefs of Staff Committee dated 26.8.43.
11 PRO AIR 24/259 HQBC ORB Appendices showing aircraft detailed for that night's operations, subsequently cancelled; also PRO AIR 14/3106 Signals from HQs Nos 1, 3 and 6 Groups re this cancelled operation.
12 PRO DEFE 2/458 Minutes of 1st *Starkey* conference held 7.7.43 added that Eaker 'had expressed his point of view to Higher Authority in strong terms'.

13 PRO AIR 14/3442 Report on 8th US Bomber Command operational sorties, period to 0730 hours 1.9.43.
14 PRO AIR 14/3735 identifies operations by seven task forces of US heavy bombers in conjunction with *Starkey*, 9.9.43.
15 Ibid.
16 Ibid.
17 PRO AIR 14/2692 Combined BC ORS and AWAS Report, Appendix A.
18 PRO AIR 40/905 Reports by USAAF Bombardment Groups carrying out Mission 55 on 9.9.43.
19 PRO AIR 14/2692 Combined BC ORS and AWAS Report details results of 'an attempt made to determine the separate results of the various types of attack'.
20 PRO AIR 24/259 Photo-Interpretation Report No. SA 558 dated 13.9.43, refers to 250 lb GP half-hour delay bombs and 98 and 180 Squadron ORBs specify 500 lb bombs with same delay; these appear to be the only mention of delayed-action high explosives being used against the six codenamed gun batteries in Boulogne area, 8.9.43/9.9.43.
21 PRO AIR 14/2692 Combined BC ORS and AWAS Report, Para 12.
22 Ibid, Para 14.
23 *No. 2 Group Official History*, Michael J.F. Bowyer, which provides the statistic that Spitfires flew 786 sorties, calls the results of *Starkey* 'extremely disappointing'.
24 PRO AIR 24/259 Bomber Command Intelligence Report No. 3689 dated 10.9.43 includes Fighter Command summary of activity for 9.9.43, which reports total of 2,006 sorties flown.
25 PRO AIR 40/905 Reports by USAAF Bombardment Groups carrying out Mission 55 on 9.9.43 identify this as No. 387 Group aircraft with five crew members killed and one injured; crash put down to poor visibility.
26 *D-Day, June 6, 1944, The Normandy Landings*, Richard Collier.
27 *The Canadian Army 1939–1945*, Col. C.P. Stacey.
28 PRO DEFE 2/566 Air Force Operation Order for Culminating Phase names SS *Victoria*, SS *Canterbury* and SS *Isle of Thanet* among participating ships.
29 PRO WO 205/449 No. 11 Group Synopsis of Operations for 24 hours ended 0600 hours 10.9.43, Para 2A(i) notes that after aerial reconnaissance about 0700 hours, enemy made no attempt to attack either with bombers or fighters and no long-range guns were fired.
30 *No. 2 Group Official History*, Michael J.F. Bowyer, describes 88 Squadron efforts to trail smoke over HQ ship when crossing Channel.
31 PRO WO 205/449 No. 11 Group Synopsis of Operations credits 65 Squadron with FW 190 and 122 Squadron with two Me 109s; losses sustained by 122 and 331 Squadrons.
32 Ibid, attributes cancellations of late afternoon series of attacks to 'bad' weather.
33 *The Times*, 10.9.43, carrying report by its aeronautical correspondent writing from Folkestone on 9.9.43.
34 PRO WO 205/449 No. 11 Group Synopsis of Operations refers only to Mustang sorties; however, 541 Squadron ORB (PRO AIR 27/2013) shows a Spitfire, EN 669, having photographed Calais, Boulogne and Dunkirk during Sortie E174 – and other Spitfires covering Cherbourg, Dieppe and aerodromes near Paris.
35 PRO AIR 27/2013 541 Squadron ORB entries for period 3.9.43/9.9.43; then bad weather ended sorties.
36 PRO WO 205/449 Immediate Interpretation Report No. K1715 dated 10.9.43, distribution list including Air Ministry and Cabinet war rooms as well as HQ Fighter Command and US 8th Air Support Command.
37 PRO AIR 20/4801 Air Force Commander's Report, Para 97 calls this loss among unescorted aircraft penetrating as deep as Brussels 'the outstanding feature' of aerial tactical reconnaissance during *Starkey*.

Chapter Thirteen

1 *Nos villes dans la tourmente* (illustrated booklet published 1944).
2 Ibid.

 3 Ibid.
 4 Ibid.
 5 Ibid.
 6 *Le Télégramme* newspaper, 11.9.43.
 7 Radio Paris text, *Le Télégramme*, 14.9.43.
 8 *Sous la botte allemande*, Guy Bataille.
 9 Archives at Le Portel Town Hall: Letter to M. le Curé dated 9.6.44.
10 *Dictionnaire de la Seconde Guerre Mondiale*, Larousse.
11 *Sous la botte allemande*, Guy Bataille.
12 *La tragédie du Portel, 4, 8, 9 septembre 1943*, 40th anniversary booklet.
13 *La Voix du Nord* newspaper, 3.1.45.
14 Archives at Le Portel Town Hall: Letter to Mayor dated 4.1.45.
15 *La Voix du Nord*, various dates.
16 Ibid.
17 Ibid.
18 Ibid.
19 Ibid.
20 Interview with M. Jean-Pierre Blond.
21 *La Voix du Nord*, various dates.
22 Ibid.
23 Ibid.
24 Archives at Le Portel Town Hall: Letter to M. Roger Berrier, Architecte Urbaniste, dated 10.1.45.
25 Ibid.
26 *La Voix du Nord*, 31.8.45.
27 Archives at Le Portel Town Hall: four-column alphabetical list dated 20.1.48.
28 *CHP Notes et Documents*, July 1989, article tracing history of Boulogne airport.
29 *La Voix du Nord*, 12/13.9.93.
30 *CHP Notes et Documents*, August 1986, article signed Alfred Dumont.
31 *CHP Notes et Documents*, August 1985, article recalling reconstruction of Le Portel church.
32 Citation, see plate section.
33 *La tragédie du Portel*: see Preface by Mayor.
34 Inteview with M. Jean-Pierre Blond.
35 *La tragédie du Portel*: Prof. Jones' letter dated 23.12.80, while at Department of Natural Philosophy, Aberdeen University.
36 *La Voix du Nord*, 10.9.93.
37 Correspondence with M. Laurent Feutry.

Chapter Fourteen

 1 PRO AIR 20/4801 Air Force Commander's Report, 11G/S500/111/Ops dated 16.9.43, Appendix B shows 1,957 RAF aircraft and 1,063 USAAF aircraft operating on final day of *Starkey* (three times daily average).
 2 Ibid, Appendix C gives 69 aircraft (64 crew) lost by No. 11 Group and 15 aircraft (41 crew) by No. 2 Group; while USAAF lost 8 Marauders and 107 Fortresses (of which only 10 were lost when operating under protection of No. 11 Group fighters).
 3 Ibid, Para 4 recalls that Air Plan was designed to bring GAF to action over several weeks prior to *Starkey* D-Day, or failing that, to destroy his aircraft on ground.
 4 Ibid, Appendix D.
 5 *La tragédie du Portel*, 40th anniversary booklet.
 6 PRO AIR 14/2991 Briefing details include Plan of Attack against 'Special Targets' in Boulogne-sur-Mer area (zero hour subsequently amended to 2200 hours).
 7 PRO AIR 14/3411 BC ORS Final Reports on Night Raids, September 1943 to May 1944, also says intercepted wireless traffic indicated that one gun, possibly flak, had been hit.
 8 PRO AIR 14/3012 BC ORS Report B173 reference BC/S29734/24/ORS dated 25.9.43.

9   Interview with aircrew member of 35 Squadron.

10 PRO AIR 14/2692 Combined BC ORS Report No. S126 and AWAS Report 52 dated 17.3.44 opens stating photo-reconnaissance cover showed direct hits on one gun in a primary target and one in a subsidiary target, with two other subsidiary guns probably damaged.

11 *Bombing 1939–45*, Karl Hecks.

12 PRO AIR 25/156 No. 8 Group ORB Appendices, *Precision*, September 1943, summarizing operations, training activities, organizational matters and decorations awarded for gallantry.

13 PRO AIR 14/2940 Weekly reports for aircrews – summary of operations by Bomber Command for week ending 12.9.43.

14 PRO AIR 14/2692 Combined BC ORS and AWAS Report, Para 23.

15 Ibid, Para 2.

16 Interview with aircrew member of 35 Squadron.

17 PRO AIR 14/2991 Documents accompanying special target plot of night photographs show prints received from Pathfinders in No. 8 Group (9 Halifaxes) and from Main Force bombers in No. 1 Group (20 Wellingtons), No. 3 Group (89 Stirlings), No. 6 Group (10 Wellingtons), No. 91 Group (14 Wellingtons), No. 92 Group (15 Wellingtons) and No. 93 Group (21 Wellingtons) – total of 178 aircraft from the 239 Halifaxes, Stirlings and Wellingtons carrying out effective sorties; handwritten figures show 85 aircraft in Phase I and 90 in Phase II 'were estimated, from the photographic evidence, to have bombed within one mile of the aiming point'.

18 PRO AIR 14/526 No. 3 Group Monthly Summary of Events, 1.8.43 to 31.8.43, Paras 29 and 31 report average error now standing at 195 yards in competition bombing in this group, with 15 Squadron topping the table with 159 yard error and individual best effort an average of 132 yards.

19 PRO AIR 14/2991 Plots for 300 Squadron put C-Charlie closest – within ¼ mile; while among No. 18 OTU crews, R-Roger was plotted on AP.

20 PRO AIR 14/3012 BC ORS Report B173 Para 8 shows that more than 80 per cent of the 180 photos plotted were within a mile: 89 photos in Phase I, 91 photos in Phase II.

21 PRO AIR 14/3012 BC ORS Report B173 Para 13 goes on to report that all backers-up except one bombed on those reds and 'an excellent concentration of TIs was achieved within 500 yards of the aiming point' (Phase II *Andante*).

22 PRO AIR 14/2692 BC ORS Report S109 dated 25.10.43 Paras 14(i) and 15.

23 PRO AIR 14/2692 Combined BC ORS and AWAS Report, Air Warfare Analysis Section Bomb Plot, Fig. I; and PRO AIR 40/312 Preliminary Survey of Bombing Attacks – *Operation Starkey*, dated 9.11.43.

24 PRO AIR 20/4801 Air Force Commander's Report, Para 119.

25 PRO AIR 8/1202 Most Secret cypher telegram Concrete No. 831 sent 10.9.43 from Chiefs of Staff to Prime Minister (attending Quebec Conference).

26 PRO AIR 20/4801 Air Force Commander's Report, Paras 63 and 65 (where it should be noted that in Saunders' report there are quote marks round 'area' when referring to this bombing).

27 Ibid.

28 Ibid.

29 PRO WO 106/4241 Encl 1A Military Force Commander's Report 21A Group/00/12/Ops is Appendix B to Air Marshal Sir Trafford Leigh-Mallory's Report to COSSAC dated 29.9.43.

30 Ibid, Naval Force Commander's Report No. 0850/5 dated 15.9.43 is Appendix A to Air Marshal Sir Trafford Leigh-Mallory's Report to COSSAC dated 29.9.43.

31 Ibid, Air Marshal Sir Trafford Leigh-Mallory's Report to COSSAC dated 29.9.43 Paras 5 and 20.

32 Ibid, Para 20.

33 PRO AIR 22/408 US 8th Air Force Semi-monthly Report, Bombing Results 1/15.9.43, describes coastal defence targets attacked as 'dispersed and extremely small' (a comment as appropriate in night bombing as for the Americans bombing by day).

34 *The Army Air Forces in World War II – Vol 2, Europe: Torch to Pointblank* (April 1942 to December 1943).

35 PRO AIR 20/4801 Air Force Commander's Report, Para 117.

36 PRO FO 898/373 records that 'it will be very much appreciated' if newspapers will refrain from publishing stories likely to excite public speculation of that kind.

37 PRO AIR 20/4801 Air Force Commander's Report, Para 121.

Chapter Fifteen

1 *Sous la botte allemande*, Guy Bataille.

2 *CHP Notes et Documents*, July 1983, article signed Jean Bouveur.

3 *CHP Notes et Documents*, July 1992, Lucien Vasseur article on German fortifications, Le Portel, 1940/4. Relying on the best available intelligence, *Starkey* planners were understandably mistaken about this and other German firepower, as Guy Bataille explained during a meeting with the author on 6 July 1996. Based on Bataille's personal experience and his study of post-war documentation, there is no doubt that coastal artillery positions the length of the Pas de Calais were in a state of flux throughout the years of occupation. Guns were removed as needs changed so there may have been replacements of a different calibre or no replacements at all. Also, an absence of suitable shells meant that some guns were inactive for long periods, and so not always the threat they seemed to be. Apparently, the German guns in this most heavily defended part of France originated in as many as seventeen countries – Cap d'Alprech even boasted British Vickers armament (see p. 50) – and keeping them all functioning all the time was an impossibility. Nonetheless, Allied planning would take no chances and assumed a worst-case scenario.

4 *La Voix du Nord*, 10.9.93.

5 *The Second World War*, Vol II, Winston S. Churchill, who added that the centre of Coventry was shattered, its life for a spell completely disrupted and four hundred people were killed.

6 *The Bomber Command War Diaries*, Martin Middlebrook and Chris Everitt.

7 *L'aube de la libération*, Guy Bataille.

8 *The Bomber Command War Diaries*, Martin Middlebrook and Chris Everitt.

9 Ibid.

10 PRO AIR 41/41 Appendix J-1 shows 534 tons of HE (and 982 tons of incendiaries) dropped night of 30/31.5.42 with 469 people killed according to German ARP records – 58 *Wehrmacht*, 27 Civil Defence and 384 civilians.

11 *The Times*, 10.9.43, reported that Whirlwind and Typhoon bombers struck at gun positions at Hardelot (12 of each at 0830 and 0900 hours respectively although they 'did not seriously damage their dispersed targets' – PRO AIR 40/312 Preliminary Survey of Bombing Attacks – *Operation Starkey*, dated 9.11.43).

12 *Le Télégramme*, 14.9.43.

13 Interview with members of Duval family.

14 GSGS 4040 Sheet 49 Reproduced and annotated in plate section.

15 PRO AIR 20/4801 Air Ministry signal AX993 sent 27.8.43; also see Target Pinpoints for *Religion* and *Andante*, detailed as Appendix I.

16 PRO WO 106/4241 Encl 22C Letter BC/S30324/Ops to COSSAC dated 11.8.43 uses this figure as premise when assessing bombing effort necessary to neutralize Pas de Calais coastal batteries.

17 PRO AIR 27/1788 405 (RCAF) Squadron ORB also describes weather conditions on 8.9.43 – cloud increasing from 8/10 to 10/10, dispersing after dark, with visibility moderate to good; winds light south-south-westerly veering north-westerly and becoming calm during evening, then light variable. During attack, crews reported no cloud with ground haze in target area (with bright moonlight/half moon setting 0015 hours according to other sources).

18 PRO WO 205/449 Immediate Interpretation Report No. K1715 dated 10.9.43.

19 PRO FO 898/319 shows that an initial quantity of 100,000 copies was considered insufficient and that by 8.6.42 as many as 240,000 copies had been collected by Air Ministry.

20 Interview with members of Duval family and subsequent correspondence. It has to be said, however, that another equally reliable source, also in a written statement to the author, dismisses these reports as *un bobard* (a colloquial term meaning 'a tall story'). This correspondent questions its veracity by recalling that during the occupation 'the Germans were very mistrustful and very well organized against spies infiltrating their ranks, especially their front-line strength'.

21 *Sous la botte allemande*, Guy Bataille.

22 Interview with members of Le Portel association of civilian war victims.

23 PRO AIR 40/904 and 905 provide detailed reports of Marauder operations on 8.9.43 and 9.9.43 including damage from AA fire and fact that both days RAF Spitfire squadrons provided protective umbrella over target area against German fighters (though USAAF gunners had occasion to fire on one FW 190 and four Me 109s).

24 PRO AIR 14/2692 Combined BC ORS Report S126 and AWAS Report 52 dated 17.3.44, Para 2 Table 1 shows 500 yards was average aiming error when 18 USAAF Marauders attacked in face of medium flak; and 1,200 yards when RAF Mitchells and Venturas attacked against intense flak.

25 PRO AIR 20/4801 Air Force Commander's Report, 11G/S500/111/Ops dated 16.9.43, Para 65 shows quotation marks round the word 'area'.

26 Correspondence with Guy Bataille – he quotes from a letter he received from Prof. Jones.

27 PRO AIR 20/4776 Oboe result assessments during bombing operations against targets in Forêts de Mormal, Raismes and Hesdin show individual errors between 10 and 150 yards.

28 PRO AIR 14/2692 Combined BC ORS and AWAS Report Para 17 says provision of adequate marking was rendered difficult by fact that for two of the three Oboe channels the angle of cut was much too low and for the third it was only just good enough (so for each Phase, three Mosquitoes (including reserve) would track with Oboe and three with Baillie beam).

29 PRO AIR 20/4736 Minute Sheet from DD Radar 1 to DB Ops dated 14.8.43 says BC ORS now examining proposal to use Baillie beam for tracking and Oboe for releasing when attacking 'very short range' targets (the less sophisticated and apparently less-rated Baillie being resurrected after early use end 1941 and early 1942).

30 PRO AIR 20/4776 Oboe results during bombing operations against Forêt de Raismes, 3.9.43, state this TI jettisoned owing to faulty release gear.

31 PRO AIR 14/2692 Combined BC ORS and AWAS Report, Para 19 states that attack on *Religion* was 'largely determined' by this salvo; while at *Andante* the 'long stick of reds attracted most of the Main Force and backers-up'.

32 Ibid, Para 23.

33 Ibid, Para 19 notes that 'as a natural consequence' of markers being scattered (the split red salvo on *Andante*), bombing was also scattered.

34 PRO AIR 8/1202 Signal A201 from 'Bomber' Harris to VCAS Air Ministry sent 25.8.43 Part I Para 1.

35 *The Times*, 23.8.43, quoting from Soviet fortnightly review 'War and the Working Class'.

36 Ibid, quoting Mrs Churchill in radio broadcast to Britain.

37 Towns targeted for 'Nickelling' operations can be listed by cross-checking Bomber Command, Group, squadron and unit documents.

38 *CHP Notes et Documents*, July 1992, Lucien Vasseur article on German fortifications, Le Portel, 1940/4, states that there were 'only two killed and five injured' at Fort de Couppes during bombardment.

39 PRO AIR 27/1352 218 Squadron ORB provides hitherto unpublished details regarding *Glimmer*, which has been mentioned in various books.

40 *The D-Day Encyclopaedia*, Edited by David G. Chandler and James Lawton Collins.

41 *The Bomber Command War Diaries*, Martin Middlebrook and Chris Everitt.

BIBLIOGRAPHY

Arnaud, Dominique, *Le Guide du Boulonnais et de la côte d'Opale*, La Manufacture, 1988

Barker, Michael, with Paul Atterbury, *The North of France*, The Heyford Press, 1990

Bataille, Guy, *L'aube de la libération*, Coubron, Pierru, 1973

Bataille, Guy, *Sous la botte allemande*, Coubron, Pierru, 1973

Bowyer, Michael J.F., *2 Group RAF: a complete history, 1936–1945*, Faber, 1974

Brown, Anthony Cave, *Bodyguard of Lies, Vol I*, Harper & Row, 1975

Chandler, David G., with J.L. Collins (eds) *The D-Day Encyclopaedia*, Simon & Schuster, 1994

Churchill, Winston S., *The Second World War, Vol II*, Cassell, 1948–54

Collier, Richard, *D-Day, June 6, 1944, The Normandy Landings*, Cassell, 1992

Cruickshank, Charles, *Deception in World War II*, OUP, 1981

Duval, Gabriel, *Nos ancêtres, étude généalogique*, Le Flobard, 1965

Foot, M.R.D., *The Special Operations Executive 1940–6*, University Publications of America, 1984

Freeman, R.A., *Airfields of the Eighth Then and Now*, After the Battle magazine, 1978

Handel, M.L. (ed.), *Strategic and Operational Deception in the Second World War*, Frank Cass, 1987

Hartcup, Guy, *The Challenge of War*, David & Charles, 1970

Hastings, Max, *Bomber Command*, Michael Joseph, 1979

Haswell, Jock, *The Intelligence and Deception of the D-Day Landings*, Batsford, 1979

Hecks, Karl, *Bombing 1939–45*, Robert Hale, 1990

Howard, Sir Michael, *British Intelligence in the Second World War, Vol 5*, HMSO, 1990

Lisiewicz, M. (ed.), *Destiny Can Wait: The History of the Polish Air Force in Great Britain*, Heinemann, 1949

Mallory, Keith, with Arvid Ottar, *Walls of War, Military architecture of two world wars*, Astragal Books, 1973

Masterman, Sir John, *The Double-Cross System*, Yale UP, 1972

Middlebrook, Martin, with Chris Everitt, *The Bomber Command War Diaries*, Viking, 1985

Morgan, Lt-Gen. Sir Frederick (COSSAC), *Overture to Overlord*, Hodder & Stoughton, 1950

Moyes, Philip J.R., *Bomber squadrons of the RAF and their aircraft*, Macdonald & Jane's, 1964

Munson, Kenneth, *Aircraft of World War II*, Ian Allan, 1962

Musgrove, Gordon, *Pathfinder Force*, Macdonald & Jane's, 1976

Partridge, Colin, *Hitler's Atlantic Wall*, DI Publications, 1976

Saunders, Hilary St G., *Royal Air Force, 1939–1945, Vol 3, The Fight is Won*, HMSO, 1975

Sawyer, Gp Capt. Tom, *Only owls and bloody fools fly at night*, Goodall Publications, 1985

Stacey, Col C.P., *The Canadian Army 1939–1945*, King's Printer, Ottawa, 1948

Stafford, David, *Britain and European Resistance 1940–45, A Survey of the Special Operations Executive*, Macmillan with St Antony's College, Oxford, 1980

Taylor, John W.R. (ed.), *Combat Aircraft of the World*, G.P. Putnam's Sons, New York, 1969

Verley, André, *Histoire du Portel et des Portelois*, Le Syndicat d'Initiative, Le Portel, 1963

Verrier, Anthony, *The Bomber Offensive*, Macmillan, 1968

Webster, Sir Charles, with Noble Frankland, *History of the Second World War, The Strategic Air Offensive against Germany 1939–1945*, HMSO, 1961

Webster, G.J., *Codenames of World War II (1939–45)*, Thesis submitted for a Fellowship of the Library Association, 1986

Weinberg, Gerhard L., *A World at Arms*, Cambridge University Press, 1994

Chronique de la France et des Français, Larousse, Jacques Legrand Editions, 1987
Dictionnaire de la Seconde Guerre Mondiale, Jean Dumont, 1971
Dictionnaire des communes du Pas-de-Calais, Louis Joseph Harbaville, 1992
Encyclopaedia of the Second World War, Longman's, 1994
Military Airfields in the British Isles, 1939–45, D. Willis & B.R. Hollis, 1987
The Army Air Forces in World War II, Vol 2, Europe, Torch to Pointblank (August 1942 to December 1943), The University of Chicago Press, 1949
The Illustrated History of World War II, Temple Press/Aerospace, 1986
The RCAF Overseas –The First Four Years, Oxford University Press, Toronto, 1944–9

INDEX